PHILOBIBLON,

A

TREATISE ON THE LOVE OF BOOKS,

BY RICHARD DE BURY,

BISHOP OF DURHAM, AND LORD CHANCELLOR OF ENGLAND.

FIRST AMERICAN EDITION,

WITH THE

LITERAL ENGLISH TRANSLATION OF JOHN B. INGLIS.

COLLATED AND CORRECTED, WITH NOTES,

BY SAMUEL HAND.

ALBANY:
JOEL MUNSELL.
MDCCCLXI.

TO THE

HON. ROBERT S. HALE,

ONE OF THE REGENTS OF THE UNIVERSITY

OF THE STATE OF NEW YORK,

THIS EDITION

OF THE

PHILOBIBLON OF DE BURY,

IS MOST RESPECTFULLY DEDICATED,

BY HIS FRIEND,

THE EDITOR.

EDITOR'S PREFACE.

My first intention in undertaking an American edition of this curious little work, was to accompany the text with a careful translation. On consideration, however, I concluded that the object attained would hardly repay the labor requisite to such a performance. The book is one which, it is not likely, will be much read but by scholars and bibliophilists, to a majority of whom a translation would be of little interest. To those who desire any translation, that of Inglis, which appeared in 1832, and though objected to by some critics as generally clumsy and in places spiritless, is on the whole honest and close to the sense of the original, it was thought would sufficiently answer all needful purposes. In the present edition it has, therefore, been placed opposite the text. Wherever it materially varies from it, I have endeavored to point out the discrepancy in the notes, and refer to the different reading of the original from which the translation was made.

A French translation of this work by M. Cocheris, member of the Imperial Antiquarian Society of France, was published at Paris in 1856. M. Cocheris has prefaced his edition with an introduction consisting of three distinct parts; biographical, bibliographical and critical. These prefaces, illustrated with notes, are all spirited, and exhibit much learning and research. Believing that they would add much to its value and interest, I have translated and prefixed them to this edition. The French translation itself was also copiously annotated. Translations of all of these notes, believed to be important or interesting, have been made and are to be found in the following pages.

It is of course impossible for one who attempts to edit a work of this kind in our country, possessing no great libraries or repositories of manuscripts to be consulted, to correct any errors of the text by comparison. Conjectural emendations are generally so unsatisfactory, except when suggested by editors of far more genius and scholarship than belongs to me, that I have entirely refrained from inflicting them upon the reader. I have therefore contented myself with placing in this edition the text most recently revised and collated.

That of the French edition has been adopted with a translation of the very full notes made by the French editor, exhibiting the various readings. The manuscripts and editions to which he had access and with which he collated it, are enumerated in the bibliographical preface. I have endeavored to follow that text carefully and accurately, and believe that few errors will be found.

Original notes of my own I have also inserted in the book occasionally, though sparingly.

The notes of Inglis to his English translation have also been nearly all preserved.

It is hoped that this humble attempt to bring to the knowledge of American readers, a quaint and beautiful little treatise upon a subject so interesting, written so many centuries ago, and by a man who played so distinguished a part in his time, as a prelate, a statesman, and a scholar, will commend itself to our reading men, and that the faults of the editor may not have so far marred the author, as to preclude the former from at least toleration if not pardon, and the latter from a just appreciation. I shall have accomplished my highest wish in regard to the book, if I in any degree succeed in rescuing from comparative forgetfulness in these modern times, a performance so truly excellent and in its day so wonderful.

SAMUEL HAND.

ALBANY, July 20, 1861.

ERRATA.

Page 16, line 1, for *Un* read *A*.
" 33, note *a*, for *Theodules* read *Theodulus*.
" 33, " (f), for *Conduiie* read *Conduite*.
" 77, " *a*, for *Attinam* read *atteriam*.
" 96, " *a*, for *honorum* read *honorem*.
" 104, " *b* should be omitted, see note 7 same page.

CONTENTS.

INTRODUCTION.

BIOGRAPHICAL NOTICE.

THE author of *Philobiblon* was born in the year 1287,[1] at Bury St. Edmonds,[2] in the county of Suffolk, England. His father, a knight of Norman descent, Richard d'Angerville,[3] dying in middle life, the young Richard was entrusted to the care of his maternal uncles, who were descended from the illustrious family of Willoughby. The inclinations displayed by him from infancy induced his guardians to send him to Oxford, there to finish his studies, and thus was given to him the opportunity of developing all the resources of his intellect and precocious learning.

Esteemed by his teachers, beloved by his fellow students, he succeeded not only in keeping at a distance envy, that stain upon the most brilliant reputations, but in drawing upon himself the notice of the king, who chose him to be the tutor of the prince of Wales, his son, so celebrated under the name of Edward the Third.

1 And not in 1281, as M. Suard assures us in the article that he has devoted to Bury in the *Biog. Univ.* (See the article Aungerville, vol. III, p. 71.)

2 *Burg*, *borough*, *bury*, *burc*, *beri*, is a word found in all languages of the Indo-Germanic family. One finds it in Hindostanee under the form *puri;* in Persian, it is *burk;* in Turkish, *burk;* in Ancient German, *purc;* in Greek, πυργος; in low Latin, *burgus;* in French, *bourg.* In general it signifies; an agglomeration of inhabitants, and more particularly, a fortified place. In 925 Bury was called Bederiksworth, and it was not until 200 years later that it received the name of St. Edmond's Bury. (See *An Illustration of the Monastic History and Antiquities of the town and abbey of St. Edmond's Bury*, by Richard Yates, 1 vol., fol , London, 1805.)

3 The MSS. have it, Awngeville, Aungerville, Almgerville and Muiegerville. Lord Campbell calls it Angraville, but we believe the true name should be written Angerville.

The duties of this office, which demanded more sagacity than learning, Richard de Bury knew how to discharge with prudence and tact. Although familiarity with the great is often fraught with hidden dangers, and brings frequent misfortunes and rarely great honors, he had the wisdom to avoid the former, and neglected nothing to secure the latter.

He had learned that to succeed at the court of the feeble Edward II, it was necessary to conceal his preferences and to preserve an absolute neutrality, lest a flattery addressed to the favorite of to-day, should appear an insult to him of to-morrow. This policy of pursuing a strict middle course amid circumstances constantly changing, so easily carried out in our days, then demanded the profoundest sagacity, and the most experienced sometimes became victims of their very silence. Bury on one occasion deviated from this course, and would have inevitably lost his influence, had not the party, which he too openly served, obtained the control of affairs.

It was at the time when Queen Isabel, who had become embroiled with Spencer, betook herself to Paris, to weave under the protection of her royal brother, Charles the Fair, that perfidious net, entangled in which, the favorite was about to lose his life, Edward II his crown, and she herself, her honor. Richard de Bury was then treasurer of the king in Gascony. As soon as he was apprised of the arrival of the queen, he hastened to join her, and to offer to her the considerable sums which he had collected in his province, as treasurer of the king of England, and which were, by her, readily accepted. This conduct, blamable in certain aspects, displeased the lieutenant of Edward in Gascony, who was probably of Spencer's party. He believed it his duty to punish the disloyal treasurer, and therefore pursued him at the head of twenty-four lances to the very gates of Paris. But, as we have seen, Bury had already sent the money to the queen, and fearing that his person might be seized, had concealed himself in the campanile of the Franciscans.[4]

After seven days of voluntary imprisonment, he quitted his belfry, and was able, thanks probably to the queen, to live in Paris without fear, awaiting the issue of events which were preparing, and of which preparation, it is certain, he was not ignorant.

On the 14th of January, 1327, Edward II was deposed, and his son Edward III ascended the throne. This revolution established on a sure basis the fortunes of our bibliophilist. He was immediately appointed steward of the palace, treasurer of the wardrobe,[5] and afterwards, in 1329, keeper of the privy seal.

The next year he was sent ambassador to the Holy See. The autograph letter, which the king on this occasion addressed to Pope John XXII, reflects as much honor upon the sovereign who wrote it, as upon the ambassador whom it accredited. The attention of the Holy Father was called to the assiduous care which had been bestowed upon Edward himself, from infancy, by Bury; and in asking for him the benefices which Gilbert of Middleton, archdeacon of Northampton, had possessed in the churches of Hereford, London, and Chichester, the king adds: "We recommend to your Holi-"ness this clerk, the more particularly, because we "know him to be a man wise in counsel, remarkable for "the purity of his life and conversation, endowed with "a knowledge of letters, and prudent in action."

Such praises, coming from the mouth of a king, would naturally attract to their object the favor of the pontiff, who failed not to give him a brilliant reception. Richard de Bury was bound to represent his sovereign with becoming magnificence. On the day of his entry, he was

4 The church of the Cordeliers no longer exists. It was situated upon the Place de l'Ecole de Medicine.

5 It was as treasurer that he assisted on the 15th of January, 1329, at the delivery of the great seal by the king to the bishop of Lincoln. (See Rymer, *Fœdera*, etc., vol. II, part II, p. 754.) He resigned this office on the 24th Sept. of the same year, and the inventory of the crown jewels, which he prepared on that occasion, is very important for the sumptuary history of the middle ages. It has been published in the xth volume of the *Archæologia*.

followed by twenty clerks and thirty-six equerries, dressed in rich and gorgeous robes. This audience cost him five thousand marks, but he received the title of chaplain of the pope,[6] and the promise of the first bishopric vacant in England.

He must have returned home in 1331, for, on the 25th of October of that year, the king wrote to the pope concerning his mission, which seems to have had a most prosperous issue;[7] and on the 2d of February, 1332, he was appointed one of the examining commissioners of the royal bursars of the University of Canterbury.[8] Nevertheless, he did not long remain at the court, but again, in the following year, departed on a new mission to the pope. This was of short duration, and he was on his way back to London, when, in the month of September, the bishop of Durham died. The decease of this prelate, leaving a see vacant, gave to the king the opportunity of recompensing one of the most worthy of his subjects, and to the pope, of redeeming his promise. The appointment of Richard de Bury seemed therefore certain.

It was very nearly defeated, however, and in this manner. The bishops were at that time elected, and the elections were to be perfectly free, according to a provision of the Great Charter, which the king had, on his accession, sworn to observe; but the oath was a political one, and being such, it was rarely kept inviolate, so that in effect, the election, almost invariably, was in accordance with the royal wishes, which are very likely to be manifested in such matters.

At the death of Louis de Beaumont, however, the

6 In the bull of John XXII, dated in the month of July, 1333, he is called a dean of the church of Wales and chaplain of the pope.

7 See the passage of this letter in which the king expresses his satisfaction at the happy issue of this mission: De gratiosa et felici expeditione dilectorum et fidelium nostrorum magistri Ricard De Bury et Antonii de Pesaigne, militis, quos nuper ad vestræ sanctitatis præsentiam pro quibusdam nostris secretis negotiis transmisimus, et laudabili consilio quod nobis, super certis articulis quos iidem nuncii nostri vestræ mansuetudini exposuerunt, ex parte nostra, vestra paterna circumspectio dignata est impartiri quas valemus et sufficimus Vestræ Beatitudini gratiarum referimus actiones. (See Rymer, *Fœdera*, etc., tom. II, part II, p. 287.)

8 See Rymer, *Fœdera*, etc., tom. II, part II, p. 831.

king seems to have authorised the election without, in any special manner, indicating his own preference as to the successor. A vote was therefore taken, and the name of Robert de Graystanes, doctor of theology and subprior of Durham, leaped from the urn. This election was declared and approved by the archbishop of York, who granted to the new bishop letters of proclamation, and appointed the 9th of November as the day of his confirmation.

While this was passing at York, the king wrote to the prior and chapter of Durham in favor of Richard of Bury. The newly chosen bishop, who was ignorant of the designs of his sovereign, came to him at Lugatersal to inform him of his election. If Edward was surprised at this news, the prelate was not less astonished, when he heard the king answer: "We have learned that our "lord the pope had intended this bishopric for our be- "loved servant Messire Richard de Bury, and, as we "are unwilling to offend the holy father, we refuse to "confirm your election."[9] Far from being intimidated by this reply, Robert lost no time, and before the letters of the king arrived at Durham, he had procured himself to be consecrated at York, installed at Durham, received the oath of fealty from his vassals and returned to Edward to obtain his temporalities.

This noble courage, which was prompted by the justice of his cause, could not but prejudice it. In the eyes of power, his boldness became presumption, even insolence, perhaps. It is not then surprising that the king should have denied him the interview which he sought, and made answer through his treasurer, that there never had been seen a bishop consecrated without the permission of his sovereign.

Robert de Graystanes returned to Durham, but when he arrived there, the clerks of his competitor, instructed by special orders, occupied the episcopal seat, and the

9 The King here did not tell the truth, for it was he who had interceded with the pope on this occasion, and not the pope with him. See, on this matter, Bzovius, who gives a long eulogy upon Richard de Bury. (*Annalium ecclesiasticarum.* tomus XIV, Colon. Agrippa, 1618, folio, col. 694.)

archbishop of York himself, who had consecrated him, was compelled to annul the first election, and absolve the inhabitants of Durham from their oath of fealty. Robert at length comprehended that he could make no further resistance, and that under such circumstances, to yield was the only course which remained to him.[10]

Richard de Bury, who on this occasion might have played a much nobler part, was consecrated on the 19th of December, 1333, in the Abbey of the Black Monks of Chertsey, by John Stratford, archbishop of Canterbury. On the 5th of June, 1334, the day of his installation by the prior of Durham, William Cowton, he gave a grand feast, at which the king and queen of England, the queen mother, the king of Scotland, two archbishops, five bishops, and the great English and Scottish lords were present. This entertainment must have made at that time a great noise, for all the national chronicles have preserved for us accounts of it. He had been appointed treasurer of the kingdom, some days before, but he did not long retain this important office, having been called to the highest dignity of the state, that of lord high chancellor of England.[11]

The questions which were then occupying the attention of the ministers were of the gravest importance. Edward sought, on the one hand, to subject Scotland, and on the other, to prosecute his claims to the crown of France. No one could more thoroughly comprehend these two subjects than Bury. As bishop of Dur-

10 Robert de Graystanes has left us a chronicle, in which he gives an account of this election in very moderate terms. The reflections suggested to him by this right of reserve, by which the pope can with a single word stop an election, are very judicious. The English boldness shows itself for an instant, and one feels that the monk of the 14th century might well have been the reformer of the 15th. When this distinguished man died, Bury was himself very much affected. (See upon the subject, the chronicle of Rob. de Graystanes and that of William de la Chambre.) Wharton says that he died of chagrin on account of the defeat to which he was obliged to submit on this occasion. (See *Appendix ad historiam litterariam, G. Cave*, etc., Oxonii, 1743, fol., p. 33, col. 2.)

11 The act of delivery of the great seal was on the 28th September, 1334, and Lord Campbell, in his *Lives of the Chancellors*, adopts this date. Nevertheless, his appointment might be put some days earlier, for in a royal decree, by virtue of which he is charged to inquire, with two other commissioners, into the troubles which had arisen in the university of Oxford, he is named as bishop of Durham and chancellor of England. (See Rymer, *Fœdera*, etc., tom. II, part II, p. 892.)

ham, a city situated upon the frontiers of Scotland, he must have reflected, with all the sagacity which he so well knew how to use, upon the means of combatting and conquering the great difficulties, which would present themselves in the accomplishment of the royal will. As ambassador, he had completely surveyed France from one end to the other; he knew the men of that country, and he knew in whom, among them, confidence could be placed. His cool and impartial character, and the horror of war which he openly professed, counterbalanced the factious influence of Robert d'Artois, who, to accomplish his revenge, was flattering the boundless ambition of Edward. This intimate acquaintance with the affairs, therefore, rendered the presence of Bury necessary in the ministerial councils, and the king on this occasion could not have made a more judicious choice. This confidence in the sagacity of his old tutor, the king never lost, since, when the deliberation was brought at length to a close, and the moment for action had arrived, he withdrew the great seal from the hands of his chancellor, in order that he might defend abroad the national interests as ambassador, which as minister he had advised upon at home.

In effect, Richard de Bury returned the seals[12] to the king on the 6th June, 1335, and departed the next year for Paris to initiate negotiations[13] in regard to the projected crusade to the Holy Land, but this enterprise appears to have been impracticable, and the conferences were broken off almost immediately. His presence being no longer necessary at the court of Philip VI, he proceeded to Flanders, traveled in that country, Hainault and Germany, and settled the terms of a treaty of alliance between his master and the counts of Hainault Namur, the marquis of Juliers, and the dukes of Brabant[14] and Guelders.

12 The great seal was given up on the 6th of June, 1335.

13 See in Rymer's *Fœdera*, tom. II, part II, p. 941, the letter of appointment dated July 6th, 1336, and those ordering payment to Bury of the expenses of this embassy.

14 In the treaty concluded on the

Hardly had he returned to Durham, where he was busying himself with the government of his diocese and procuring the confirmation of certain ancient rights and privileges of his church,[15] when, under new orders from the king, he assisted, as commissioner of the government, at the assemblies held at York,[16] Stamford,[17] and Newcastle upon Tyne,[18] to discuss Scottish affairs. These debates occupied him the greater part of the year 1337, and he only quitted them to return to France as ambassador.[19]

This mission must have been very disagreeable to him, for, far from carrying propositions for peace, he bore a declaration of war; and war was, by his calm and lofty mind, regarded as an awful scourge, fatal to the progress of knowledge. It could not have been but from devotion to his sovereign, or to enjoy, once more, the pleasure of beholding Paris, the paradise of the universe, as he was accustomed to call it, that he, a prince of the church, enlightened partizan of peace, and friend of letters, was able so far to sacrifice all his personal feelings, as to declare a war of which ambition was the sole cause, and which not even the most brilliant successes could justify.

At the commencement of hostilities, he returned to England, and withdrew to his diocese, watching the shifting changes of that bloody drama, to which, con-

22d of June, 1339, between Edward III and John, Duke of Brabant, Richard de Bury is made one of the pledges on the part of the king. (See Rymer, *Fœdera*, tom. II, part II, p. 1083.)

15 Edward III remitted to the examination of the officers of the exchequer the rights and privileges claimed by the bishop of Durham. (See a letter of 18th March, 1337, inserted in the *Fœdera* of Rymer, tom. II, part II, p. 961.) They were afterwards confirmed, but William de Chambre, who so informs us, does not mention the date of this confirmation.

16 See in Rymer a letter of the 24th of March, 1337, vol. II, part II, p. 963.

17 See in Rymer another letter of 28th of June, 1337, vol. II, part II, p. 979.

18 See in Rymer another letter of 6th Oct., 1337, vol. II, part II, p. 1000.

19 The first order of departure was dated on the 11th June, 1338 (See Rymer, vol. II, part II, p. 1044), the order of embarkation, on the 23d of June of the same year (See Rymer, vol. II, part II, p. 1045), the letters of safe conduct, the same day (See Rymer, vol. II, part II, p. 1043), but at the moment of departure the powers of the ambassador were revoked (See a letter of 22 July, 1338, in Rymer, vol. II, part II, p. 1051), and Bury did not actually leave until the 15 of November, 1338. (See Rymer, vol. II, part II, p. 1065.)

trary to his own inclinations, he had set his name as author.

The victories gained by the English must have pleased his national pride, and caused the fears which he had entertained, of a descent upon England, to vanish.[20]

He was enjoying, then, perfect tranquillity, when David Bruce suddenly crossed the frontiers of England, laid waste Northumberland, took Durham by assault and besieged Salisbury.[a] Brought to a stand before this fortress, he soon found himself under the necessity of retreating and entrenching himself in the inaccessible forests of Gideon, where he awaited the enemy. But Edward did not care to make war upon the king of Scotland. He preferred to return to France, and ordered the bishop of Durham to conclude a truce for two years,[21] which was soon after extended.[22]

This negotiation was the last public act of Richard de Bury. From this time, he withdrew himself entirely from the world, to live only for and in the midst of his books, sources of all his joys, and for which he had always preserved the warmest attachment. He took advantage of this repose to describe the numerous causes which had produced in him this irresistible desire, and it is the history of this ardent passion which he has bequeathed to us under the title of *Philobiblon*.

This treatise may be called his literary testament, for

a M. Cocheris has evidently blundered here in topography. Bruce never could have reached Salisbury. In one of his irruptions he beseiged the earl of Salisbury in Northumberland, and this must be the origin of the mistake. I have been unable to find in Holinshed, Laigh, Tytler or Aickman any mention of this foray; nor do I find in any gazetteer or other work on the border counties of England or Scotland any notice of the forests of Gideon.—*Ed.*

20 It is almost certain that he did not anticipate Edward's success in France, for in a pastoral letter which he addressed to the priests of his diocese, ordaining that thanksgivings be offered in honor of the naval victory of Ecluse, there is perceptible amidst the most lively joy, the greatest astonishment. (See this letter in the 31st volume of the Surtees collection entitled: Depositions and other ecclesiastical proceedings, 1311 to the reign of Elizabeth, edited by Raine, 1 vol. in 8vo. London, 1845, p. 16.)

21 See a letter of 3d April, 1342, which instructed Richard de Bury and certain other persons to treat with David de Brus. (Rymer, *Fœdera*, tom. II, part II, p. 1191.)

22 See a letter of the 18th August, 1345, in which Bury is named by the king one of the commissioners to preserve the truce concluded with the Scotch, and to settle all questions which may arise in relation thereto. (See Rymer, vol. II, part II, p. 1230.)

he died soon after its completion, on the 14th of April, 1345. He was borne from Auckland, the episcopal residence, on the 22d of the same month, and buried, with great pomp, in the cathedral church of Durham, at the northern corner of the chapel of St. Mary Magdalen. A magnificent marble tomb, now unfortunately destroyed, upon which he was sculptured as clothed in pontifical robes and surrounded by the twelve apostles, marked his last resting place.[23] The church of Durham, as was then the custom, inherited the two horses which transported him to the church, his mule,[24] his sacred ornaments,[25] and his seals.[26]

As to his library, it was, according to the last wishes of the testator, removed to Oxford to the college of Durham, known at the present time as Trinity college. He had prepared an accurate catalogue of it, which up to this time has never been discovered.

The books were at first carefully preserved and fastened with chains, and it was not until the reign of Henry VIII, that they were taken from their shelves and went to enrich the collections in the Baliol college of Duke Humphrey and the physician George Owen.[27]

23 See the description of this monument in the beginning of the chronicle of William de Chambre, published by the Surtees society at London and Edinburgh in 1839, in 8vo, p. 127, et seq.

24 See the *Historiæ Dunelmensis scriptores tres*, Appendix CXXXII, Surtees society's publications.

25 The sacred ornaments possessed by Richard de Bury were very numerous and very rich. They may be seen described in detail in a volume of the publications of the Surtees society, entitled: *Wills and Inventories illustrative of the history, manners, language, statistics, etc., of the Northern Counties of England, from the 11th century downwards*, part I, ch. xvii, p. 25.

26 The custom at Durham then was, that the bishops offered at their deaths, *ad feretrum sancti Cuthberti*, the seals of silver which they used to seal their acts. These seals were then broken in pieces, *sigilla fracta per particulas*, before the officers of the chapter, who consulted upon the use to which they should be put.

The offering of these seals was made at the offertory, and they recited in honor of the dead bishop five *paters* and one *salutatio angelica*. After the offertory, the priest who held the seals handed them to the artificer to be broken up.

Richard de Bury appears to have used two seals. The first is of ordinary form, but the other may be regarded as a *chef d'œuvre* of engraving, and in examining it we cannot fail to admire the taste which governed its design.

Of these two seals, the chapter decided that one should be converted into a cup. This was actually done, and they engraved upon the foot of it the following inscription:

RI. Dunelmensis, quarti, natu Buriensis, hic ciphus
insignis fit præsulis ex tetra sigillis.

27 *Historia et antiquitates universitatis Oxoniensis*, duobus voluminibus comprehensæ. Oxonii, e theatro Sheldoniano, 1674, fol., lib. II, p. 48.

Habent sua fata libelli!

Cotemporary chronicles confirm the favorable impressions of Bury's character, which the perusal of his book will produce. A prelate, pious and charitable, a statesman wise and skillful, a bibliophilist learned and enthusiastic, heknew how to render himself beloved, not for his honors nor his fortune, but for the valuable qualities which distinguished him at once, as a man of God, a man of the state and a man of learning. Surrounded by friends and men of letters,[28] he delighted to discuss some obscure point of philosophy, and, in this, worthy disciple of Aristotle, he failed not to be the first in the assault. His taste for books was but a natural consequence of his ardor for study, and the passion which urged him continually to new acquisitions, was but an imperious desire to enlarge the circle of his acquaintances.

To this passion he owed the honor of the friendship of Petrarch, with whom he became acquainted at Avignon, and not at Rome, as has been affirmed by all his biographers.[29] The existence of this intimacy,

28 Among the distinguished men who habitually enjoyed the company of Richard de Bury, the chronicles mention Thomas Bradwardin, archbishop of Canterbury, Richard Fitz Ralph, archbishop of Armagh, Richard Bentworth, bishop of London, William Seagrave, bishop of Chichester, and Robert Holcot, doctor of theology. This last, very well known by the commentaries upon several books of the Bible which he has left, is regarded by some critics as the author of *Philobiblon*. (See the Bibliographical notice, p. 15.)

29 This friendship with Petrarch, and his mission to the pope, have caused his biographers to suppose that he had visited Italy. They should nevertheless remember, that at the time Richard was ambassador to the Holy See, the pope was at Avignon, where Petrarch lived. As to what he himself says, in his VIIIth chapter, about his mission to the holy father, *ad sedem Romæ*, he is to be understood, I apprehend, as meaning the Roman court, and not the court at Rome. The Roman court could be perfectly well understood as referring to the suite of the pope, wherever it happened to be, whilst the court of Rome has a sense very much more restricted. Besides there can be no doubt in the matter, since John XXII never was in Italy, whatever Mr. Merryweather may say, who seems in his *Bibliomania* to vouch the contrary. Indeed, this error of the English bibliophilist is unhappily not the only one which occurs in his book, and it is deplorable that a work, filled with so much valuable matter as this, should swarm with the grossest and even incredible blunders, to such a degree that even the Latin texts, which are quoted, are sometimes unintelligible. As for instance, in place of *ad librorum latebras libere perscrutandas*, he has *ad libros latebras libere perscruta tandas*; for *percrebuit*, *percreluit*; for *volatilis*, *volatitis*; for *cupiditate languescere*, *cupidite las vestere*. We could easily increase the list, and to amuse my readers, tell them of *nobilissimos monasterios*, of *jucebant*, of *amor excitet* for *amor extaticus*, but the enumeration would be too long, and in making errata, we prefer to confine ourselves to our own; *suum cuique*.

which a similarity of sentiments and tastes had produced, is proven by a letter of the great poet, in which he speaks of Bury as *vir ardentis ingenii.*[30] In reading this letter, one cannot refrain from drawing a comparison between these two great minds. The former, opposing to the gross sensualism of the Romance of the Rose his platonic passion, which he felt for Laura; the latter, offering in contrast to the materialism of the 14th century his noble and unconquerable love of books. Both determined enemies of war and despotism, both enthusiastic friends of peace and liberty, and both leaving to posterity, as a memorial of their attachment to letters, the one to the Republic of Venice, the other to the University of Oxford, the wandering divinities of antiquity, which they had adored during their lives, and which the world did not learn to venerate, until long after they were dead.

30 See the passage of the letter entitled *Tule sive Tyle insula*, and which is very interesting, as it contains the judgment of the greatest writer of the fourteenth century upon a man, who, though born and educated in England, as he himself remarks, was nevertheless one of the most praiseworthy *literati* of his time: "Indocti "ipsum insulæ nomen ignorant: liter- "atis utique clarum nomen insulæ "est: insula vero ipsa non minus ig- "nota, quam vulgo. *Mihi quidem de* "*hac re cum Richardo, quondam Ang-* "*lorum regis cancellario, sermo non* "*otiosus fuit, viro ardentis ingenii nec* "*litterarum inscio, et qui, ut in Bri-* "*tannia genitus atque educatus, abdita-* "*rumque rerum ab adolescentia supra* "*fidem curiosus, talibus præsertim* "*quæstiunculis enodandis aptissimus* "*videretur.* Ille autem, seu quia sic "speraret, seu quia puderet ignoran- "tiam fateri (qui mos hodie multorum "est, qui non intelligunt, quanta mo- "destiæ laus sit homini nato, nec "nosse omnia volenti profiteri in- "genue se nescire, quod nesciat) seu "forte, quod non suspicor, quia hujus "mihi arcani notitiam invideret, re- "spondit, certe se dubitationi meæ "satisfacturum, sed non priusquam "ad libros suos, quorum nemo copi- "osior fuit, in patriam revertisset. "Erat enim, cum in amicitiam ejus "incidi, tractandis domini sui nego- "tiis, apud sedem apostolicam pere- "grinus, ea scilicet tempestate, qua "inter præfatum dominum suum et "Francorum regem prima diuturni "belli semina pullulabant, quæ cru- "entam messem postea protulere. Nec "dum repositæ falces, aut clausa sunt "horrea; sed cum promissor ille meus "abiisset, sive nihil inveniens, sive "noviter injuncti pontificalis officii "gravi munere distractus, quamvis "sæpe literis interpellatus, exspecta- "tioni meæ non aliter quam obstinato "silentio satisfecit. Ita mihi Tyle "amicitia Britannica nihil notior facta "est," etc. (See Franc. Petrarchæ philosophi oratoris et poetæ *Epistolarum* libri XVII, apud Samuelem Crispinum, 1601, 1 vol. 8vo, page 80.)

BIBLIOGRAPHICAL NOTICE.

NOTWITHSTANDING the reputation of *Philobiblon* in the fourteenth century, the manuscripts are not so numerous as would be supposed. There exists in the British Museum one of the fifteenth century in the Harleian library,[1] another in the Cottonian,[2] under the title, *Ricardi de Aungerville Philobiblon.* According to the author of the Catalogue of MSS. of England and Ireland, there exists a manuscript of the work in the Bodleian[3] library (Digby Collection, No. 147); one in the library of Norfolk, at Gresham college, at London[4] (No. 325); one in that of Sidney Sussex, at Canterbury[5] (No. 16); another in that of the college of St. Benedict, in the same city[6] (No. 280); another in that of the college of the Holy Trinity at Oxford[7] (No. 24); and another in that of the college of St. John the Baptist, in the same city[8] (No. 9.) The library of Bishop Cosin, at Durham,[9] that of the dukes of Burgundy,[10] at Brussels, and that of Basle,[11] contain each a copy, all of the 15th century. The Imperial library at Paris possesses three manuscripts of this work. These are those which I

1 See *Cat. Lib. MSS. Biblioth. Harl.*, tom. II, p. 10, No. 3224.

2 MS. P. 158, Cl. Faustina, Cottonian library.

3 See *Cat. Lib. MSS. Angliæ et Hibernæ*, Oxoniæ, 1697, fol., tom. I, part I, p. 84, No. 1748.

4 Ibid, II, I, 81, No. 3224.

5 Ibid, I, III, 103, No. 706.

6 Ibid, I, III, 141, No. 1547.

7 Ibid, I, III, 96, No. 312.

8 Ibid, I, II, 59, No. 1747.

9 This manuscript is in octavo, endorsed VVI. It is a collection containing: 1st. Novum testamentum angliæ versum; 2d. Anticlaudianus; 3d. Alanus de planctu naturæ; 4th. Papa stupor mundi; 5th. Philobiblon Ricardi Almgerville cognominati de Buri quondam episcopi Dunelmensis. The editor of the catalogue thus describes it: "Tractatus hi scripti sunt lineis "continuis, literis mediocribus, acutis, "non malis; ante annos circa 300 fuit "Geo. Davenport." (See *Catalogue of the Library of Durham Cathedral, at various periods from the conquest to the dissolution, including catalogues of the library of the abbey of Hulne, and of the MSS. preserved in the library of bishop Cosin at Durham*, London, 1838, 8vo, p. 177.)

10 See *Cat. des MSS. de la Biblioth. Roy. des Ducs de Bourgogne*, Brussels, 1842, tom. I, p, 15, No. 738.

11 It is a MS. in 4to, endorsed A6. See Hænel. *Cat. MSS.*, col. 527.

have collated with the printed text and of which I have made use in my various readings.

The first is a small quarto, bound in wood, covered with parchment, upon which may still be seen the marks of clasps. It makes part of the *fonds* St. Victor and bears the number 797. It is a collection of theological treatises. The *Philobiblon* occupies the first 45 folios, and the writing is less ancient than that of the succeeding works. After the *amen*, we read: "Hunc "librum acquisivit Monasterio Sancti Victoris prope "Parisius frater Johannes La Masse, dum esset prior "ejusdem ecclesiæ."

The second is a folio, bound in red morocco, of which the lids are ornamented with the shield of France, and upon the back of which are seen L, interlaced, and the title: *Remigius in apocalyps. et alia opusc. variorum.* It, in fact, contains this treatise, as well as some homilies, sermons, &c. It originally bore the number 4107, and now it makes part of the Ancient Latin *fonds* under the number 2454.

The third is of the fourteenth century, and is written upon parchment. It is a folio MS., bound in red morocco, with the arms of Colbert upon the sides. In the library of this minister it bore the number 2167; now it is in the Imperial library, in the same *fonds* as the preceding, and is marked 3352 C.

Another manuscript, which seems very important, formerly belonged to Fabricius. It shows the date of the completion of *Philobiblon*, and we should rejoice that this celebrated bibliographer has preserved for us this sentence:[12] "*In manuscripto codice hujus philo-* "*biblii quod habeo,*" says he, "*leguntur hæc verba.* "Explicit Philobiblon domini Ricardi de Muiegervile, "cognominati de Bury, quondam episcopi Dimelmensis. "Completus autem tractatus iste in manerio nostro de "Aukelande XXIV die Januarii, anno domini millesimo "trecentesimo XLIII, ætatis nostræ quinquagesimo octavo.

12 See Fabricius, *Bibl. Lat. mediæ et infimæ ætatis*, lib. II, tom. II, p. 307, col. 2

"præcise completæ; pontificatus vero nostri anno undecimo finiente, ad laudem Dei feliciter."

According to the description which Mr. Merryweather has given of the manuscript of the Cottonian library, I am inclined to believe that it is the same as that of Fabricius, but as I have not seen it, it is impossible for me to establish their identity.

To conclude, there are two other manuscripts to which are attached a peculiar interest, as they deprive Richard de Bury of the honor of having composed the *Philobiblon.*

The first of these manuscripts is at the college of Corpus Christi at Oxford,[13] under the number 1634. One observes upon it the following note: *Philobiblon R. de Bury, quem librum compilavit Rob. Holcot ordinis Prædicatorum, sub nomine dicti episcopi.* The second is found at Venice,[14] and is entitled: *Philobiblon magistri Roberti Holkoth, Angli, ordinis Prædicatorum.*

As Holcot was a black friar, Echard has not failed to profit by the note of the first manuscript and the title of the second, in drawing from them a conclusion favorable to the literary history of the Dominicans.[15] It is certainly impossible to prove beyond question the title of Richard de Bury to the authorship of this work, but I believe nevertheless that Echard and his partisans, Leland and Fabricius, have deceived themselves in this matter, and that they have not thoroughly read the *Philobiblon;* otherwise they would have noted the character essentially autobiographic of its composition, and would have taken good care not to add to the literary laurels of Holcot, at the expense of Bury.

Holcot was one of the most intimate acquaintances of the Bishop of Durham; he may have copied many times the work of his friend and even set his own name to it. An *Ego Holcot scripsi* would be enough to cause a scribe,

13 See *Cat. lib. MSS. Angl. et Hibern.* fol., Oxoniæ, 1667, tom. I, part II, p. 53.

14 See *Bibliothecæ Venetæ manuscr. pub. et priv., quibus diversi scriptores hactenus incogniti recensentur*, opera Jacobi Phillippi Thomasini, Utini, 1650 4to, p. 27.

15 See *Scriptores ordinis Prædicatorum recensiti notisque historicis et criticis illustrati*, etc., fol., 1719, tom. I, p. 631, art. Holkot.

some time afterwards to believe himself authorized to write a note similar to that which is found upon the manuscript of the college of Corpus Christi, at Oxford, and thus to originate, through his ignorance, the idea of a pseudonym.

The ancient editions of the *Philobiblon* are not less rare than the manuscripts.

The first edition was in 1473. It is a small, thin book in octavo of 48 folios, having 26 lines of gothic writing upon each page. Below the *amen*, one reads: *Explicit Philobiblon sci. liber de amore librorum. Colonie impressus, anno domini M.CCCC.LXXIII.*

The Imperial library possesses in its reserve two copies of this edition,[16] and it is to the courtesy of M. Ravenel that I owe the privilege of examining this precious bibliographic treasure, unknown to Panzer and Quetif.

Ten years later, in 1483,[17] the brothers, John and Conrad Hust, printed at Spire a new edition, which seems to be much more rare than the preceding one, for no public depository at Paris[18] contains it. According to M. J. Ch. Brunet, this edition is a small gothic quarto of 39 leaves of 34 lines to the page. It has for title:[19] *Richardi de Buri dilmelmensis episcopi, Phylobyblon, de querimoniis librorum, omnibus litterarum amatoribus perutile. Spiræ, per Johannem et Conradum Hust, inclytæ Spirensis urbis librariis, MCCCCLXXXIII.*

Two new editions appeared at Paris in the year 1500, one under the direction of Jean Petit, the other of Badius Ascensius. The first is entitled simply: *Richardi de Bury Philobiblon;* the second: *Richardi de Bury Philobiblon, sive de amore librorum et institutione bibliothecarum tractatus. Parisiis*, 1500.

16 There are wanting the 10th and 15th leaves in one of the copies.

17 Peignot, in his *Repertoire Bibliographique* (p. 379), reads 1473, and inquires, in consequence, which of the two editions has priority over the other. Had he read the two editions he would not have committed this error.

18 See Maittaire, *Annal. Typogr.*, tom. III, p. 22. It was already very rare in the time of Oudin, who says, in speaking of it: "*Cujus exemplaria* "*hodie rarissima sunt.*" (See Cas. Oudini, *Commentarius de scriptoribus ecclesiæ antiquis*, etc., tom. III, col. 937.)

19 See *Manuel du Libraire*, tom. I, p. 502, ed. 1842.

In 1599 Thomas James published a fifth edition at Oxford, with a title very much more extended: *Philobiblon Richardi Dunelmensis, sive de amore librorum, et institutione bibliothecæ, tractatus pulcherrimus. Ex collatione cum variis manuscriptis editio jam secunda; cui accessit appendix de manuscriptis Oxoniensibus, omnia hæc, opera et studio T. I. novi coll. in alma academia Oxoniensi socii. B. P. N. Non quæro quod mihi utile est, sed quod multis. Oxoniæ, excudebat Josephus Barnesius*, 1599. This edition is a quarto, and prefaced by a letter full of sense and spirit from Thomas James to the celebrated Thomas Bodley.

According to Fabricius, the *Philobiblon* was printed the following year at London. This edition, concerning which all the bibliographers are silent, seems to be very rare. If it exists, it is the last one in which this work has been published separately from others. In fact, from this time, it is no where to be found, except in the collections of Goldast[20] and of Maderus.[21] These two collections and the edition of Thomas James have been the most instrumental in giving extended circulation to the *Philobiblon* during the course of the sixteenth and seventeenth centuries. It is moreover mentioned by many authors of that age in their writings. William Fabricius gives almost the same title to his dialogue[22] upon sacred and profane literature, which he dedicated to

20 This collection is entitled: *Philologicarum* epistolarum centuria una diversorum arenatis literis doctissimorum virorum, in qua veterum theologorum, jurisconsultorum, medicorum, philosophorum, historicorum, poetarum, grammaticorum, libris difficillimis locis vel emendantur vel illustrantur: insuper Richardi de Buri, episcopi Dunelmensis, etc., *Philobiblon*.........omnia nunc primum edita ex bibliotheca Melchioris Haiminsfeldii Goldasti, etc. Francofurti, anno 1610, 8vo, pp. 400.

21 See the title of this collection: *De Bibliothecis* atque archivis virorum clarissimorum libelli et commentationes, cum præfatione de scriptis et bibliothecis antediluvianis. Antehac edidit Joachimus Joan. Maderus secundam editionem curavit I. A. S. D. Helmstadii, 1702, 4to. The *Philobiblon* is found in a supplement to this work, entitled: De Bibliothecis nova accessio collectioni Maderianæ adjuncta a I. A. S. D. Helmstadii, 1703.

22 See the title of this work: Gulielmi Fabritii Lodunatis canonici Pyctaviensis *Philobiblius*, sive dialogus de studio divinarum et humanarum literarum, ad eruditissimum virum Gulielmum Budæum libellorum supplicum in regia magistrum-Pyctavii, ex officina Marnesiorum fratrum, 1536, 4to.

William Budæ.[a] G. Salden,[23] Lomeier,[24] and Herm. Conringius,[25] cite it many times. Naudé gives extracts[26] from it, and Ant. Possevin,[27] Richard Smith,[28] Du Boulay,[29] Wood,[30] Barnes,[31] Cas. Oudin,[32] Tanner,[33] Fabricius,[34] Moreri,[35] each dedicate to it a special article in their respective works.

In our days, Surtees,[36] Petit-Radel,[37] Hallam,[38] Dibdin,[39] Lud. Lalanne,[40] the *Archæologia*,[41] the *Serapeum* and the *American Publishers' Circular*,[42] have recalled

a In the edition published by Bohn, London, 1748, Bury is spoken of at pp. 29 and note, 185, and 186 and note.—*Ed.*

23 See Gulielmi Saldeni, Ultrajectini, *De libris* varioque eorum usu et abusu libri duo, cum indicibus necessariis. Amstelodami, 1686, 8vo, p. 265.

24 See Johannis Lomeieri ecclesiastæ Zutphaniensis, *De Bibliothecis* liber singularis, apud Mader. Collect. access. Helmst., 1705, p. 222.

25 See Hermanni Conringii *De Bibliotheca* augusta, quæ est in arca Wolfenbuttelensi ad illustr. et generosum Joan. Christ. L. Bar. a Boineburg Epistola, qua simul de omni re bibliothecaria disseritur. Apud Maderum, *De Bibliothesis*, etc., Helmst., 1702, p. 190.

26 *Advis pour dresser une bibliotheque*. 2d edition, Paris, 1664, 8vo, p. 97, and Gabr. Naudæi parisiensis, *Dissertatio* de instruenda bibliotheca, etc., a Gallico in Latinum idioma translata. Apud Mad. *Collect. Access.*, Helmst., 1703, p. 110.

27 See Ant. Possevini mantuami, societ. Jesu, *Apparatus sacri*, Colonia Agrippa, 1608, fol., tom. II, p. 323.

28 See *Florum historiæ eccles. gentis Angl.* libri VII, fol., Parisiis, 1654, p. 313.

29 See *Historiæ universitatis Parisiensis*, auct. Cæsare Egassio Bulæ, tom. IV, Parisiis, fol., p. 988.

30 See *Historia et antiquitates universitatis* Oxoniensis, 2 vols. fol., Oxon., 1674–1675, tom. II, p. 48.

31 See *The History of that most Victorious Monarch, Edward First*, King of England and France, etc., etc., Cambridge, 1688, fol., p. 83, 114, 120 and 328.

32 See *Comment. de Scriptoribus* ecclesiæ antiquis illorumque scriptis, etc., Lipsiæ, 1722, tom. III, col. 936.

33 See *Bibliotheca Britannico-Hibernica*, sive de scriptoribus, etc., Lond., fol., 1748.

34 See *Bibliotheca Latina* mediæ et infimæ ætatis, 6 vols. 4to, Patavi, 1754, tom. I, p. 307.

35 The *Historical Dictionary*, or the curious mingling of sacred and profane history, etc., by Louis Moreri. Paris, 1759, fol., tom. I, art. *Aungerville*.

36 The *History and Antiquities* of the County Palatine of Durham, by Robert Surtees, London, 1816, 3 vols., fol., tom. I.

37 *Researches upon Ancient and Modern Libraries*, down to the foundation of the Mazarin library, Paris, 1819, 8vo, p. 133 and 258.

38 *L'Europe au moyen age*, translated from the English of Henry Hallam, by Borghers and P. Dudouit, 4 vols., 8vo, Paris, 1837, tom. V, p. 143.

39 Dibdin, *Bibliomania*, p. 247.

40 *Curiosites Bibliographique*, Paris, 1845, 8vo, p. 198, et seq.

41 *Archæologia*, or miscellaneous tracts relating to antiquity, published by the Society of Antiquaries, 34 vols., 4to, London, 1770–1852, toms. X and XXVII.

42 *American Publishers' Circular and Literary Gazette*, New York, 1855, vol. I, No. of the 8th December, article entitled: Books before printing.

to the minds of bibliophilists the existence of this singular treatise, which has not failed to receive the honor of an English translation.

This translation, which seems at present to be very rare, is unknown to most amateurs. I have made every effort in my power to procure it, but unfortunately have not succeeded. Lord Campbell says, in speaking of it: "I have chiefly followed an English translation, pub-"lished anonymously in the year 1832; printed for "that very worthy bookseller, my friend, Thomas Rodd, "Great Newport street."[43] By whom was it made? Lord Campbell does not seem to know, and it would have been impossible for me to state, had not the *spirituel* Charles Knight, in his last work, entitled: *The Old Printer and the Modern Press*,[44] mentioned both the translation and the name of the translator, John B. Inglis.[45] This translation, which probably would have been very useful to me to consult, is indeed so little known, that a celebrated English bibliophilist, Thomas Lowndes, has not mentioned it in the article which he has devoted to Richard de Bury.[46] He names only the edition published at Oxford in 1599, and announces that there would shortly appear a new edition, which would be accompanied by notes, various readings, and an English translation, by Mr. Edward R. Poole; "A new edition," he says, "of this curious tract is preparing for publication, "with an English translation, notes, and various read-"ings, by Edward R. Poole, B. A." We believe we can assert that this last has never appeared.

43 *Lives of the Chancellors*, vol. I, p. 219.

44 London, 1854, 12mo.

45 According to Charles Knight, the title of the translation is: *Philobiblon, a treatise of the love of books, by Richard de Bury, translated by John B. Inglis, London*, 1832. I have since found, in the Bibliomania of Merryweather, the same information.

46 See *The Bibliographer's Manual of English Literature*, etc., London, Pickering, 1834, vol. I, p. 309, col. 1.

CRITICAL NOTICE.

THE *Philobiblon* of Richard de Bury is what is called by the English in our days an *autobiography*. It is perhaps the first literary monument of the middle ages of this kind, in which the author intermingles his own thoughts and the incidents of his life; a particular by no means the least original of those which characterize this singular book, which we now lay before the public.

Without being one of those men whom nature creates in times not fitted for them, Richard de Bury, nevertheless, seems to merit higher eulogies than all other writers of his country, we had almost said, of his age. His work, it is true, is filled with conceits, and one undoubtedly finds there an affectation in the language, which was so much the fashion at a later period, at the court of Elizabeth; but if the form is occasionally absurd, the substance is creditable, and worthy of our admiration.

It is one of the greatest merits of our author, that he recognized the downward tendency of his age, and has described it. In his prologue, he shows us students discouraged by poverty, abandoning letters for the mechanical arts, and seeking that fortune which science so rarely bestows. He points out to us that aptitude for trade which had already begun to influence the English character, which would one day be the source of England's wealth. To combat this unworthy inclination, he strives to infuse into students his own passion for books; he endeavors to prove to them that books are above all the things of earth, above the king, wine, and women. We doubt whether those to whom he addressed himself were sufficiently wise to share so exclusive an enthusiasm.

We prefer the comparison which he institutes between books and professors. "They are masters," says he, "who instruct us without birch or ferule, without "clamor or without rage, without clothes, and without "fee. If we approach them, we do not find them asleep; "if we interrogate them, they do not conceal their ideas; "if we mistake them, they do not grumble; if we com-"mit a blunder they do not mock us."[1] One cannot fail to observe in this comparison, a satire pointed at his teachers. If, as we see from the above, he had not forgotten their conduct, the following passage shows that he as clearly remembered their lèssons: "The truth," he says, "presents itself to our minds without interruption, "in a permanent manner, and passing by the spiritual "path of the eyes into the vestibule of common sense "and the entrance hall of the imagination, it penetrates "into the palace of the understanding, and there allies "itself with memory to engender the eternal truth of "thought."[2]

These two extracts suffice to show the quintessential language of our bibliophile. His style, which he says was formed in the modern school, sometimes brilliant, abounding in metaphor and vigorous, but always clerical and mystical, errs oftenest in childish elaboration of trifling conceits and playing upon words, a surfeit of superfluous quotations, and a turgidity sometimes ridiculous and so excessive as to weaken itself, as says Montaigne, by its own extravagance.

He demonstrates the unspeakable value of books but to draw therefrom this ruinous consequence: "Except "from fear of being cheated by the booksellers, we "should recoil from no sacrifice whatever, where the "occasion seems favorable; for, if wisdom," adds he, "an infinite treasure in the eyes of men, gives them "their value and that value is too great to be expressed, "it is impossible their price should be too high."[3]

1 See the *Philobiblon*, chap. I.

2 Ibid.

3 See the *Philobiblon*, chap. III.

What a charming conclusion! And does it not deserve that in our age, in which celebrities are created expressly that statues may be erected to them, the booksellers should unite in raising one to the author of so worthy a maxim?

The fourth chapter is undoubtedly the most important of the *Philobiblon*. It is a striking picture of the moral and intellectual degradation of the regular clergy of the fourteenth century, a picture unhappily too faithful, in which the disorderly manners prevalent in the monasteries, and the ignorance and indolence of their inmates are set forth with as much force as originality.

Whatever may be our preconceived desire to find this an exaggerated description, we cannot forget that these accusations are not made by a Guillaume de Lorris, a John de Meun, a Gautier Map or a Langland, but by a man of rank, a learned ecclesiastic; in a word, a prelate, who occupied in the political world a position at least equal to that which he had attained in the church. Accordingly, the doubt which we feel in reading the satires of those first named can no longer exist, when we listen to the lamentations of the latter. Besides, the value we put upon an assertion is always proportioned to the esteem we have for its author, and in this case, we cannot question the elevated sentiments which inspired the pious bishop in making his accusations. As he cannot, however, keep his style up to the height of his indignation, it results that the reader is rather amused than moved, and smiles when he ought to censure.

It is impossible, in truth, not to be diverted by his unhappy history of a book, as related by itself. Its misfortunes in the monasteries; the hate which woman, *bestia bipedalis*, bears it; its miserable condition; its maladies; the operations to which it is compelled to submit by the commentators, the translators, and the plagiarists, make up the incidents of this comic and witty account, as quaint in its style as in its ideas, and portraying with happy correctness the gross manners which it is forced to paint.

The two following chapters are a continuation of his diatribes against the monks, and he is not less severe in his criticism of their moral imperfections than he had been in rebuking their idleness. He is filled with indignation at their Epicurean life; he exposes the joys entirely earthly of their monachal estate, and he cannot pardon them for preferring wine to study, "the *Liber* "*Bacchus* to the *Liber Codex*." He conjures them to change their lives, to give better examples to youth, to the end that it may become "Socratic in its morals and peri-"patetic in its doctrine." Could a partisan of Plato and Aristotle close his peroration better?

But from these upbraidings and exhortations, he is diverted by a consideration of the disasters which war and despotism bring upon letters and books. He deplores with bitterness the irreparable losses occasioned by the bloody contests of the ancient world, and invokes for his own times the god of peace. It is in reading this chapter, where the author collects together examples from pagan and Judaic antiquity, that one may exclaim with Dibdin: "What can be more delightful to a lover of his "country's intellectual reputation than to find such a "character as De Bury, in such an age of war and blood-"shed, uniting the calm and mild character of a legislator "with the sagacity of a philosopher, and the elegant-"mindedness of a scholar."[4]

Chapter viii is unquestionably the most interesting, as it gives to us a view of the author himself. It is the part of *Philobiblon* really autobiographic. There only can we appreciate the character of the bibliophilist; there the full expression of his love for books bursts forth; and there, in spite of himself, he makes known to us, what we would never have dared to affirm of ourselves—that any means whatever seemed to him justifiable in acquiring them. Where he frankly avows that

4 Dibdin, *Bibliomania*, 3d ed., London, 1842, p. 168.

he was sufficiently powerful to injure or protect, is it not made evident that his passion hurried him to the point of transgressing, when necessary, the laws of honesty?

The chronicler has preserved for us the record of one of these extortions, if one may give a name so severe to the result of one of his compromises with heaven and his conscience.

While he was keeper of the privy seal, Richard de Wallingford, abbot of St. Albans, instituted a suit against the inhabitants of that borough to recover certain properties which the monks claimed as belonging to them. Richard de Bury assisted the latter with all his influence, and judgment was rendered in their favor. The abbot immediately convened the chapter, and detailed the secret services which the keeper of the privy seal had performed for them on this occasion. He gave them to understand that it was impossible not to recompense him, and that the only means to render themselves agreeable to him were to present him with some of the manuscripts in the library of the convent, and to permit him to purchase such of them as he desired. The chapter agreed with the abbot and offered to Bury a Terence, a Virgil, a Quintilian and the treatise of St. Jerome against Rufinus. The volumes sold to him were thirty-two in number, and were purchased for fifty pounds.[5] This transaction unfortunately did not please all the monks of the convent, and some of them not unreasonably denounced it on the ground that to aggrandize its domains, the abbot plundered the convent of its literary treasures. But these remonstrances were in vain, and Richard de Bury retained possession of his manuscripts.

This method of forming a library is sufficiently common among bibliophilists, and Naudé, in his *Advis*

5 The British Museum possesses a manuscript containing the *Ententicus* of John of Salisbury, where may be read this note: Hunc librum fecit dominus Symon, abbas Sancti Albani, quem postea venditum domino Ricardo de Bury, episcopo Dunelmensi, emit Michael, abbas Sancti Albani ab executoribus prædicti episcopi. A. D. 1345. (See Warton, *Hist. of English Poetry*, p. cxlvii; Merryweather, *Bibliomania in the Middle Ages*, etc., 1 vol., 12mo., London, 1849, p. 71 et seq.)

pour dresser une bibliothèque, far from censuring, on the contrary recommends it. "The third means of collect- "ing books," says he, "is one of those practiced by "Richard de Bury, bishop, high chancellor and trea- "surer, which consists in publishing and making known "to every one the love which one has for books, and "the great desire that possesses one to collect a library, "for this being made generally and widely known, it is "unquestionable that if he who has this design, is in "sufficient credit and authority to be of service to his "friends, there will be none of them who will not be "eager to present to him the most curious books which "fall into their hands; who will not very willingly give "him access to the libraries of themselves and their "friends; who, in short, will not aid and contribute to "his purpose, everything within their power. All "which is very well remarked by the said Richard de "Bury in his own words, which I the more willingly "here transcribe, as his book is very rare and one of "those which is being lost by our negligence."[6]

In the chapters which follow, Richard de Bury endeavors to demonstrate the superiority of the ancients over the moderns. He labors to prove that the most perfect models are found in antiquity, and that the poets and fabulists ought not to be censured for the faults of which they are accused.[7] He is of the opinion of Lafontaine:

Une morale nue apporte de l'ennui,
Le conte fait passer le precepte avec lui.

The importance which he gives to the Greek language, is a fact which we cannot silently pass over. It is by no means the least of his merits in our eyes, that he was able so clearly to perceive the unquestionable influence, not only of the Hellenic genius upon the Roman mind, but also of its philosophy upon the Christian religion.

6 See *Advis pour dresser une bibliotheque*, presente a Monseigneur le president de Mesme, par Naude, seconde edition, revue, corrigee et augmentee, Paris, 1664, 8vo, p. 97.

7 See *Philobiblon*, chap. xiii.

"What," says he, "would their Sallust, their Cicero, "their Boëtius, their Macrobius, their Lactantius, the "whole Latin cohort in fine, have produced, had they "not been acquainted with the labors of the Athenians "and the master pieces of the Greeks? Jerome, skilled "in the three languages of scripture, St. Ambrose, St. "Augustine who nevertheless avows his hatred of the "Greek literature, and even St. Gregory, who posi-"tively affirms that he knew nothing of it, would have "certainly contributed little to the doctrine of the "church, had they not borrowed from the more learned "Greeks."[8]

This taste for both Greek and Roman antiquity, which shows itself so clearly and decidedly at the commencement of the fourteenth century, is a proof the more, that the classic writers were during the middle ages far more widely studied than is generally believed. And here it may be permitted us to remark, that there has not been a sufficiently just appreciation of the literary epochs, the little revivals, if we may so express ourselves, which flashed up, at intervals, during the middle ages. Like every great revolution, the grand revival of letters was but the result of a train of events commencing long before, and it is not just to say that at that moment antiquity was discovered as if by magic. Antiquity had never been lost. It had only been little attended to and often misunderstood. For our ancestors Scipio was a knight clothed in armor, the lance in his hand, helmet upon his head; Cicero an advocate of Parliament; Virgil a minstrel. They could not imagine other manners, other customs, other dresses, than their own. This mode, little critical, of looking upon antiquity, would naturally hinder them from comprehending it, as it should be comprehended. Nevertheless this disturbing influence did not entirely shut them out from a knowledge of the *chefs d'œuvre* which they had in their possession. In an age much nearer to us,

8 Ibid, chap. x.

Athalia in a hoop petticoat did not hinder the spectators from applauding the dramas of Racine, and we still profoundly admire, despite the anachronisms of costume, the *Nozze di Cana* of Paul Veronese.

It would be, moreover, unjust to judge of the knowledge of antiquity in the middle ages from the numerous commentaries upon Aristotle, Hippocrates and Galen, which encumber the shelves of our libraries. These are often but exercises from the copy books of scholars, and consequently cannot serve as a guide in coming to any accurate conclusion upon so important a point of literary history.

In examining the treatises of professors then high in public estimation and the letters of the most celebrated authors, we find traces of a sounder judgment, and one, which although led astray by false ideas, often gives proofs of sufficiently solid erudition.

In the ninth century, the attention of the select few were turned towards antiquity. In his description of the library of York cathedral, the celebrated Alcuin[9] enumerates the classic authors then most esteemed.

Illic invenies veterum vestigia Patrum
Quidquid habet pro se *Latio Romanus* in orbe.
Græcia vel quidquid transmisit clara *Latinis :*
Hebraicus vel quod populus bibit imbre superno
Africa lucifluo vel quidquid lumine sparsit.
Quod Pater *Hieronymus*, quod sensit *Hilarius*, atque
Ambrosius præsul, simul *Augustinus*, et ipse
Sanctus *Athanasius*, quod *Orosius* edit avitus :
Quidquid *Gregorius* summus docet, et *Leo* papa ;
Basilius quidquid, *Fulgentius* atque coruscant.
Cassiodorus item, *Chrysostomus* atque *Johannes*.
Quidquid et *Althelmius* docuit, quid *Beda* magister,
Quæ *Victorinus* scripsere, *Boëtius :* atque
Historici veteres, *Pompeius*, *Plinius*, ipse
Acer *Aristoteles*, rhetor quoque *Tullius* ingens.
Quid quoque *Sedulius*, vel quid canit ipse *Juvencus*,
Alcuinus et *Clemens*, *Prosper*, *Paulinus*, *Arator*,
Quid *Fortunatus*, vel quid *Lactantius* edunt :

9 See B. Flacci Albini seu Alcuini *Opera*, 1777, fol., tom. II, p. 257, col. 1, *Poema de pontificibus et sanctis ecclesiæ Eboracensis.*

Quæ *Maro Virgilius*, *Statius*, *Lucanus*, et *auctor*
Artis grammaticæ vel quid scripsere magistri;
Quid *Probus* atque *Focas*, *Donatus*, *Priscianusve*,
Servius, *Euticius*, *Pompeius*, *Comminianus*.
Invenies alios perplures, lector, ibidem
Egregios studiis, arte et sermone magistros,
Plurima qui claro scripsere volumina sensu:
Nomina sed quorum præsenti in carmine scribi
Longius est visum, quam plectri postulet usus.

Loup de Ferriere,[10] Raban Maur,[11] Freculphus[12] and Photius fill their works with quotations from the Greeks and Latins, quotations the more precious that they bring to our knowledge, oftentimes, works now destroyed or lost. Thus in the tenth century, the learned Sylvester II speaks of the *Republic* of Cicero, which, four hundred years later, Petrarch laments that he could not bring again to light.[13]

What has been said of civilization, may be applied to the progress of scholarship. It advances in a spiral line. In truth, at the moment when it seems to revive and arrive at a certain degree of development, it, all at once, swerves from its course and vanishes. One would say that intellect, exhausted by its very fecundity, refused to conceive or produce.

After the ninth century, a decline makes itself perceived, though not so universal as might be supposed;[14] and it was not until the twelfth century that literary research again came into favor.

Pierre le Chantre, Peter of Blois, and the celebrated John of Salisbury, added to the list of authors already known, Herodotus, Tibullus, Quintus Curtius, Esop,

10 Cicero, Sallust, Virgil, Horace, Cæsar, Trajan, Pompey, Valerius Maximus, Quintilian, Suetonius, Aulus Gellius, Servius, Macrobius, Cassiodorus, Boetius, Priscian. (See Petit-Radel, *Researches in the Libraries of Paris*, 1819, 8vo.)

11 Homer, Aristotle, Cato, Ennius, Plautus, Lucretius, Varro, Ovid, Persius, Lucan, Pliny, Statius, Josephus, Juvenal, Martial, Apuleius.

12 Dion Cassius, Plato, Cornelius Nepos, Pomponius Mela, Tacitus, Ptolemy, Eusebius of Cæsarea, Justin, Egesippus, Tatianus, Clement of Alexandria, Archelaus, Anatolius of Alexandria, etc.

13 See Gerberti, *Epistola*, XXXVII, p. 681.

14 See, on this subject, a very interesting note of the learned Dom. Petri in his report of a literary mission to England, pamph. 8vo, p. 11.

Isocrates, Petronius, Epictetus, etc. The convent of Citeaux possessed at that time a *Corpus Poetarum*,[15] which comprised, beside the Latin poets, a translation in Latin verse of parts of the *Iliad*, a circumstance which is opposed to the belief generally held, that the West had no knowledge of the poems of Homer until the fourteenth century, through the labours of Petrarch and the translations of Leontus-Pilate. William of Meerbeke, a Dominican, who lived at the close of the twelfth century, was a Grecian, Latinist and Arabist.[16] Geoffrey of Waterford and Vitellion, his cotemporaries, also possessed a knowledge of these three languages, and the latter even goes so far as to characterize them respectively, as verbose, involved, and poor. "Libros "itaque veterum tibi super hoc negotio perquirenti "occurrit tædium verbositatis arabicæ, implicationis "græcæ, paucitas quoque enarrationis latinæ,"[17]

But an incident which manifests in a striking manner the false ideas of antiquity entertained by some minds, and which, at the same time, illustrates the humorous side of English character, has been preserved to us in the account of Gervais de Tilbury, according to whom, an English traveller came to demand of Roger, king of Sicily, permission to take home the bones of Virgil, that he might interrogate them concerning magic.[18]

Virgil and magic, what a strange and absurd collocation of words and ideas! but yet what a characteristic jumble! How natural in an age when Cupid, graven on an antique, is taken for the archangel Michael and surrounded in consequence by a biblical inscription, *Ecce mitto angelum meum*,[19] and when Socrates, having upon his head Minerva's helmet, is transformed into a

15 This MS. is in the library of Dijon. See *Journ. des Sav.*, year 1839, p. 42.

16 See *Hist. Litt.*, vol. XXI.

17 See Vitellionis περι οπτικῆς quam vulgo perspectivam vocant, lib. x, Nuremburg, 1535, fol.

18 *Otia imperialia* inter Liebnitzii *Scriptores Brunsvic.* etc., etc., fol., vol. I, p. 1002.

19 Seal of the abbot of the monastery of St. Stephen of Caen.

Holy Virgin, with the inscription, *Ave Maria, gratia plena!*[20]

Antiquity and sorcery, paganism and the Bible, nothing could be more characteristic of an age when Plato is reconciled with Aristotle, and the latter disguised by Avicenna and Averroes serves the defenders of Christianity as a champion!

In spite of this confusion which prevailed in its ideas, the thirteenth century felt nevertheless the effects of the revival of the twelfth. The study of antiquity became popular in the narrow circle of the men of letters of that time, and one encounters in their writings, at every step, evident traces of its powerful influence upon their intellects.

Thus Vital de Blois employs himself upon the *Aulularia* and *Amphytrion* of Plautus;[21] William of Blois imitates a poem of Menander newly translated into Latin;[22] and Geoffrey of Waterford translated into French Dares and the Roman history of Eutropius.[23] Under this influence, Philip Gautier, in his *Alexandriad*, a metrical version of Quintus Curtius, attempts to imitate Lucan;[24] the historian Rigord commences his chronicle with quotations from Virgil and Horace,[25] and Guillaume le Breton, in his *Phillipiad*, takes Ovid as a model.[26] Basingstoke made a voyage to Athens to learn Greek, and his countryman Robert Grossetete, the celebrated bishop of Lincoln, imported Greek manuscripts from Athens to form a magnificent library,[27] which he afterwards presented to the Franciscans at Oxford. He has left us, as proofs of his learning, translations of Dionysius the Areopagite, Damascenus and Suidas.

20 Seal of the church of Noyon.

21 *Hist. Litt. de la France*, tom. XXII p. 40.

22 Ibid, vol. XXII, p. 52.

23 Ibid, vol. XVI, p. 141, and vol. XX, p. 216.

24 This poem, which was many times reprinted in the sixteenth century, had great success during the middle ages. See *Hist. Litt. de la France*, vol. XVI, and Fabricius, *Bibl. Latin, mediæ et infimæ ætatis*, lib. III.

25 See *Rec. des Histor. de France*, tom. XXVII, p. 1.

26 See Ibid, p. 117.

27 See R. Bacon, *De Utilitate Scientiarum*, cap. xxxix.

Without enlarging upon Papias and Guiot de Provins, who in his *Bible* cites certain of the ancient writers, we will mention the anonymous author of the *Vocabula a Poetis Usurpata*,[28] and, above all, Vincent de Beauvais, the great encyclopædist of the thirteenth century, who was acquainted with almost all the writers of antiquity.[29] But the learning of Vincent de Beauvais was not then common, and his contemporary scholars had not generally pushed their studies so far. The fable entitled *Le Department des Livres*, which we insert here, will show that, on the contrary, the works of the ancients were then far from constituting the majority of classic books.

Chascuns enquiert et veut savoir
Que je ai fet de mon avoir,
Et comment je suis si despris
Que n'ai chape ne mantiau gris,
Cote, ne sorcot, ne tabart,
Tout est alé à male part.
Li tremeriaus[30] m'a abatu,
Par ma folie ai tout perdu,
Tout mon avoir et toz mes livres
Grant pieça que j'en sui delivres.
En duel ai torné mon revel,
Quar je cuit que il n'aist chastel
En France que je n'i alaisse,
Et de mes livres n'i lessaisse.
A Gandelus lez La Ferte
La lessai-je mon *A B C*
Et ma *patenostre* à Soisson,
Et mon *Credo* à Monloon,

28 MS. de la Biblioth. imper. No. 7598 (*anc. fonds latin*).

29 Greek authors (books attributed to Mercurius Trismegistus, Æsculapius, Musæus, etc.), Hesiod, Homer, Alcman, Esop, Thales, Anaximenes, Empedocles, Ocellus Lucanus, Æschylus, Anaxagoras, Protagoras, Gorgias. Archytas of Tarentum, Herodotus, Sophocles, Euripides, Socrates, Democritus, Hippocrates, Xenophon, Ctesias, Plato, Speusippus, Eudoxus, Pytheas, Aristotle, Demosthenes, Xenocrates, Menander, Theophrastus, Metrodorus, Epicurus, Zeno, Diocles, Praxagoras, Erasistratus, Heraclitus, Euclid, Aratus, Eratosthenes, Hipparchus, Polybius, Panætius, Nicander, Posidonius.

Latin authors: Plautus, Ennius, Cæcilius, Accius, Terence, Cato the elder, Julius Cæsar, Cicero, Nigidius, Cornelius Nepos, Varro, Gallus, Tibullus, Virgil, Horace, Ovid, Manilius, and Vitruvius.

As to the later Greek and Latin writers, the list would be too long, and the reader is referred to vol. XVIII of the *Hist. Litt. de la France*, p. 483, whence we have taken the list of names cited above.

30 Game of hazard.

Et mes *set siaumes* à Tornai
Mes *quinze siaumes* à Cambrai,
Et mon *sautier* à Besençon,
Et mon *kalendier* à Dijon.
Puis m'en revint par Pontarlie ;
Iluec vendi ma *litanie*,
Et si bui au vin mon *messel*,
A la ville où l'en fet le sel
Aus espices à Monpellier
Lessai-je mon *antefinier ;*
Mes *legendes* et mon *greel*[31]
Lessai-je à Dun le Chastel.
Mes *livres de Divinité*
Perdi à Paris la cite,
Et cels d'*art* et cels de *fisique*,
Et mes *conduis*[32] et ma *musique*,
Grant partie de mes auctors
Lessai à Saint-Martin à Tors :
Et mes *doves* est á Orliens,
Et mes *chacones* à Amiens :
A Chartres mes *Théodeles*[33]
A Roen mes *Aviones.*[34]
Mes *Ovides* est à Namur,
Ma philosophie à Saumur,
A Bouvines delez Dinant
La perdi-je *Ovide le grant.*
Mi *regiment* sont à Bruieres,
Et mes *gloses* sont à Maisieres.
Mon *Lucan* et mon *Juvenal*
Oubliai-je à Bonival.
Estace le grant et *Virgile*
Perdi aus dez à Abevile.
Mes *Alixandres* est à Goivre,
Et mon *Grecime*[35] est à Auçoirre,
Et mon *Thobie* est à Compiengne,
Ne cuit que je jamès le tiengne,
Et mon *doctrinal* est à Sens.
La perdi-je trestout mon sens.
Ainsi com je vous ai conté,
Jamés ne seront racheté
Mi livre en trestoute ma vie,
Toute ai perdu ma clergie

31 Grail.

32 Canticles.

33 Theodulus, a moralist, author of a Latin poem upon truth and falsehood.

34 Avienus, a fabulist.

35 A grammatical work, called *Græcismus*, by Eberhard de Bethune.

Se je ne truis aucune gent
Qui me doingnent de lor argent,
Autrement ne les puis ravoir!
Or li doinst Diex sens et savoir,
Qui m'en donra par tel convent,
Se je revieng en mon couvent,
Je ferai proier en chapitre
Que Diex set pechiez li acquite.*a*

a Of this curious old poem, if so it may be called, I have made the following translation, rather a free, and in some parts I will admit, a conjectural one, but retaining the sense and form of the original with tolerable accuracy.

Every one asks and desires to know
What I have done with my goods,
And how I have become so destitute
That I have neither cope, nor grey cloak,
Nor coat, nor surcoat, nor tabard.
All is gone to the devil;
The dice have ruined me wholly.
By my folly I have lost all,
All my goods and my books.
It is a long time since they disappear'd.
My revelling has turned to grief,
For I think there is no chateau
In France where I have not been,
And left there some of my books.
At Gandelus near La Ferte,
Left I my A B C,
And my paternoster at Soissons,
And my credo at Monlon,
And my *Seven Psalms*(a) at Tournay;
My *Fifteen Psalms*(b) at Cambray,
And my Psalter at Besancon,
And Calendar at Dijon.
Then I returned by Pontarlie
There I sold my Litany,
And I so drank up my Missal.
At the town where they make the salt
With spices, at Montpelier,
Left I my Antiphoners,(c)
My legends(d) and my grailes(e)
Left I at Dun le Chastel.
My books of divinity
Lost I at Paris the city.
And those of art and physic,
And my canticles and music,
Great part of my authors
Left I at St. Martin le Tours;
And my *doves* is at Orleans,
And my *chacones* at Amiens.
At Chartres my Theodules,
At Rouen my Avienus;
My Ovid at Namur;
My Philosophy at Saumur;
At Bouvines near Dinant
Lost I Ovid the Great;
My *regiments*(f) at Bruyeres,
And my glosses at Maissieres;
My Lucan and my Juvenal
I forgot at Bonival;
Eustatius the Great and Virgil
Lost I in play at Abbeville.
My Alexander is at Goivre,
And my Græcismus at Auçoirre,
And my *Thobie* at Compiengne,
I do not think I shall ever again have it.
And my Doctrinal at Sens,
There lost I all my sense.
Thus as I have told you,
Never will be returned to me
My books in all my life.
I have lost all my clergy.
If I do not find somebody
Who will give me of their money,
Otherwise I cannot recover them.
Now then, may God give to him sense and knowledge
Who will lend me on this agreement,
That when I return to my convent
I will pray in the chapter
That God may pardon his sins. *Ed.*

(a) Seven Penitential Psalms; they are the 6th, 25th, 32d, 35th, 38th, 51st and 130th.

(b) The gradual psalms; that is, from the 120th to the 135th, so called according to some authorities because they were sung on the fifteen steps of Solomon's Temple. Psalmi graduales—qui ad quinque parvas horas congrue distribuuntur in quotidiano officii Dei paræ. See ORTIGUE, DICT. DE PLAIN-CHANT.

(c) An Antiphoner is a book of anthems to be sung with responses, and is mentioned in Chaucer as a school book of his time.

This litel childe, his litel book lerning
As he sate in the scole at his primere
He ALMA REDEMPTORIS herde sing
As children lered hir ANTIPHONERE.
CANT. TALES, V, 13, 446.

See DIBDIN'S BIBLIOMANIA, 115, n.—ED.

(d) A Legend, an Antiphonayre, a Gralle and Psalter were the books appointed to be kept in every parish church of the province of Canterbury by Robert Winchelsea. See Ibid, n. 115.—ED.

e() A Gradale, or Grail, is a book containing the office of sprinkling the holy water: the beginning of the mass, or the offices of the Kyrie, with the verses of GLORIA IN EXCELSIS: the GRADALES, or what is gradually sung after the epistles; the hallelujah and tracts, the sequences, the creed to be sung at mass, the offertories, the hymns holy, and Lamb of God, the Communion. See Ibid, 150.—ED.

(f) Rules, Regulations, "Conduite."i

This indifference in regard to books, which characterizes the author of this story, we find more general than ever during the fourteenth century.[36] The character of this century is extremely difficult to analyze. It was an era of immaturity, strife, fusion, oscillation, reaction and compromise. In the political world feudalism falls, while the *third estate* begins to rise; in religion, schism and the immorality of the clergy pave the way for reform. Political prejudices favor the general indifference. All is either in embryo or in decay.

If you compare the productions of this age with those of the preceding, you cannot fail to remark a sensible decline in all branches of human knowledge. The most celebrated theologians of the fourteenth century do not approach Saint Bonaventure, Saint Thomas Aquinas, William de Saint-Amour, Hugh of Saint-Cher and Robert Sorbonne. No scholar succeeds to Vincent de Beauvais or Brunetto Latini. The pulpit is not deserted, but the preachers who occupy it have not the eloquent tones of St. Francis d'Assise, of St. Antony of Padua, of St. Hyacinthe, and of the credulous J. de Voragine. The civilians display in their writings neither the peculiar originality of P. de Beaumanoir and Pierre des Fontaines, nor the classic science of Accursius. In spite of the efforts of Bradwardin, Dondi, and Wallingford, mathematics, chemistry, and astronomy, which, thanks to Roger Bacon, Fibonacci and William d'Auvergne, had made some progress, are abandoned, or transformed into alchemy and astrology. Even the scholastic philosophy ends with Occam, its brilliant but last defender.[37] Language alone has made great progress, and Froissart shields with his great reputation the melancholy age in which he lived.

The study of antiquity sustained itself but feebly in the midst of such a chaos. Some writers, nevertheless, like Petrarch and Richard de Bury, labored to

36 See Meon, *Nouv. rec.*, vol. I, p. 404, and *Hist. Litt. de la France*, vol. XXI, p. 99 (article by Leclerc).

37 See Haureau, *Upon the Scholastic Philosophy*. vol. II, p. 41, *et seq.*

extend it. So Peter Bercheur translated by order of king John the decades of Titus Livy,[38] Phillippe de Vitri, bishop of Meaux, made a translation of the *Metamorphoses* of Ovid, and Simon of Hesden brought into general notice the works of Valerius Maximus.

These translations, then entirely novel, which served to diffuse in some degree a knowledge of the history and literature of ancient times, were due to the influence of the *Romance of the Rose* and the *Speculum*,[39] two encyclopædias very dissimilar, the one for the use of general readers, the other for the learned only; twin-born, but neither, the ripened product of the twelfth century revival.

Had not Thomas Aquinas and Vincent de Beauvais been preaching friars, we might have attributed to their order, that remarkable indifference to the study of the classics, which shows itself in the fourteenth century. The statutes of the Dominicans prohibited them, in fact, from studying pagan books: " *In libris gentilium* "*philosophorum non studeat, et si ad horam suscipiat* " *seculares scientias non addiscat, nec artes quas liberales* " *vocant.*" This very explicit article is followed by another which exhorts them to read none but theological writings: " Sed tantum *libros theologicas tam juvenes* " *quam alii legant.*" And, to conclude, a third points out the Bible and the scholastic histories and the sentences as the only works to which they ought to apply themselves: " *Statuimus ut quælibet provincia fratribus suis missis ad* " *studium ad minus in tribus libris tenentur providere* " *videlicet in biblia, historiis scholasticis et sententiis et* " *ipsi in his tam in textu quam in glosis studeant et intend-* " *ant.*"

Such rules for men who were to become professors and writers, if strictly obeyed, must have had a disastrous influence, and could have been in no respect similar to those which Vincent de Beauvais and St. Thomas

38 At the same period the *Decades* of Livy were translated into the Spanish by P. Lopez d'Ayala, who brought them from Italy.

39 The *Speculum Historiale* was translated for the use of Jeanne of Burgundy, first wife of Philip of Valois.

Aquinas observed, in acquiring the knowledge which has rendered them so celebrated.

But the question which we raise here, it is necessary to admit, is very difficult of examination, and not one which can be thoroughly discussed and resolved in a few pages. It is a fact, certain and undeniable, that there was a decline, and that it was remarked by the writers of that age.

"We see in these sad times, the palladium of Paris "overturned, Paris where cools or rather is frozen up "almost entirely the noble ardor of the schools, the light "whence formerly illuminated every part of the world "with its rays. The pens of all the scribes already lie "idle; the race of books is no longer propagated; and "there is no one who seeks to be regarded as a new "author: *Nec est qui incipiat novus auctor haberi*."[40]

If the perusal of the *Philobiblon* is instructive having regard to the literary history of the age in which it was composed, it is not less so in the eyes of bibliographers. In the chapter entitled "*de ordinatione provida "qualiter libri extraneis concedantur*,[41] the author establishes certain rules to facilitate the loan of books to strangers. The question as to the best manner of lending out books, which is still the despair of librarians, Bury solves by a system of pledges. If one asks of you a book, says Bury, lend it to him, but demand a pledge in exchange, and let that which he pledges be of greater actual value than that of the book.

Whence did Bury obtain this system, still used at Oxford? Was it the result of his own invention? Or was it a reminiscence of what he had seen practiced elsewhere? This, as a question of bibliographical history, is sufficiently important to be answered, and we very naturally put it to ourselves.

If, as editor of the *Philobiblon*, we regret to deprive Richard de Bury of the honor of having first estab-

40 See *Philobiblon*, chap. IX.

41 This precious document is found in a manuscript of the Imperial library (fonds de Sorbonne No. 1280, fol. 9). It was shown to us by our brother and friend Mr. Vallet de Viriville.

lished rules for the management of a library, we are nevertheless as Frenchmen, happy to restore to our finest literary institution, the University of Paris, what properly belongs to it. It is, in fact, to the Sorbonne that we are indebted for the first rules for the organization of a library.

These regulations,[42] entitled *De libris et de librariis*, were put in force in 1321, some years before Richard de Bury came to Paris. They are perhaps more minute than those of the bishop of Durham, but do not materially differ from them. The first article prescribes a system of pledges,[43] and the second directs the election of the custodians or librarians by the *socii*. These two fundamental articles are to be found in R. de Bury's scheme and are its essential features. It is therefore quite impossible not to perceive the imitation. It is, besides, easy to explain this borrowing by Bury from the Sorbonne. His literary taste, and the high position which he occupied in the political world, gave him easy access to this institution, where, once admitted, he would not fail to visit the library and learn from its officers the rules for its management. Besides, these rules were the result of the joint labors of several of the professors, among whom was his compatriot, Thomas of England (Thomas de Anglia), and Bury could not have visited the Sorbonne without conversing with him concerning them.

With the chapter which contains his library regula-

42 Observe the wording of this article: "Ut nullus liber præstetur extra "domum alieni nec socio nec extraneo "sub juramenta, nisi super vadium, "amplius valens et in re quæ servari "potest, puta, auro, argento vel libro "et hæc vadia serventur in cista ad "hoc deputata."

43 It is even probable that he refers to the library of the Sorbonne, when he says: *ibi bibliothecæ jucundæ supra cellas aromatum redolentes* (*Philobiblon*, chap. viii.) The anonymous author of a *factum* of the University, published in 1678, against the precentor of the cathedral, concerning the right which he claimed of establishing grammar schools (second part, p. 84), refers to the visits made by R. de Bury to the Sorbonne. "R. de Bury," says he, "in former times ambassador "from the king of England, took a "singular pleasure in visiting the uni- "versity." *Quantus impetus voluptatis lætificavit cor nostrum quoties paradysum mundi Parisiis visitare vacavimus*, etc. But in the ninth chapter he deplores the abuses which were creeping into the study of the humanities and of grammar which were cultivated only "for the purpose of sooner "obtaining a degree, and by means of "the degree a benefice." *Prisciani regulas et Donati statim de cunis erepti, et sic celeriter ablactati pertingunt categorias et perihermenias*, etc.

tions the *Philobiblon* properly ends, but the author seems to have thought that the students, who, through his generosity, were in future to reside at his college, and make use of his books, owed him at least a prayer. Notwithstanding the pains taken by him in its composition, we doubt, considering its length, whether it has often been repeated. Let us hope that the bibliophilist who has inherited but this little work, will be willing, more grateful than those to whom our author addressed himself, to cherish the memory of an honest and generous writer to whom he owes the only treatise ever written upon the love of books, and which strangely enough appeared at a period when they were so little prized.

PHILOBIBLON,

A TREATISE

ON THE LOVE OF BOOKS.

PHILOBIBLON,

TRACTATUS PULCHERRIMUS DE AMORE LIBRORUM.

PROLOGUS.[1]

UNIVERSIS Christi fidelibus, ad quos præsentis scripturæ tenor pervenerit, Richardus de Buri, miseratione divina Dunelmensis episcopus, salutem in Domino sempiternam, piamque ipsius præsentare[2] memoriam jugiter[3] coram Deo, in vita pariter et post fata.

Quid retribuam Domino pro omnibus quæ retribuit mihi? devotissime[4] investigat psalmista, rex invictus[5] et eximius prophetarum. In qua quæstione gratissima, semetipsum redditorem voluntarium, debitorem multifarium, et sanctiorem[6] optantem consiliarum recognoscit; concordans cum Aristotele philosophorum principe, qui omnem[7] de agibilibus quæstionem consilium probat esse *tertio et sexto Ethicorum.*

Sane si propheta tam mirabilis,[8] secretorum præscius divinorum, præconsulere volebat tam sollicite, quomodo grate possit gratis data[9] refundere, quid nos rudes regratiatores, et avidissimi receptores, onusti divinis beneficiis infinitis poterimus dignius[10] velle? Procul dubio deliberatione sollerti et circumspectione multiplici, invi-

1 In the ms. 797, St. Victor, it is entitled: *Incipit prologus Philobiblon;* in the Oxford ed., 1599: *Præfatio auctoris ad lectorem;* in the Frankfort ed., 1610, and Helmstadt, 1702: *Richardi de Buri episcopi Dunelmensis Philobiblion, prologus.*

2 *Repræsentare*, Ox. ed.

3 This word is omitted in the ed. of 1500.

4 *Devotissimis*, ms. 797; *devotissimus*, ed. 1500, 1610 and 1702.

5 *Inunctus*, Ox. ed.

6 *Saniorem*, ed. 1473.

7 *Ad omnem*, Ox. ed,

8 *Mirabilis futurus, præscius divinorum*, Ox. ed.

9 *Grata*, Ox. ed.

10 *Digne*, mss. and Ox. ed.

PHILOBIBLON.[a]

HERE BEGINNETH THE PROLOGUE TO A TREATISE UPON THE LOVE OF BOOKS.

TO all the faithful in Christ, to whom the tenor of this present writing may descend, Richard de Bury, by divine commiseration Bishop of Durham, wisheth eternal health in the Lord, as also to present a pious memorial of himself before God, while he yet liveth, and likewise after his decease.

The invincible king, psalmist, and greatest of prophets, most devoutly asks, "What can I render to the "Lord for all that he hath conferred upon me?" In which most grateful question he recognizeth in himself the willing retributer, the multifarious debtor, and the most soundly discerning counsellor; agreeing with Aristotle, the prince of philosophers, who proves the whole question about things practicable, to be deliberate choice.[1]—*Ethics*, book III and VI. Truly, if so admirable a prophet, having a foreknowledge of divine secrets, was willing thus earnestly to premeditate upon the manner in which he might acceptably return gifts by thanks, what more worthily shall we, who are rude thankers and most eager receivers, laden with infinite divine benefactions, be able to resolve upon? Without doubt, in anxious deliberation and increased circumspection, the septiform spirit[2] being first invoked, so that an illuminating fire may burn in our meditation, we ought most

a *Philobiblon*, ed. Cologne, 1473, Oxford, 1599; *Philobiblion*, Paris, 1500. If the first was the author's own word, it ought not to be altered.—*Inglis*.

1 The references by figures in this translation are to the notes of Mr. Inglis at the end of the work.

tato primitus[1] spiritu septiformi, quatenus in nostra meditatione ignis illuminans exardescat, viam impedibilem[2] prævidere[3] debemus attentius, quo largitor omnium de collatis muneribus suis, sponte veneretur reciproce, proximus relevetur[4] ab onere, et[5] reatus contractus per peccantes quotidie eleemosinarum remediis redimatur.[6]

Hujus ergo[7] devotionis monitione præventus[8] ab eo qui solus bonam hominis et prævenit voluntatem et perficit, sine quo nec sufficientia suppetit cogitandi;[9] cujus, quicquid boni fecerimus, non ambigimus esse munus, diligenter tam penes nos, quam cum aliis inquirendo discussimus, quod inter diversorum generum pietatis officia primo gradu placeret Altissimo, prodessetque potius ecclesiæ militanti. Et ecce mox[10] nostræ considerationis[11] aspectibus grex occurrit scholarium elegorum, quin potius electorum in[12] quibus Deus artifex et ancilla natura morum optimorum et scientiarum celebrium plantaverunt radices; sed[13] ita eos[14] rei familiaris oppressit penuria, quod obstante fortuna contraria, semina tam[15] fecunda virtutum, in inculto juventutis agro, roris debiti non rigata favore, arescere compelluntur. Quo[16] fit, *ut lateat in obscuris condita virtus clara,*[17] ut verbis alludamus Boëthii et ardentes lucernæ non[18] ponuntur sub modio, sed itaque[19] præ defectu olei penitus exstinguuntur: sic ager in vere floriger ante messem exaruit; sic frumenta in lolium, et vites degenerant in libruscas, ac sic in oleastros olivæ silvescunt, marcescunt omnino tenellæ trabeculæ, et qui in fortes columnas ecclesiæ poterant excrevisse, subtilis ingenii capacitate dotati, studiorum gymnasia derelinquunt. Sola invidia[20]

1 *Invocato prius*, ms. 2454.
2 The mss. have it, *viam non impedibilem*, and the Ox. ed., *viam non redibilem*.
3 *Providere*, mss. and Ox. ed.
4 *Reveletur*, ed. 1500, 1610 and 1702.
5 Omitted in the ed. 1500, 1610 and 1702.
6 *Redimant*, ed. 1702.
7 *Igitur*, Ox. ed.
8 *Præventi*, mss. and Ox. ed.
9 *Cogitandi solo modo*, ms. 797,; *solummodo*, ms. 2454, and Ox. ed.
10 Omitted in the Ox. ed.
11 *Cogitationis*, Ox. ed.
12 *Cum*, ms. 2454.
13 *Scilicet*, ed. 1500, 1610 and 1702.
14 This word is not found in the mss. nor in the Ox. ed.
15 Omitted in the Ox. ed.
16 *Quibus*, Ox. ed.
17 *Clara tenebris*, ms. 2454.
18 *Nunc*, ms. 2454.
19 Omitted in ms. 797 and ed. 1500; in ms. 2454, in Frankfort ed. 1610, and Helmstadt, 1702, *scilicet* replaces *sed itaque*. *Sed pro defectu*, in Ox. ed.
20 *Inedia*, mss. and Ox. ed.

attentively to look forward to the unbeaten way in which the Dispenser of all things would willingly be reciprocally venerated on account of his gifts conferred upon us. Let our neighbor be relieved of his burthen, and the guilt daily contracted by our sins be redeemed by the remedy of alms.

Forewarned, therefore, by admonition of this devotion, by him who alone anticipates and perfects the good will of man (without whom no sufficiency of thinking in any way suggests itself, of whom we doubt not is the reward for whatever good we shall have done), we have diligently discussed within ourselves, and also inquired of others, which amongst the duties of the various kinds of piety might be in the first degree pleasing to the Most High, and best promote the church militant. And behold a herd of outcast rather than of elect scholars meets the views of our contemplation,[3] in whom God the artificer, and Nature his handmaid, have planted the roots of the best morals and most celebrated sciences. But the penury of their private affairs so oppresses them, being opposed by adverse fortune, that the fruitful seeds of virtue, so productive in the unexhausted field of youth, unmoistened by their wonted dews, are compelled to wither. Whence it happens, as Boëtius says, that bright virtue lies hid in obscurity, and the burning lamp is not put under a bushel, but is utterly extinguished for want of oil.[4] Thus the flowery field in spring is plowed up before harvest; thus wheat gives way to tares, the vine degenerates to woodbine, and the olive grows wild and unproductive. The slender beams which might have grown into strong pillars of the church entirely decay.[a] Men endowed with the capacity of subtle wit, relinquish the schools of learning, violently repelled by the sole envy of a stepmother from the nectareous cup of philosophy, having first tasted of it, and by the very taste become more fervently thirsty. Fitted for

[a] According to the text, this should be: And those who might grow to be strong pillars of the church, endowed with new intellect abandon the schools. Envy alone, acting the part of a stepmother, they are repelled, etc.—*Ed.*

novercante, repelluntur[1] a philosophiæ nectareo poculo violenter, quam primo gustaverunt, ipso[2] gustu ferventius sitibundi, liberalibus artibus habiles, et scripturis tantum dispositi contemplandis, orbati necessariorum subsidiis, quasi quadam apostasiæ specie, ad artes mechanicas, propter victus solius suffragia, ad ecclesiæ dispendium et totius cleri vilipendium, revertuntur. Sic mater ecclesia pariendo filios, abortire compellitur, quinimo ab utero fœtus informis menstruose[3] dirumpitur, et pro paucis minimisque quibus contentatur natura, alumnos amitit egregios postea promovendos in[4] pugiles, fidei et athletas. Heu quam repente tela succiditur, dum texentis manus orditur! Heu quod sol eclipsatur in aurora[5] clarissima et planeta progrediens regiratur retrograde, ac naturam et speciem veræ stellæ prætendens, subito decidit[6] et fit assub! Quid poterit pius homo intueri miserius? Quid misericordiæ viscera penetrabit acutius? Quid cor congelatum intus[7] in calentes guttas resolvit[8] facilius? Amplius[9] arguentes a sensu contrario, quantum profuit toti reipublicæ Christianæ, non quidem Sardanapali deliciis, neque Cresi divitiis enutrire[10] studentes, sed melius mediocritate scholastica suffragari pauperibus, ex eventu præterito recordemur. Quot oculis vidimus, quot ex scripturis collegimus, nulla[11] suorum natalium claritate fulgentes, nullius hæreditatis successione gaudentes, sed tantum proborum virorum pietate suffultos, apostolicas cathedras meruisse? Subjectis fidelibus præfuisse probissime? Superborum et humilium[12] colla jugo ecclesiastico subjecisse et procurasse propensius ecclesiæ libertatem?

Quamobrem perlustratis humanis egestatibus usquequaque, caritativæ considerationis intuitu, huic tam caliginoso[13] generi hominum, in quibus tamen tanta

1 *Refelluntur*, Ox. ed.
2 *Proprio*, ed. 1500, 1610 and 1702.
3 *Monstrose*, Ox. ed.
4 *Et*, Ox. ed.
5 *Aura*, Ox. ed.
6 *Decidens fit assub*, Ox. ed.
7 *Ut intus*, mss. and Ox. ed.
8 *Guttas effundat resolvet*, ms. 2454; *Resolvet*, Ox. ed.
9 *Amplius ergo*, ed, 1500, 1599, 1610 and 1702.
10 *Enervare*, mss. and Ox. ed.; *Enarrare*, ms. 3352c.
11 *Nulla ex suorum*, Ox. ed.
12 *Sublimium*, mss. and Ox. ed.
13 *Tandem calamitoso*, mss. 797, 3352c, and Ox. ed.; *tam calamitoso*, ms. 2454.

the liberal arts, and equally disposed to the contemplation of scripture, but destitute of the needful aid, they revert, as it were, by a sort of apostacy, to mechanical arts solely for the sake of food, to the impoverishment of the church, and the degradation of the whole clerical profession. Thus the mother church conceiving sons, is compelled to miscarry, if indeed some monstrous misshapen abortion is not torn from her womb; and instead of the few and the smallest with which she is by nature contented, she sends forth egregious bantlings, and finally promotes them as the athletæ and champions of the faith. Alas, how quickly the web is cut up, while the hand of the weaver is yet at work! How soon the sun is eclipsed in the clearest sky, and the progressing planet becomes retrograde! How suddenly the meteor,[5] exhibiting the nature and appearance of a real star, falls down; for it is formed from below. What can the pious man more pitifully behold? What can more keenly penetrate the bowels of compassion? What more readily dissolve a heart, though hard as an anvil, into the warmest tears?

Arguing further on the contrary side, let us call to mind from the events of former times, how greatly it profited the whole Christian republic, not indeed to enervate students by the luxuries of Sardanapalus, nor yet by the riches of Crœsus, but rather to support the poor in scholastic mediocrity. How many have we seen, how many have we collected from writings, who, not being distinguished by brilliancy of birth, nor boasting of hereditary succession, but supported alone by the piety of just men, have deserved the apostolical chair, and most honorably presided over its faithful subjects, have subjected the necks of the proud and exalted, to the ecclesiastical yoke,[6] and easily procured the liberty of the church!

Wherefore, taking a thorough survey of human wants, with a view of charitable consideration for this obscure class of men, in whom, however, such great hopes of

redolet spes profectus ecclesiæ, præelegit peculiariter nostræ compassionis affectio pium ferre præsidium, et eisdem non solum de necessariis victui verum multo magis[1] de libris utilissimis[2] studio providere. Ad hunc effectum acceptissimum, coram Domino,[3] nostra jam ab olim[4] vigilavit intentio indefessa. Hic quidem[5] amor exstaticus, tam potenter nos rapuit, ut, terrenis aliis abdicatis, ab animo acquirendorum librorum solummodo flagremus[6] affectu. Ut ergo[7] nostri finis intentio tam posteris pateat quam .modernis, et ora loquentium perversa, quantum ad nos pertinet, obstruamus perpetuo, tractatum parvulum[8] edidimus, stilo quidem levissimo modernorum. Est enim ridiculum[9] rhetoricis, quando levis materia scribitur grandi stilo.[10] Qui tractatus, amorem quem ad libros habuimus, ab excessu purgabit, devotionis intentæ propositum propalabit, et circumstantias facti nostri, per viginti divisi[11] capitula, luce clarius enarrabit. Quia vero de amore librorum principaliter disserit, placuit nobis, more veterum Latinorum, ipsum græco vocabulo *Philobiblion*[12] amicabiliter[13] nuncupare.

1 *Etiam* in place of *multo magis*, ms. 2454.
2 *Utilissimo*, Ox. ed.
3 *Deo*, Ox. ed.
4 *Jam absolvi vigilavit*, Ox. ed.
5 *Quidem* is omitted in the mss. and Ox. ed.
6 *Flagraremus*, mss. and Ox. ed.
7 *Igitur*, mss. 2454, 3352c and Ox. ed.
8 *Parvulinum*, mss. 797, and 3352c.
9 *Ridiculosum*, mss. 797, 3352c, and Ox. ed.
10 *Describitur stilo*, ms. 3352c and Ox. ed.
11 *Divisus*, mss. and Ox. ed.
12 *Philobiblon*, Ox. ed.
13 *Amabiliter*, mss. and Ox. ed.

Explicit Prologus.

advantage to the church are felt, the bent of our compassion has peculiarly predisposed us to offer our pious aid; and not only to provide them with necessary food, but, what is more, with the most useful books for study. For this purpose, most acceptable to the Lord, our unwearied attention hath already been long upon the watch. This ecstatic love hath indeed so powerfully seized upon us, that, discharging all other earthly pursuits from our mind, we have alone ardently desired the acquisition of books. That the motive of our object, therefore, may be manifest as well to posterity as to our contemporaries, and that we may, in so far as it concerns ourselves, forever close the perverse mouths of talkers, we have drawn up a little treatise, in the lightest style indeed of the moderns (for it is ridiculous in rhetoricians to write pompously when the subject is trifling), which treatise will purge the love we have had for books from excess, will advance the purpose of our intense devotion, and will narrate in the clearest manner all the circumstances of our undertaking, dividing them into twenty chapters. But because it principally treats of the love of books, it hath pleased us, after the fashion of the ancient Latins, fondly to name it by a Greek word, *Philobiblon*

Here endeth the Prologue.

CAPITULUM PRIMUM.

DE COMMENDATIONE SAPIENTIÆ ET LIBRORUM IN QUIBUS SAPIENTIA HABITAT.[1]

THESAURUS desiderabilis sapientiæ et scientiæ, quem omnes homines per instinctum naturæ[2] desiderant, cunctas mundi transcendit divitias infinite: cujus respectu lapides pretiosi vilescunt: in[3] cujus comparatione argentum lutescit, et aurum obryzum exigua fit arena: cujus splendore tenebrescunt visui sol et luna: cujus dulcore mirabili[4] amarescunt gustui mel et manna.

O valor sapientiæ non marcescens ex tempore, virtus virens assidue, omne virus evacuans ab habente![5] O munus cœleste liberalitatis divinæ, descendens a Patre luminum, ut mentem rationalem provehas usque ad[6] cœlum! Tu es intellectus cœlestis alimonia, quem qui edunt, adhuc exurient, quem qui bibunt, adhuc sitient, et languentium[7] animas harmonia lætificans, quam qui audit, nullatenus confundetur. Tu es morum moderatrix et regula, secundum quam[8] operans non peccabit, *Per te reges regnant et legum conditores justa decernunt.* Per te deposita rusticitate naturæ,[9] elimatis ingeniis atque linguis,[10] vitiorum sentibus coeffossis[11] radicitus, apices consequuntur honorum[12] fiuntque patres patriæ et comites principum, qui sine te conflassent lanceas in ligones et vomeres, vel cum filio prodigo pascerent fortasse sues.[13]

Quo namque sic[14] lates potissime multum,[15] prælec-

1 The rubric of ms. 797, and the title of the chapter in the Oxford edition is: *Quod thesaurus sapientiæ potissime sit in libris.*

2 *Naturæ scire desiderant*, Ox. ed.

3 This word is not in the mss., nor in the Ox. ed.

4 *Admirabili*, ms. 2454.

5 *Omne virus evacuans ab habente* omitted in the Ox. ed.

6 *In*, ms. 2454; *Usque cœlum*, ms. 3352c.

7 *Languentis animæ*, ms. 797, and Ox. ed.

8 *Quem*, ed. 1500.

9 *Ruditate nativa*, mss. and Ox. ed.

10 *Signis*, ms. 797.

11 *Effossis*, ms. 2454; *Confossis*, ms. 3352c.

12 *Honoris*, mss. and Ox. ed.

13 *Forte sues*, mss. and Ox. ed.

14 *Namque sic* not in mss. or Ox. ed.

15 *Multum* omitted in Ox. ed.

CHAPTER I.

ON THE COMMENDATION OF WISDOM, AND OF BOOKS IN WHICH WISDOM DWELLETH.

THE desirable treasure of wisdom and knowledge, which all men covet from the impulse of nature, infinitely surpasses all the riches of the world; in comparison with which precious stones are vile, silver is clay, and purified gold grains of sand; in the splendor of which the sun and moon grow dim to the sight; in the admirable sweetness of which, honey and manna are bitter to the taste. The value of wisdom decreaseth not with time; it hath an ever-flourishing virtue that cleanseth its possessor from every venom. Oh celestial gift of divine liberality, descending from the Father of Light to raise up the rational soul even to heaven! Thou art the celestial alimony of intellect, of which whosoever eateth shall yet hunger, and whoso drinketh shall yet thirst; a harmony rejoicing the soul of the sorrowful, and never in any way discomposing the hearer. Thou art the moderator and the rule of morals, operating according to which, none will err. By thee kings reign, and lawgivers decree justly. Through thee, the rusticity of nature being cast off, wits and tongues being polished, and the thorns of vice utterly eradicated, the summit of honor is reached, and they become fathers of their country and companions of princes, who, without thee, might have forged their lances into spades and plowshares, or perhaps have fed swine with the prodigal son. Where then, most potent, most longed-for treasure, art thou concealed? and where shall the thirsty soul find thee? Undoubtedly, indeed, thou hast placed thy desirable tabernacle in books, where the Most High, the Light of Light, the Book of Life, hath established thee. There

te[1] thesaure? et ubi te invenient[2] animæ sitibundæ? In libris quidem[3] procul dubio posuisti tabernaculum desiderabile[4] tuum, ubi te fundavit Altissimus, lumen luminum, liber vitæ. Ibi namque[5] te omnis, qui petit, accepit:[6] qui quærit, invenit, et pulsantibus[7] citius aperietur. In his Cherubin alas suas extendunt, et intellectus studentium ascendunt,[8] et a polo usque ad polum prospiciunt[9] a solis ortu usque ad occasum,[10] ab aquilone et mari.[11] In his comprehensibilis[12] ipse Deus altissimus apprehensibiliter continetur et colitur; in his patet natura cœlestium, terrestrium et infernorum; in his cernuntur jura, quibus omnis regitur politia, hierarchiæ cœlestis distinguuntur officia, et dœmonum tyrannides describuntur, quos[13] nec ideæ Platonis exsuperant, nec Cratonis[14] cathedra continebat.

In libris mortuos quasi vivos invenio: in libris futura prævideo: in libris res bellicæ disponuntur: de libris prodeunt jura pacis. Omnia corrumpuntur et tabescunt in tempore: Saturnus quos generat, devorare non cessat: quoniam[15] mundi gloriam operiret oblivio, nisi Deus mortalibus librorum remedia providisset. Alexander[16] orbis dominator,[17] Julius orbis et urbis invasor, qui et in arce et arte[18] primus, in unitate personæ assumpsit imperium, fidelis Fabricius et Cato rigidus, hodie caruissent memoria, si librorum suffragia defuissent. Turres ad terram sunt dirutæ,[19] civitates eversæ putredine perierunt[20] triumphales. Nec quicquam reperiet rex vel papa, quo perenniter[21] privilegium conferatur commodius[22] quam per libros. Reddit[23] vicissitudinem liber

1 *Præeffecte*, ms. 797.
2 *Reperient*, mss. and Ox. ed.
3 *Quidem* not in mss. nor Ox. ed.
4 *Desiderabile*, is also wanting.
5 *Namque*, is also wanting.
6 The words *petit et accepit* are not in the ed. of 1473.
7 *Pulsantibus improbe*, mss. and Ox. ed.
8 *Ut intellectus studentis ascendat*, mss. and Ox. ed.
9 *Polo ad polum prospiciat*, Ibid.
10 *Ortu et occasu*, mss. and Ox. ed.
11 *Aquilone ad meridiem*, ed. 1702.
12 *Incomprehensibilis*, mss. 2454, 3352c and Ox. ed.
13 *Quas*, Ox. ed.
14 Ms. 797 has it *Catonis;* Thomas James, in his Oxford edition, quotes it differently.
15 *Omnem*, mss. and Ox. ed.
16 *Alexander Macedo orbis*, ms. 2454.
17 *Domitor*, mss.
18 *Qui et Marte et arte*, mss. and Ox. ed.
19 *Dejectæ*, Ox. ed.
20 *Perierunt, formice triumphales*, mss. and Ox. ed.
21 *Reperit rex vel papa, quo perhennitatis*, mss and Ox. ed.
22 *Commodius* omitted in ed. of 1702.
23 *Reddit auctori*, mss. and Ox. ed.

then all who ask receive, all who seek find thee, to those who knock thou openest quickly. In books cherubim expand their wings, that the soul of the student may ascend and look around from pole to pole, from the rising to the setting sun, from the north, and from the sea. In them the Most High incomprehensible God himself is contained and worshipped. In them the nature of celestial, terrestrial and infernal beings is laid open. In them the laws by which every polity is governed are decreed, the officers of the celestial hierarchy are distinguished, and tyrannies of such demons are described as the ideas of Plato never surpassed, and the chair of Crato never contained.

In books we find the dead as it were living; in books we foresee things to come; in books warlike affairs are methodized; the rights of peace proceed from books. All things are corrupted and decay with time. Saturn never ceases to devour those whom he generates; insomuch that the glory of the world would be lost in oblivion if God had not provided mortals with a remedy in books. Alexander the ruler of the world; Julius the invader of the world and of the city, the first who in unity of person assumed the empire in arms and arts;[a] the faithful Fabricius, the rigid Cato, would at this day have been without a memorial if the aid of books had failed them. Towers are razed to the earth, cities overthrown, triumphal arches mouldered to dust; nor can the king or pope be found, upon whom the privilege of a lasting name can be conferred more easily than by books. A book made, renders succession to the author: for as long as the book exists, the author remaining αθαvατος, immortal, cannot perish;[b] as Ptolemy witnesseth in the prologue of his *Almagest*, he, he says, is not dead, who gave life to science.

What learned scribe, therefore, who draws out things

a This translation differs slightly from the original and was probably from the *Marte et arte* text.—*Ed.*

b Here also the translation is similar to the Oxford edition.—*Ed.*

factus, ut, quamdiu liber supererit, actor[1] manens athanatos nequeat interire, teste Ptolemæo in prologo Almagesti: *non fuit*, inquit *mortuus, qui scientiam vivificavit.* Quis igitur infinito thesauro librorum[2] doctus scriba profert nova et vetera, per quodcunque alterius speciei pretium limitabit? Veritas vincens super omnia, quæ regem vinum et mulieres supergreditur,[3] quam amicis præhonorare beneficium[4] obtinet sanctitatis: quæ est via sine[5] devio et vita[6] sine termino, cui sacer Boëthius attribuit[7] triplex esse, in mente, voce et scripto. In libris videtur manere[8] utilius et fructificare fecundius ad profectum. Nam veritas[9] vocis perit cum sonitu: veritas mente latens est sapientia absconsa[10] et thesaurus invisus: veritas vero quæ lucet in libris, omni se disciplinali sensui manifestare desiderat. Visui dum legitur: auditui dum[11] auditur, amplius vero et tactui[12] se commendat quodam modo, dum transcribi se sustinet, colligari, corrigi et servari. Veritas enim mentis[13] clausa licet sit possessio nobilis animi, tamen cum[14] caret socio, non constat esse jucundam,[15] de qua nec visus judicat nec auditus. Veritas vero vocis soli patet auditui, visum latens, qui plures nobis differentias rerum ostendit,[16] affixaque subtilissimo motui incipit et desinit quasi simul.[17] Sed veritas scripta libri non successiva sed permanens palam se præbet aspectui, et per spirituales vias oculorum veluti vestibula ad sensus communis[18] et imaginationis atria transiens, thalamum intellectus ingreditur, in cubile memoriæ se recondens, ubi æternam mentis congenerat veritatem.

1 *Auctor*, mss. and Ox. ed.
2 *Librorum de quo scriba doctus*, mss. and Ox. ed.
3 *Mulierem superare dicitur*, Ox. ed.
4 *Officium*, mss. and Ox. ed.
5 *Quæ est et via sive*, mss. and Ox. ed.
6 *Via*, ed. of 1702.
7 *Tribuit*, ms. 2454.
8 *Maturare*, ms. 2454.
9 *Virtus*, mss. and Ox. ed.
10 *Abscondita*, Ox. ed.
11 *Cum*, ms. 2454.
12 *Amplius et tactu*, ms. 797; *Amplius et tactui*, mss. 2454, 3352c and Ox. ed.
13 *Veritas cunctis*, ms. 797; *Veritas mentis*, mss. 2454, 3352c and Ox. ed.
14 *Quia tamen caret*, mss. 797, 3352c and Ox. ed.; *Que tamen caret*, ms. 2454.
15 *Jucunda*, mss. and Ox. ed.
16 *Monstrat*, mss. 797, 3352c and Ox. ed.
17 *Similiter*, Ox. ed.
18 *Et per sphærulas pervias oculorum, vestibula sensus communis*, mss. 797 and 3352c; *Et per spirituales pervias oculorum, vestibula sensus communis*, ms. 2454; *Et per sphærulas pervias oculorum, vestbiula*, (*seu vestigia*) *sensus communis*, Ox. ed.

new and old from an infinite treasury of books, will limit their price by any other thing whatever of another kind? Truth overcoming all things, which ranks above kings, wine and women, to honor which above friends obtains the benefit of sanctity, which is the way that deviates not, and the life without end; to which the holy Boëtius attributes a threefold existence, in the mind, in the voice, and in writing, appears to abide most usefully and fructify most productively of advantage in books. For the truth of the voice perishes with the sound. Truth latent in the mind, is hidden wisdom and invisible treasure; but the truth which illuminates books desires to manifest itself to every disciplinable sense, to the sight when read, to the hearing when heard: it, moreover, in a manner commends itself to the touch, when submitting to be transcribed, collated, corrected, and preserved. Truth confined to the mind, though it may be the possession of a noble soul, while it wants a companion and is not judged of, either by the sight, or the hearing, appears to be inconsistent with pleasure. But the truth of the voice is open to the hearing only, and latent to the sight (which shows us many differences of things fixed upon by a most subtle motion, beginning and ending as it were simultaneously). But the truth written in a book, being not fluctuating, but permanent, shows itself openly to the sight, passing through the spiritual ways of the eyes, as the porches and halls of common sense and imagination; it enters the chamber of intellect, reposes itself upon the couch of memory, and there congenerates the eternal truth of the mind.

Lastly, let us consider how great a commodity of doctrine exists in books, how easily, how secretly, how safely they expose the nakedness of human ignorance without putting it to shame. These are the masters who instruct us without rods and ferules,[7] without hard words and anger, without clothes or money. If you approach them, they are not asleep; if investigating you interrogate them, they conceal nothing; if you mistake

Postremo pensandum quanta doctrinæ commoditas sit in libris quam facilis, quam arcana, quam tuto[1] libris humanæ[2] ignorantiæ paupertatem sine verecundia denudamus. Hi sunt magistri, qui nos instruunt sine virgis et ferula, sine verbis et cholera,[3] sine pannis et pecunia. Si accedis, non dormiunt, si inquirens interrogas, non se abscondunt, non remurmurant, si oberres, cacchinos nesciunt, si ignores. O libri soli liberales et liberi,[4] qui omni petenti tribuitis, et omnes manumititis vobis sedulo servientes! Quot[5] rerum millibus typice viris doctis recommendamini,[6] in scriptura modo[7] divinitus inspirata. Vos enim estis profundissimæ sophiæ fodinæ: ad quas sapiens filium suum mittit, ut inde thesauros effodiat, *Proverbiorum secundo*[8]; vos putei aquarum viventium, quos pater Abraham primo fodit, Isaac eruderavit, quosque nituntur obstruere Philistini,[9] *Genesis vicesimo sexto.* Vos estis revera spicæ gratissimæ, plenæ granis, solis apostolicis manibus confricandæ, ut egrediatur cibus gratissimus[10] famelicis animabus; *Matth.* xii. Vos estis urnæ aureæ, quibus manna reconditur atque petræ mellifluæ, imo potius favimellis, ubera uberrima lactis vitæ, promptuaria semper plena. Vos lignum vitæ, atque quadripartitus fluvius paradisi, quo mens humana pascitur et aridus intellectus imbuitur et rigatur. Vos arca Noæ et scala Jacob, canalesque quibus fœtus intuentium coloratur.[11] Vos lapides testimonii, et lagenæ servantes lampades Gedeonis, pera David, de qua limpidissimi lapides extrahuntur, ut Goliath prosternatur. Vos estis aurea vasa templi, arma clericorum militiæ, quibus tela nequissimi destruuntur, olivæ fecundæ, vineæ Engadi, ficus sterilescere nescientes, lucernæ ardentes,[12] et optima quæque scripturæ libris adaptare poterimus, si loqui libeat figurate.

1 *Toto*, ed. 1702.
2 This word is not found in ms. 2454.
3 *Hi libri sunt magistri qui nos instruunt sine virgis et cholera*, Ox. ed.
4 *O liberales et libri qui*, ms. 2454.
5 *Qui*, ms. 2454.
6 *Commendamini*, ed. 1702.
7 *Scriptura nobis*, mss. and Ox. ed.
8 *Quinto*, ed. 1500, 1610 and 1702.
9 *Palestini*, mss. and Ox. ed.
10 *Sanissimus*, mss. 797 and 3352c; *Suavissimus*, ms. 2454 and Ox. ed.
11 *Colorantur*, mss. and Ox. ed.
12 *Ardentes, semper in manibus, prætendendæ*, mss. and Ox. ed.

them, they never grumble; if you are ignorant, they cannot laugh at you.

You only, oh books, are liberal and independent. You give to all who ask, and enfranchize all who serve you assiduously. How many thousands of things do you typically recommend to learned men, in writing after a divinely inspired manner; for you are the deepest mines of wisdom, to which the wise man sent his son, that he might thence dig up treasure. *Prov.* ii. You are the wells of living water, which the patriarch Abraham first dug, and Isaac again cleared out after the Philistines had endeavored to fill them up. *Genesis*, xxvi. Truly you are the ears filled with most palatable grains, to be rubbed out by apostolical hands alone, that the most grateful food for hungry souls may come out of them. *Matth.* xii. You are golden urns in which manna is laid up, rocks flowing with honey, or rather indeed honey-combs; udders most copiously yielding the milk of life; store-rooms ever full; the tree of life, the four-streamed river of Paradise, where the human mind is fed, and the arid intellect moistened and watered; the ark of Noah, the ladder of Jacob, the troughs by which the fœtus in those who look upon them is colored, the stones of the covenant, and the pitchers preserving the lamps of Gideon; the bag of David from which polished stones are taken that Goliah may be prostrated. You, oh books, are the golden vessels of the temple, the arms of the clerical militia with which the missiles of the most wicked are destroyed; fruitful olives, vines of Engaddi, fig-trees knowing no sterility; burning lamps to be ever held in the hand. And, if it please us to speak figureatively, we shall be able to adapt the best sayings of every writing whatever to books.

a To all the best things in the scriptures we could compare books, if, etc., is according to the text.—*Ed.*

CAPITULUM II.

CAPITULUM AUTEM ISTUD SECUNDUM CANIT QUOD LIBRI DIVITIIS ET DELICIIS CORPORALIBUS SINT PRÆPONENDI.[1]

SI quodlibet[2] juxta gradum valoris gradum mereatur amoris, valorem vero librorum ineffabilem persuadet præsens[3] capitulum, non tamen[4] liquet lectori, quid sit[5] concludendum probabiliter. Non enim demonstrationibus in morali materia utimur, recordantes, quoniam disciplinati hominis est certitudinem quærere, sicut rei naturam perspexerit tolerare, Aristotele philosopho[6] attestante *Ethicorum primo*, et *Metaphysicæ secundo*:[7] quoniam nec Tullius requirit Euclidem, nec Euclidi Tullius facit fidem. Hoc revera sive logice sive rhetorice suadere conamur, quod, quæcunque divitiæ vel deliciæ cedere debent libris in anima spirituali, ubi spiritus, qui est charitas, ordinat charitatem. Primo quidem, quia in libris sapientia continetur[8] plus, quam omnes mortales comprehendunt;[9] sapientia vero divitias vilipendit,[10] sicut capitulum antecedens allegat. Præterea Aristoteles *De Problematibus* III,[11] *problemate* 10, istam determinat quæstionem, *propter quid antiqui in gymnasticis*[12] *et corporalibus*[13] *agoniis præmia statuerunt potioribus, nullum unquam*[14] *præmium sapientiæ decreverunt?*

1 *Qualis amor libris rationabiliter debeatur*, mss. 797, 3352c and Ox. ed.
2 *Quidlibet*, Ox. ed.
3 *Præcedens*, mss. and Ox. ed.
4 *Capitulum palam liquet*, mss. and Ox. ed.
5 *Sit inde concludendum*, mss. and Ox. ed.
6 *Tolerare archiphilosopho attestante*, mss. and Ox. ed.
7 *Et metaphysicæ secundo* is omitted in the mss. and Ox. ed.
8 *Continetur potissime plus*, mss. and Ox. ed.
9 *Mortales naturaliter comprehendant*, mss. and Ox. ed.
10 *Parvipendit*, mss. 797 and 2454, and Ox. ed; *Comprehendit*, ms. 3352c.
11 *Problematibus, particulo* 30, mss. 797, 3352c and Ox. ed.
12 *Antiqui pro gymnasticis*, mss. and Ox. ed.
13 *Temporalibus* ed. 1702.
14 *Uni*, ed. 1702; *Uno*, ed. 1610.

CHAPTER II.

SHOWETH THAT BOOKS ARE TO BE PREFERRED TO RICHES AND CORPORAL PLEASURES.

IF anything whatever, according to a degree of value, deserves a degree of love, the present chapter truly proves the ineffable value of books, though its conclusions may probably not appear clear to the reader; for we do not make use of demonstration in moral subjects, seeing that it is the business of a moral man to seek for certainty accordingly as he may have perceived the nature of the subject to bear it, as the archphilosopher witnesseth, *Ethics* I; *Metaph.* II: for Tully neither requires Euclid, nor does Euclid put faith in Tully. But this indeed we endeavor either logically, or rhetorically to inculcate, that riches and pleasures of every kind ought to give way to books in a spiritual mind, where the spirit, which is charity, ordaineth charity.

In the first place indeed, because more wisdom is contained in books than all mortals comprehend; and wisdom holds riches in no esteem, as alleged in the preceding chapter. Moreover Aristotle (*Problems*, sect. 30, dis. 11) determines this question, viz.: Upon what account did the ancients chiefly appoint prizes for gymnastic and corporal exertions, and never decree any reward for wisdom? Which question he thus solves. In gymnastic exercises, the reward is better and more eligible than that for which it is given; but it is evident, nothing is better than wisdom, wherefore no reward could have been assigned to wisdom;[8] therefore neither riches nor pleasures are more excellent than wisdom. Again, that friendship is to be preferred to riches, none but a fool will deny; to this the wisest of men bears witness. But the archphilosopher honors

Hanc quæstionem ita solvit:[1] *in gymnasticis exercitiis præmium est melius et eligibilius illo pro quo datur. Sapientia autem nihil melius esse constat*[2] *quamobrem sapientiæ nullum potuit præmium assignari.* Igitur[3] nec divitiæ nec deliciæ sapientiam[4] antecellunt.

Rursus amicitiam divitiis præponendam esse solus negabit insipiens, cum sapientissimus hoc testatur; amicitiæ vero veritatem archiphilosophus[5] præhonorat, et verus Zorobabel omnibus anteponit. Subsunt igitur deliciæ[6] veritati. Veritatem vero potissime et tuentur et continent satis[7] libri, imo sunt veritas ipsa scripta, quia[8] pro nunc librorum asseres librorum non asserimus esse partes. Quamobrem divitiæ subsunt libris, præsertim cum pretiosissimum genus divitiarium omnium sint amici, sicut *secundo de Consolatione* testatur Boëthius: quibus tamen librorum veritas est per Aristotelem præferenda.[9] Amplius vero cum[10] divitiæ ad solius corporis subsidia primo et principaliter pertinere noscantur: veritas[11] vero librorum sit perfectio rationis, quæ *bonum humanum* proprie nominatur.

Ergo[12] apparet, quod libri homini ratione utenti sunt divitiis cariores. Præterea enim illud, quo[13] fides defenditur[14] commodius, dilatatur[15] diffusius, prædicatur[16] lucidius, diligibilius debet esse fideli. Hoc autem est librorum[17] veritas libris[18] inscripta, quod evidentius figuravit Salvator quando contra tentationem[19] præliaturus viriliter se scuto circumdedit veritatis, non cujuslibet sed[20] scriptæ,[21] scriptum est præmittens, quod vivæ vocis articulo erat prolaturus;[22] *Matth.* iv. Rursus igitur[23] felicitatem nemo dubitat esse divitiis[24] præpon-

1 *Hanc responsione tertia ita solvit*, mss.
2 *Potest*, mss. and Ox. ed.
3 *Ergo*, mss. and Ox. ed.
4 *Animam*, ed. 1702.
5 *Ieraphilosiphus*, mss. and Ox. ed.
6 *Ergo divitiæ*, mss. and Ox. ed.
7 *Sacri*, mss. and Ox. ed.
8 *Quoniam*, mss. and Ox. ed.
9 *Præponenda*, ms. 2454.
10 *Amplius cum*, mss. and Ox. ed.
11 *Virtus*, mss. 2454, 3352c and Ox. ed.
12 *Ergo* omitted in mss. and Ox. ed.
13 *Præterea quo*, ms. 2454; *Præterea illud quo*, Ox. ed.
14 *Defenderetur*, mss. and Ox. ed.
15 *Dilataretur*, mss. and Ox. ed.
16 *Prædicaretur*, mss. and Ox. ed.
17 *Librorum* omitted in mss. 797, 3352c and Ox. ed.
13 *Libris* omitted in ms. 2454.
19 *Tentatorem*, mss. and Ox. ed.
20 *Imo*, mss. and Ox. ed.
21 *Scripturæ*, Ox. ed.
22 *Vocis oraculo fuerat probaturus*, mss. and Ox. ed.
23 *Autem*, mss. 787, 3352c. *Ergo*, ms. 2454. *Etiam*, Ox. ed.
24 *Dubitat præponendam*, ms 787. *Dubitat divitis præponendam*, ms. 2454.

truth above friendship; and the ancient Zorobabel gives it precedence over all things; therefore pleasures are inferior to truth. But the sacred books most powerfully preserve and contain the truth; they are assuredly the written truth itself; for upon this occasion we do not assert the main beams of the books to be parts of books, wherefore riches are inferior to books, more especially as the most precious of all kinds of riches are friends (witness Boëtius *De Consolatione*, book II), to which, however, the truth of books is preferred by Aristotle. But, further, as riches are primarily and principally acknowledged to pertain to the aid of the body only, and as the truth of books is the perfection of reason, which is properly named the good of mankind; so it appears that books to a man using them with reason are dearer than riches. Again, that by which the faith is most conveniently defended, most widely diffused, and most clearly preached, ought to be most beloved by a faithful man; and that is the truth of books, inscribed in books; which our Saviour most evidently figured when, manfully fighting against temptation, he covered himself with the shield of truth, not indeed of writing of any sort; but premising, that what he was about to declare by the sound of his living voice, was also written. *Matth.* iv.

Again, therefore, nobody doubts that happiness is to be preferred to riches, for happiness is consistent with the operation of the most noble and divine power we possess, namely, when the intellect is entirely at leisure for the contemplation of the truth of knowledge, which is the most delectable of all operations according to virtue, as the prince of philosophers[a] determines in the Nicomachian *Ethics*, book X, on which account philosophy also appears to possess admirable delights from its purity and stability, as the same author states in the sequel. But the contemplation of truth is never more

a Aristotle is inserted in one text, but not in Oxford ed. See note 2, p. 60.—*Ed.*

endam. Consistit enim[1] felicitas in operatione nobilissimæ et divinioris potentiæ quam habemus, dum videlicit intellectus vacat totaliter veritati sapientiæ contemplandæ, quæ est delectabilissima omnium operationum secundum virtutem, sicut princeps philosophorum Aristoteles[2] determinat *quarto*[3] *Ethicorum;* propter quod et philosophia videtur habere admirabiles delectationes, puritate et firmitate, ut ibidem[4] scribitur consequenter. Contemplatio autem veritatis nunquam est perfectior quam per libros, dum actualis imaginatio continuata per[5] actum intellectus, super visas veritates non sustinet interrumpi. Quamobrem libri videntur esse felicitatis speculativæ immediatissima instrumenta; unde Aristoteles, sol physicæ[6] veritatis, ubi de eligendis distribuit methodos,[7] docet, quod philosophari est simpliciter eligibilius[8] quam ditari, quamvis casu, ex circumstantiis[9] puta necessariis, indigenti ditari quam philosophari sit potius eligendi, *tertio Topicorum.*

Adhuc[10] cum nobis libri sint commodissimi magistri, ut præcedens assumit capitulum, eisdem non immerito tam amorem quam honorem tribuere convenit magistralem. Tandem cum omnes homines[11] natura[12] scire desiderant, ac per libros scientiam veritatis[13] præoptandam divitiis omnibus adipisci possimus, quis homo secundum naturam vivens, librorum non habeat appetitum? Quamvis vero[14] porcos margaritas spernere videamus,[15] nihil in hoc prudentis læditur opinio, quominus oblatas comparet margaritas. Pretiosior igitur est cunctis opibus sapientiæ libraria, et omnia quæ desiderantur, huic non valent comparari. *Proverbiorum tertio.* Quisquis igitur fatetur se veritatis,[16] felicitatis, sapientiæ,[17] scientiæ, vel[18] etiam fidei zelatorem, librorum necesse est[19] se fateatur amatorem.

1 *Autem*, mss. and Ox. ed.
2 *Aristoteles*, not in mss. nor Ox. ed.
3 *Decimo*, mss. and Ox. ed.
4 Omitted in the mss and Ox. ed.
5 *Per librum actum*, mss. and Ox. ed.
6 *Philosophicæ*, Ox. ed.
7 *De eligendis disciplinarum methodis*, ms. 2454.
8 *Eligibilibus*, ed. of 1702.
9 *Quamvis in casu ex circumstantia*, mss. and Ox. ed.
10 *Ad hæc*, ed. of 1702.
11 *Homines*, omitted in ed. of 1702.
12 *Naturales*, Ox. ed.
13 *Scientiam veterum*, mss.; Ox. ed.
14 *Enim*, ibid.
15 *Sciamus*, ibid.
16 *Veritatis*, omitted in Ox. ed.
17 *Sapientiæ vel scientiæ*, mss.; Ox. ed.
18 *Seu*, mss. and Ox. ed.
19 *Est ut se faciat*, ms. 3352c, and Ox. ed.

perfect than in books, as the active imagination, kept up by a book, does not permit the operation of the intellect upon visible truths to be interrupted.[a] For which reason books appear to be the most immediate instruments of speculative happiness; whence Aristotle, the sun of physical truth, where he unfolds the doctrine of objects of choice, teaches that to philosophize is in itself more eligible than to grow rich, although from necessary circumstances in the case, it may be thought more eligible for an indigent man to grow rich than to philosophize. *Topics*, III. Inasmuch, then, as books are our most convenient masters, as the preceding chapter assumes, it becomes us not undeservedly to bestow upon them, not only love, but magisterial honor.

Finally, as all men by nature are desirous of knowledge, and as we are able by books to obtain the knowledge of truth, to be chosen before all riches, what man, living according to nature, can be without an appetite for books? But although we may see hogs despise pearls, the opinion of a prudent man is in no way injured by that; he will not the less purchase proffered pearls. The library, therefore, of wisdom is more precious than all riches, and nothing that can be wished for is worthy to be compared with it. *Prov.* iii. Whosoever, therefore, acknowledges himself to be a zealous follower of truth, of happiness, of wisdom, of science, or even of the faith, must of necessity make himself a lover of books.

a This translation differs widely from the text, and requires the presence of *librum* as it is, as appears by note 5 on p. 60, in the Oxford ed.—*Ed.*

CAPITULUM III.

QUOD LIBRI SEMPER DEBENT EMI, NISI IN DUOBUS CASIBUS.[1]

CORRELARIUM nobis gratum de prælectis[2] elicimus, paucis tamen (ut credimus) acceptandum. Nullam videlicet debere caristiam hominem impedire ab emptione librorum, cum sibi suppetat, quod petitur pro eisdem, nisi ut[3] obsistatur malitiæ venditoris, vel tempus emendi oportunius exspectetur. Quoniam si sola sapientia, præcipuum facit libri,[4] quæ est infinitus thesaurus hominibus, et si valor librorum est ineffabilis, ut prædicta[5] supponunt, qualiter probabitur carum esse commercium, ubi bonum emitur infinitum? Quapropter libros libenter emendos et invite vendendos, sol hominum, Salomon nos hortatur. *Prov.* xxiii. *Veritatem*, inquit, *eme, et noli vendere sapientiam.* Sed quod rhetorice vel logice suademus, adstruamus historiis rei gestæ.

Archiphilosophus Aristoteles, quem Averroës[6] datum putat quasi regulam in natura, paucos libros Speusippi, post ipsius decessum, pro septuaginta duobus millibus sestertiis statim emit. Plato prior tempore sed doctrinis posterior, Philolai pythagorici librum emit pro[7] millibus denariorum, de quo dicitur *Timæi* dialogum excerpsisse. Sic refert A. Gellius *Noctium Atticarum, libro secundo*,[8] *capitulo* xvi. Hæc autem narrat A. Gellius, ut perpendat insipiens, quantum[9] vilipendant[10] sapientes pecuniam comparatione librorum. Et e contrario, ut omni superbiæ stultitiam cognoscamus annexam, libet[11] hic Tarquinii

1 *Qualiter in libris emendis sit pretium æstimandum*, ms. 797 and Ox. ed.
2 *Prædictis*, Ox. ed.
3 *Ut suppetatur obsistatur*, ms. 797
4 *Pretium facit libris*, Ox. ed.
5 *Præmissa*, mss. and Ox. ed.
6 *Averoys*, mss.
7 *Pro decem millibus*, mss.; Ox. ed.
8 *Libro tertio*, mss. and Ox. ed.
9 *Sicut refert A. Gellius, ut perpendat insipiens quam nichilipendant*, ms. 3352c.
10 *Quam nichilipendant*, mss. and Ox. ed.
11 *Autem*, ms. 2454.

CHAPTER III.

BOOKS OUGHT ALWAYS TO BE BOUGHT EXCEPT IN TWO CASES.

WE draw this corollary satisfactory to ourselves from what has been said, although, as we believe, but few will receive it; namely, that no expense ought to prevent men from buying books when what is demanded for them is at their command, unless the knavery of the seller is to be withstood, or a better opportunity of purchasing is expected. Because if wisdom alone, which is an infinite treasure to man, determines the price of books, and if the value of books is ineffable, as the premises suppose, how can a bargain be proved to be dear which purchases an infinite benefit. For this reason Solomon, the sun of mankind (*Prov.* xxiii), exhorts us to buy books freely and sell sparingly: he says, "Buy truth, and sell not wisdom." But what we now rhetorically and logically inculcate, we can support by histories of past events. The archphilosopher Aristotle, whom Averroës thinks was given as it were for a rule in nature, bought a few of Speusippus's books immediately after his death for 72,000 sesterces.[10] Plato, prior to him as to time, but his inferior as to doctrine, bought the library of Philolaus the Pythagorean for 10,000[a] denarii; from which he is said to have extracted the dialogue of Timæus, as Aulus Gellius relates, *Noct. Attic.* book III, c. xvi. But Aulus Gellius relates these things, that the ignorant may consider how greatly the wise undervalue money in comparison with books: and on the contrary, that we may all know the folly attached to pride, let us here review the folly of Tarquin the

a 1000 in the text. See note 7, p. 62.—*Ed.*

superbi stultitiam recensere in parvipensione[1] librorum, quam refert idem A. Gellius *Noctium Atticarum, libro primo, cap.* xix. Vetula quædam omnino incognita ad Tarquinium superbum, regem Romanorum septimum[2] dicitur accessisse, venales offerens novem libros, in quibus (ut asseruit) divina continebantur oracula, sed immensam pro iisdem poposcit pecuniam, in tantum ut rex diceret, eamdem[3] delirare. Illa commota, tres libros in ignem projecit, et pro residuis summam, quam prius, exegit; rege negante, rursos tres libros[4] in ignem projecit, et adhuc[5] pro tribus residuis eamdem[6] summam poposcit. Tandem stupefactus supra modum Tarquinius summam pro tribus gaudet exsolvere, pro qua novem poterat redemisse. Vetula statim disparuit, quæ nec prius nec postea visa fuit.

Hi sunt libri Sibyllini, quos quasi quoddam divinum oraculum, per aliquem de quindecim viris consulebant Romani, et quindecim viratus creditur officium[7] habuisse.

Quid aliter[8] hæc sibylla prophetissa tam vario[9] facto superbum regem edocuit, nisi quod vasa sapientiæ, sacri libri, omnem humanam æstimationem excedunt? Et sicut de regno Cœlorum dicitur:[10] tantum valet, quantum habes.

1 *Impensione*, Ox. ed.
2 *Sextum*, ms. 2454.
3 *Eam*, mss. 797, 2454, and Ox. ed.; *Eam diceret delirare.* ms. 3352c.
4 *Alios*, mss. and Ox. ed.
5 *Ad hæc*, ed. 1702.
6 *Primam*, mss. and Ox. ed.
7 *Originem*, mss.; *Officium originem*, Ox. ed. and ms. 3352c.
8 *Aliud*, mss. and Ox. ed.
9 *Vafro*, ms. 797 and Ox. ed.
10 *Dicit Gregorius*, Ox. ed.

Proud in undervaluing books, as the same Aulus Gellius relates it, *Noct. Attic.*, book I, c. xix. "A certain old "woman, quite unknown, is said to have come into the "presence of Tarquin the Proud, the seventh king of "the Romans, and offered him nine books for sale, in "which, as she asserted, the divine oracles were con-"tained; but she demanded such an immense sum of "money for them, that the king said she was mad. "Taking offence at this, she threw three of the books "into the fire, and demanded the sum first asked for the "rest. The king refusing, she threw three more of the "books into the fire, and still demanded the same sum "for the remaining three. At length Tarquin, being "astonished beyond measure, was glad to pay the sum "for three books for which he could have bought the "whole nine. The old woman, who was never seen "before nor afterwards, immediately disappeared." These are Sibylline books which the Romans consult as divine oracles, through one of the quindecemvir, and from them the quindecemvirate office is supposed to have had its origin. What else did this Sibylline prophetess teach the proud king by so subtle a device, but that the vases of wisdom, the sacred books, surpass all human estimation; and as Gregory says of the kingdom of heaven, "Whatsoever you may possess, that is "its value!"

CAPITULUM IV.

QUANTA BONA PROVENIANT PER LIBROS ET QUOD MALI CLERICI SUNT LIBRIS PLURIMUM INGRATI.[1]

PROGENIES viperarum, parentes proprios perimens, atque semen nequam ingratissimi cuculi, quæ[2] cum vires acceperit, virium largitricem suam nutriculam necat: sic[3] clerici degeneres erga libros. Redite prævaricatores ad cor, et quod per libros recipitis fideliter, computetis,[4] et invenietis libros, totius nobilis status vestri creatores,[5] sine quibus procul dubio defecissent[6] promotores.

Ex persona librorum.[7]

Ad nos nempe rudes penitus et inertes reptastis,[8] ut parvuli sapiebatis, ut parvuli evigilantes[9] implorastis participes fieri lactis nostri. Nos ergo[10] protinus lacrymis vestris tacti, mamillam grammaticæ porreximus exsugendam, quam dentibus atque lingua contractastis assidue, donec direpta nota barbarie,[11] nostris[12] linguis inciperetis magnalia Dei fari. Post hæc philosophiæ vestibus valde bonis, dialectica et rhetorica, quas apud nos habuimus et habemus, vos induimus, cum essetis nudi atque tabula depingenda. Omnes enim philosophiæ domestici sunt vestiti duplicibus, ut tegatur tam nuditas quam ruditas intellectus. Post hæc, ut alati more seraphico super cherubin scandentes transmisimus[13] ad

1 *Querimonia librorum contra clericos jam promotos*, mss. 797, 3352c and Ox. ed.

2 *Qui*, Ox. ed.

3 *Sunt*, mss. and Ox. ed.

4 *Et quid per libros recipitis, fideliter, computate*, Ox. ed.

5 *Vestri quodammodo creatores*, mss. 797, 3352c and Ox. ed.; *Vestri quosdam creatores*, ms. 2454.

6 *Defecissent cæteri promotores*, mss. and Ox. ed.

7 *Ex persona librorum* not in the mss. nor in Oxford ed.

8 *Reptastis ut parvuli loquebamini*, mss. 797, 3352c, and Ox. ed.

9 *Ejulantes*, mss. and Ox. ed.

10 *Vero*, mss. 797, 3352c and Ox. ed.

11 *Donec dempta nativa*, mss. 797, 2454; *Contrectastis assidue donec dempta vestra*, Ox. ed.; *Donec dempta natura*, ms. 3352c.

[Donec direpta notatur barbarie—nota barbarie—dempta vestra barbarie—babbling accents—all wrong perhaps.—*Inglis*.] *Quere*, barbara—*Ed.*

12 *Vestris*, ms. 797 and Ox. ed.

13 *Cherubin scanderetis, quadrivialium pennas vobis adjungentes, transmisimus*, mss. 797, 2454, and Ox. ed.; *Cherubin ....quatuor adjungentes transmisimus*. ms. 3352c. [*Quadruvij*

CHAPTER IV.

HOW MUCH GOOD ARISES FROM BOOKS; AND THAT THE CORRUPT CLERGY ARE FOR THE MOST PART UNGRATEFUL TO BOOKS.

A PROGENY of vipers destroying its own parents, and the cruel offspring of the most ungrateful cuckow, which, when it hath acquired strength, slays its little nurse, the liberal donor of its power; such are the degenerate clergy with respect to books. Turn to your hearts, ye prevaricators, and faithfully compute how much you have received from books,[a] and you will find books to have been in a manner the creators of your entire noble estate; without them it would certainly have been deficient of promoters. Hear them speak for themselves. Well then: When you were altogether ignorant and helpless, you spoke like children, you knew like children; and crying like children you crept towards us, and begged to be participators of our milk. We indeed, moved by your tears, instantly tendered you the paps of grammar to suck, which you firmly adhered to with tooth and tongue, till your babbling accents[11] were overcome, and you began to utter the mighty acts of God in our own language. After that we clothed you with the right comely garments of philosophy, dialectics, and rhetoric, which we had, and keep by us; as you were naked, and like tablets for painting upon: for all the inmates of philosophy are doubly clothed, that the nakedness, as well as the rudeness of their understandings may be concealed. Lastly, affixing to you the four wings[12] of the four converging

a This translation is according to the Oxford Edition (see note 4 p. 66) and differs from our text decidedly.—*Ed.*

b This sentence varies considerably from our text. It requires the *ejulantes* and *ut parvuli loquebamini* of the Oxford edition.—*Ed.*

amicum, ad cujus ostium, cum tam[1] improbe pulsaretis, tres panes[a] commodarentur intelligentiæ trinitatis, in qua consistit finalis felicitas cujuslibet viatoris. Quod si vos hæc munera non habere dixeritis, confidenter asserimus, quod vel ea per incuriam perdidistis collata, vel in principio desides respuistis oblata. Si hujusmodi videantur ingratis pusilla, adjicimus his majora. Vos estis genus electum, regale sacerdotium, gens sacra et populus acquisitionis, vos peculiarem in sortem[2] Domini computati, vos sacerdotes et ministri Dei, imo vos antonomastice ipsa ecclesia,[3] dicimini, quasi laici non sint ecclesiatici nuncupandi. Vos laicis postpositis,[b] psalmos et hymnos concinitis in cancellis, et altari Dei servitis altario[4] participantes, verum conficitis corpus Christi, in quo Deus ipse vos non solum laicis, imo paulo magis angelis honoravit. Cui enim aliquando angelorum dixit: *Tu es sacerdos in æternum secundum ordinem Melchisedech?* Vos corporis crucifixi testimonium dispensatis[5] pauperibus, ubi jam quæritur inter dispensatores, ut fidelis quis inveniatur. Vos estis pastores gregis diversi, tam exemplo quam[6] verbo doctrinæ, qui vobis tenetur rependere lac et lanam.

Qui sunt istorum omnium largitores, O clerici? Nonne libri? Reminisci libeat, supplicamus, quod per nos clericis sunt concessa egregia privilegia libertatum.[7] Per nos, siquidem vasa sapientiæ et intellectus imbuti, cathedras scanditis magistrales, vocati ab hominibus *rabbi*. Per

pennas may mean the four gospels. Arithmetic, geometry, music, astrology, are called *quadrivium* in the gloss on Boetius. *Scientiæ quadruviales* G. de Monte Rockerij. *Litteræ quadruviales, triviales, Quadrifida mathesis*, J. Stapulensis, used to express the various branches of any science, &c.—*Inglis.*]

a The three loaves This idea was taken from *Luke* xi, 5; but the 8th verse is rather against the bishop's explanation of the three loaves: "He will give him *as many* as he needeth."—*Inglis.*

b ***Postpositis***, placed behind. The reformers were very indignant at the manner in which mass is celebrated. The priest stands with his back to the people. In describing the ceremony, one of them says: "Then turning his tail to the people," or words to that effect.—*Inglis.*

1 *Dum tamen*, Ox. ed.

2 *Gens sancta, populus peculiaris in sortem*, ms. 797; *Gens sancta et populus acquisitionis, vos populus peculiaris in sortem*, Ox. ed.: *Gens sancta vos populus peculiaris*, ms. 3352c.

3 *Ecclesia Dei*, mss. 797, 3352c, and Ox. ed.

4 *Et altari deservientes, cum altario*, mss. and Ox. ed.

5 *Vos crucifixi patrimonium dispensatis*, mss. and Ox. ed.

6 *Dominici tam exemplo vitæ quam*, Ox. ed.

7 *Privilegia sacerdotum*, ms. 797.

ways,[a] that being winged in a seraphic manner you might soar above the cherubim, we transmitted you to a friend, at whose door, while you yet knocked earnestly, the three loaves of the intelligence of the Trinity, upon which the final happiness of every wayfaring man whatever depends, would be prepared for you. What if you should say, You have no such gifts; we confidently assert that you either lost them, when conferred upon you, throu carelessness, or rejected them from the beginning,[13] when offered to you, through indolence. If trifles of this kind are found disagreeable, we will add something more important. You are the elect race, the royal priesthood, the holy tribe and people of the acquisition;[14] you are held to be in the peculiar lot of the Lord, the priests and ministers of God; indeed you may be called by antonomasia the church itself, inasmuch as laymen cannot be called churchmen. You chant psalms and hymns in the chancel, and serve at the altar of God, participating with the altar, while the laity are placed behind you.[15] You concoct[b] the true body of Christ, in which God himself hath honored you, not only above laymen, but even somewhat above his angels; for to which of the angels hath he ever said, Thou art a priest for ever after the order of Melchisedech?[16] You dispense the testimony of Christ crucified to the poor. Where is it now sought for amongst the dispensers, so that any faithful man can find it?[c] You are the pastors of the flock of the Lord, as well by the example of your lives as by the words of your doctrine, which is kept by you to distribute the milk and the wool. Who, O clergy, are the liberal bestowers of these gifts? Are they not books? We beg it may please you to remember how many excellent privileges of exemption and freedom have been conceded to the clergy through us. Qualified indeed by us alone, the vessels of wisdom and intellect, you ascend the ma-

a This is not in the text, but is in the Ox. ed. See note 13, p. 66.—*Ed.*

b *Concoct* is a bad translation.—*Ed.*

c This differs from the text.—*Ed.*

nos, in oculis laicorum mirabiles, velut magna mundi luminaria, dignitates ecclesiæ, secundum sortes varias, possidetis. Per nos, cum adhuc carebatis genarum lanugine, in ætate tenera constituti, tonsuram portatis in vertice, prohibentem statum ecclesiæ sententia formidandum.[1] *Nolite tangere christos meos, et in prophetis meis nolite malignari.* Et qui eos tetigerit temere, violenter anathematis vulnere ictu proprio[2] feriatur.

Tandem ætate succumbente malitiæ, figuræ Pythagoricæ bivium attingentes, ramum lævum eligitis, et retrorsum abeuntes, sortem Domini præassumptam dimittitis, socii facti furum. Sicque[3] proficientes in pejus, latrociniis, homicidiis et multigenis impudicitiis maculati, tam fama quam conscientia tabefacta sceleribus, compellente justitia in manicis et compedibus coarctati servamini, morte turpissima puniendi. Tunc elongatur amicus et proximus, nec est, qui doleat vicem vestram. Petrus jurat se hominem non novisse: vulgus clamat justitiario: *Crucifige eum, crucifige, quoniam, si hunc dimiseris, non es amicus Cæsaris.* Jam periit omnis fuga, jam[4] ante tribunal oportet assisti, nec locus suppetit appellandi, sed solum suspendium exspectatur. Dum sic tristitia compleverit cor miseri et solæ camenæ laceræ[5] fletibus ora rigant, fit balatus[6] angustiis undique, memor nostri, et ut evitet mortis propinquæ periculum, antiquatæ tonsuræ quam dedimus, parvum præfert signaculum,[a] supplicans ut vocemur in medium et collati muneris testes simus. Tunc misericordia statim moti, occurrimus filio prodigo, et a portis mortis, servum eripimus fugitivum. Legendus liber porrigitur non ignotus, et ad modicam balbutientis præ timore lecturam, judicis potestas dissolvitur, accusator subtrahitur, mors fugatur.

a *Parvum præfert signaculum.* The benefit of clergy is alluded to. From this and what follows, it appears to have been only intended for clergymen, and not for everybody that could read, as some have supposed. A particular verse in the psalms was generally read; it is mentioned somewhere but I cannot recollect where.—*Inglis.*

1 *Prohibente statim ecclesiastica sententia formidanda*, mss. 797, 3352c, and Ox. ed.

2 *Proprio protinus*, mss. and Ox. ed.

3 *Sicque semper*, mss. 797, 3352c, and Ox. ed.

4 *Nam*, ibid.

5 *Lacrymæ*, Ox. ed.

6 *Valatus*, mss. 797, 3352c; Ox. ed.

gisterial chair, and men call you *rabbi*. Through us you are admirable in the sight of the laity, as the great luminaries of the world; and you possess the dignities of the church according to your various destinies. Constituted by us at a tender age, while you yet wanted the down upon your chins, you bore the tonsure upon your crowns, bespeaking the formidable state of the church in the decree, Touch not my anointed, and do my prophets no harm: and whoever rashly toucheth them, his own blow shall instantly recoil upon him with the wound of an anathema.

At length, falling into the age of wickedness, arriving at the double way of the Pythagoric symbol Y,[a] you choose the left-hand branch, and turning aside cast off the preassumed destination of the Lord, and become companions of thieves; and thus over progressing to worse, you are defiled by robberies, homicide, and various shameful crimes, your character and conscience being equally corrupted by wickedness. Being called to justice, you are kept bound in manacles and fetters, to be punished by a most ignominious death. Then your friend and neighbor is absent, nor is there any one to pity your fate. Peter swears he never knew the man; the mob cry out to the judge, Crucify him! crucify him! for if you discharge this man you will not be the friend of Cæsar. It is now too late to fly; you must stand before the tribunal; no place of appeal offers itself; nothing but hanging is to be expected. When sorrow and the broken song of lamentation alone shall have thus filled the heart of a wretched man;[b] when his cheeks are watered with tears, and he becomes surrounded with anguish on every side, let him remember us; that he may avoid the peril of approaching death, let him display the little token,[17] of the antiquated tonsure which we gave him,

a An allusion, says M. Cocheris, in a note to this passage, to the letter Y of Pythagoras, which represents the road of virtue and vice.—*Ed.*

b This translation requires *lacrymæ* of Ox. ed., in place of the *laceræ* of the text. The text is: While the heart of the wretched man is thus filled with sadness, and the dishevelled Muses alone weep over him.—*Ed.*

O carminis empirici mira virtus! O diræ cladis antidotum salutare! O lectio pretiosa psalterii, quæ meretur hoc ipso liber vitæ deinceps appellari! Sustineant laici sæculare judicium, ut vel insuti culleis enatent ad Neptunum, vel in terra plantati Plutoni fructificent, aut Vulcano per incendia holocausta se offerant medullata, vel certe suspensi victima sint Junoni; dum noster alumnus, ad lectionem unicam libri vitæ, pontificis commendatur custodiæ, et rigor in favorem convertitur. Ac dum forum transfertur a laico,[a] a librorum alumno clerico mors defertur.

Ceterum jam de clericis, qui sunt vasa virtutum, nos loquamur.[1] Quis de vobis pulpitum vel scabellum prædicaturus ascendit, nobis penitus inconsultis? Quis scholas lecturus vel disputaturus vel prædicaturus[2] ingreditur, qui nostris comatibus[3] non fulcitur? Primum oportet volumen cum Ezechiele comedere, quo venter memoriæ dulcescat extrinsecus.[4] Et modo sint[5] pantheræ refertæ, redoleat extrinsecus conceptorum aromatum odor suavis, ad cujus anhelitum coanhelent accedere homines, bestiæ[6] et jumenta. Sic natura nostra in vobis familiarius[7] operante latenter, auditores accurrunt benevoli, sicut adamas trahit ferrum nequaquam invite. Quinimo infinita librorum multitudo jacet[8] Parisiis vel Athenis, similiter resonant in Britannia vel in Roma. Quiescentes quippe moventur, dum ipsis loca sua tenentibus, auditorum intellectibus circumquaque feruntur. Nos denique sacerdotes, pontifices, cardinales, et papam, ut cuncta in hierarchia ecclesiastica[9] collocentur, in ordine literarum scientia stabilimus. A libris namque sumit originem, quicquid boni provenit statui clericali. Sed

a *Dum forum transfertur a laico*, in all the editions. Query, *laicus transfertur ad forum*.

"Then went he to the market place,
As fast as he could hye,
A payre of new gallows he there set up,
Beside the pillory."

The layman transferred to the market place, would be more intelligible. —*Inglis*.

1 *Vasa virtutis loquamur*, mss. 797, 3352c, and Ox. ed.

2 *Vel prædicaturus* wanting in mss. 797, 3352c, and in Ox. ed.

3 *Conatibus*, Ox. ed.

4 *Intrinsecus*, mss. and Ox. ed.

5 *Et modo sic*, ms. 2454. *Et sic more*, ms. 797, and Ox. ed.

6 *Omnes bestiæ*, Ox. ed,

7 *In nostris familiaribus*, Ox. ed.

8 *O virtus infinita librorum*, *jacent*, ms. 3352c, and Ox. ed.

9 *Ecclesiastica*, wanting in Ox. ed.

begging that we may be called in on his behalf, and bear witness to the benefit conferred.

Then moved by pity we instantly run to meet the prodigal son, and snatch the fugitive servant from the gates of death; the well known book is tendered to be read, and after a slight reading by the criminal stammering from fear, the power of the judge is dissolved, the accuser is withdrawn, death is put to flight. Oh wonderful virtue of an empiric verse! Oh salutary antidote to dire calamity! Oh precious reading of the *Psalter*, which deserves henceforth from this itself to be called the book of life! Laymen must undergo secular punishment; either being sewn up in sacks they may be consigned to Neptune; or planted in the ground may fructify for Pluto; or may offer themselves up by fire, as fattened holocausts to Vulcan; or at all events, being hanged they may be victims to Juno,[a] while our pupil, by a single reading of the book of life, is commended to the custody of the pontiff, and rigor is converted into favor. And while the bench is transferred from the layman,[18] death is averted from the clerical nursling of books.

Let us now speak of those clergy who are the vessels of virtue. Which of you ascends the pulpit or desk to preach without first consulting us? Which enters the schools either to lecture, dispute or preach, who is not enlightened by our rays?

You must first eat the volume with Ezekiel, that the stomach of your memory may be internally sweetened; and thus after the manner of the perfumed panther[b] (to the breath of which men, beasts and cattle draw near that they may inhale it), the sweet odor of your aromatic conceptions will be externally redolent. Thus our nature secretly and most intimately working within you, benevolent auditors flock about you, as the magnet attracts iron, by no means unwillingly. What though

a The pious prelate waxes merry upon so cheerful a subject.—*Ed.*

b An allusion to the idea prevailing in former times that the panther exhaled a pleasant aroma, and drawing to him by this means his prey, seized upon it.—*Pliny, Nat. Hist.* book VII, chap. xxiii.—*Ed.*

hæc hactenus. Piget[1] reminisci, quæ dedimus populo clericorum degeneri, quæ[2] magis videntur perdita, quam collata quæcumque munera tribuuntur ingratis. Deinceps insistemus parum pro[3] recitandis injuriis, quas rependunt vilipensionibus et jacturis; de quibus nec singula genera recitare sufficimus, imo vix proxima genera singularum.

In primis de domiciliis clericorum, nobis, jure hereditario, debitis vi et armis expellimur. In quodam interiori[4] cubiculo cellulas habebamus quietas,[5] sed proh dolor! his nefandis temporibus, penitus exsulantes improperium patimur extra portas. Occupant enim[6] loca nostra nunc canes et aves,[7] nunc bestia bipedalis, scilicet mulier, cujus habitatio vitabatur a clericis,[8] a qua semper super aspidem et basiliscum alumnos nostros docuimus fugiendum; quamobrem ista[9] bestia[10] nostris studiis semper æmula, nullo die placanda, finaliter nos conspectos in angulo jam defunctæ arenæ sola tela protectos, in rugam fronte collecta, virulentis sermonibus detrahit et subsannat. Ac nos in tota domus suppellectili semper vacuos hospitari[11] demonstrat, et ad unumquodque œconomiæ servitium quæritur otiosos, et mox in capitegia pretiosa, syndonem et sericum, et coccum bis tinctum, vestes et varias farraturas[a] lanam et linum consulit[12] commutandos. Et quidem merito, si videret intrinseca cordis nostri: si nostris privatis interfuisset consiliis: si Theophrasti vel Valerii perlegisset volumen, vel saltem *Ecclesiastici* xxv capitulum auribus intellectus audisset. Quapropter conquerimur de hospitiis nobis injuste ablatis, de vestibus non quidem datis, sed de datis anti-

a *Farraturas*, al. *furraturas*. It should be *forraturas*, from *fourrures*, Fr. it is so written by Ja. de Vitriaco, in *Vita Marie de Ocgines*, circa 1200, and other authorities. It properly means fur trimmings, *fourritures*.—*Inglis*.

1 *Piget enim*, mss. 797, 3352c, and Ox. ed.

2 *Quia*, ibid

3 *Parumper*, mss and Ox. ed.

4 *Expellimur, qui quondam in interiori*, mss. 797, 3352c, and Ox. ed.

5 *Quietis*, ibid.

6 *Et enim*, Ox. ed.

7 *Nunc canes, nunc aneti*, ms. 797; *Nunc canes, nunc aves*, ms. 3352c and Ox. ed.

8 *Scilicet mulier* is wanting in mss. 797, and 3352c, also in Ox. ed; the phrase is thus expressed: *Nunc bestia bipedalis cujus cohabitatio cum clericis velabatur antiquitus.*

9 *Fugere quamobrem istis*, Ox. ed.

10 *Bestia*, wanting in mss. 797, 3352c, and in Ox. ed.

11 *Super vacaneos hospitari*, mss. 797, 3352c, and in Ox. ed.

12 *Nos consulit*, ibid.

an infinite multitude of books be deposited in Paris or Athens, do they not likewise speak aloud in Britain and in Rome—for even being at rest they are moved; while confining themselves to their proper places, they are everywhere carried about to the understandings of hearers.

Finally, we establish priests, pontiffs, cardinals, and the pope, that all things in the ecclesiastical hierarchy may be set in order by the knowledge of letters; for every benefit that arises out of the clerical state has its origin in books. But even now it grieves us to reflect upon what we have given to the degenerate race of clergy, because gifts bestowed upon the ungrateful appear to be rather lost than conferred.

In the next place, let us stop a little to recite the injuries, indignities and reproaches they repay us with, of which we are not competent to recount all of every kind—scarcely indeed the first kinds of them all.

In the first place, we are expelled with heart and hand from the domiciles of the clergy, apportioned to us by hereditary right, in some interior chamber of which we had our peaceful cells: but, to their shame, in these nefarious times we are altogether banished to suffer opprobrium out of doors; our places, moreover, are occupied by hounds and hawks, and sometimes by a biped beast; woman, to wit, whose cohabitation[a] was formerly shunned by the clergy, from whom we have ever taught our pupils to fly, more than from the asp and the basilisk; wherefore this beast, ever jealous of our studies, and at all times implacable, spying us at last in a corner, protected only by the web of some long deceased spider, drawing her forehead into wrinkles, laughs us to scorn, abuses us in virulent speeches, points us out as the only superfluous furniture lodged in the whole house; complains that we are useless for any purpose of domestic economy whatever, and recommends our being bartered away forthwith for costly head-dresses, cambric, silk,

[a] *Habitatio* in the text.—*Ed.*

quitus violenter[1] manibus laceratis, in tantum quod adhæsit[2] pavimento anima nostra,[3] conglutinatus in terra est venter noster, et gloria nostra in pulverem redacta[4] est. Morbis variis laboramus dorsa lateraque: dolentes jacemus membratim paralysi dissoluti, nec est, qui cogitet, nec est, qui benigne malagma[5] procuret. Candor nativus et luce perspicuus, jam in fuscum et croceum est conversus, ut nemo medicus, qui nos reperiat, dubitet[6] ictericia nos infectos. Atteriam[7] patiuntur nonnulli de nobis, sicut extremitates retortæ insinuant evidenter. Fluvius aut[8] fumus ac pulvis, quibus infestamur assidue, radiorum visualium aciem hebetarunt, et jam lippientibus oculis ophthalmium superducunt. Ventres nostri duris torsionibus viscerum, quæ vermes edaces non cessant corrodere, consumuntur, et utriusque lateris[9] sustinemus putredinem, nec invenitur quisquam, qui cedri resina nos liniat, vel[10] quatriduano jam putrido clamans dicat, *Lazare, veni foras!* Nullo circumligantur ligamine[11] vulnera nostra sæva, quæ nobis innoxiis inseruntur atrociter, nec est ullus, qui super vulnera[12] nostra cataplasmet: sed pannosi et algidi, in angulos tenebrosos abjicimur in lacrymis, vel cum sancto Hiob in sterquilinio collocamur, vel quod nefas videtur mihi effari,[13] in abyssis abscondimur cloacarum. Pulvinar subtrahitur evangelicis supponendum lateribus, quibus primo deberent de sortibus clericorum[14] subsidia, et sic ad[15] suo famulatui deputandos prospere[16] communis victus necessariis,[17] derivari.

Rursus de alio genere calamitatis conquerimur, quæ personis nostris crebrius irrogatur injuste. Nam in servos

1 *Violentis* mss. 797, 3352c; Ox. ed.
2 *Laceratis adhæsit*, ibid.
3 *Mea*, ms. 3352c.
4 *Deducta*, mss. 797, 3352c, and Ox. [ed.
5 *Nec est qui recogitet, nec est ullus qui malagma*, mss. 797, 3352c, and Ox. ed.; *Nec est qui benigna aut maligna*, ms. 2454.
6 *Ut nemo medicus dubitet*, mss. 797, 3352c, and Ox. ed.
7 *Archeticam*, ms.; *Arthreticam*, Ox. edition.
8 *Fluvius aut* wanting in mss. 797 and 3352c, and in Ox. ed. We believe it should be *pluvia*.
9 *Lazari*, ms. 797, and Ox. ed.; *Viriusque Lazari*, ms. 3352c
10 *Vel qui*, mss. and Ox. ed.
11 *Medicamine*, mss. 797 and 3352c, and Ox. ed.
12 *Ulcera*, Ox. ed.
13 *Videtur affatu*, mss. 797, 3352c and [Ox.ed.
14 *Clericorum provenire*, ibid.
15 *Ad nos suo*, ibid.
16 *Pro semper*, ibid.
17 *Necessarius*, ibid.

twice dipped purple garments, woolen, linen and furs: and indeed with reason, if she could see the interior of our hearts, or be present at our secret councils, or could read the volumes of Theophrastus and Valerius, or at least hear the 25th chapter of Ecclesiasticus with ears of understanding.[17]

We complain, therefore, because our domiciles are unjustly taken from us—not that garments are not given to us, but that those which were formerly given are torn off by violent hands, insomuch that our souls adhere to the pavement, our belly is agglutinated to the earth, and our glory is reduced to dust (*Ps.* xliv and cxix). We labor under various diseases; our back and sides ache, we lie down disabled and paralyzed in every limb, nobody thinks of us, nor is there any one who will benignly apply an emollient to our sores. Our native whiteness, perspicuous with light, is now turned tawny and yellow; so that no medical man who may find us out, can doubt that we are infected with jaundice. Some of us are gouty,[a] as our distorted extremities evidently indicate. The damp, smoke and dust with which we are constantly infested, dim the field of our visual rays, and superinduce ophthalmia upon our already bleared eyes.

Our stomachs are destroyed by the severe griping of our bowels, which greedy worms never cease to gnaw. We suffer corruption inside and out, and nobody is found to annoint us with turpentine; or, who, calling to us on the fourth day of putrefaction, will say, Lazarus, come forth! The cruel wounds atrociously inflicted upon us who are harmless, are not bound up with any bandage, nor does any one apply a plaster to our ulcers. But we are thrown into dark corners, ragged, shivering and weeping, or with holy Job seated on a dung hill, or (what appears too indecent to be told) we are buried in the abysses of the common sewer. The supporting cushion is drawn from under our evangelical sides, from whose oracles the subsidies of the clergy ought first of

a *Attinam* probably means a wasting or wearing away; but Oxford ed. has *arthreticam*, allied to the classical word *arthritis*, meaning gout.—*Ed.*

venundamur[1] et ancillas, et obsides in tabernis absque redemptione[2] jacemus. In cellariis[3] crudelibus subdimur, ubi mactari tam pecora quam jumenta sine piis lacrymis non videmus, et ubi millesies moritur, ipso metu morimur, qui[4] in virum posset[5] cadere constantem. Judæis committimur, Sarracenis, hæreticis, et paganis, quorum semper[6] toxicum formidamus, per quos nonnullos de nostris parentibus per venenum pestiferum constat csse corruptos.

Sane nos, qui architectonici reputari debemus in scientiis, et subjectis nobis mechanicis imperamus, subalternorum[7] regimini vice versa committimur, tanquam si monarcha summe nobilis, rusticanis calcaneis substernatur. Sartor et sutor et scissor quicumque aut cujuslibet operis artifex, inclusos nos custodit in carcere, pro superfluis et lascivis deliciis clericorum.

Jam volumus prosequi novum genus injuriæ, quo tam in nostris personis lædimur quam in fama, qua[9] nihil carius possidemus. Generositati nostræ omni die detrahitur, dum per pravos compilatores, translatores, transformatores nova nobis auctorum nomina imponuntur, et antiqua nobilitate mutata, regeneratione multiplici renascentes degeneramus omnino. Sic quod vilium vitricorum[4] nobis nolentibus affiguntur vocabula, et verorum patrum nomina filiis subducuntur. Versus Virgilii adhuc ipso vivente quidam pseudoversificus usurpavit, et Martialis Coci[a] libellos Fidentinus quidam sibi mendaciter arrogavit, quem idem Martialis merito redarguit sub his verbis:

> Quem recitas, meus est, O Fidentine, libellus:
> Sed male quum recitas, incipit esse tuus.

Quid ergo mirum, si defunctis nostris auctoribus suas per nos fimbrias simiæ clericorum magnificant, cum eis-

a *Martialis Coci*, Martial the cook. The monks always call him so. It is said to have originated from a mistake in a dedication; but Martial very often speaks of cookery; this may have led somebody to speak of him in a way that a careless reader may have mistaken.—*Inglis*.

1 *Vendimur*, mss. 797, 3352c; Ox. ed.

2 *Redemptore*, ibid.

3 *Macellariis*, mss. 797, 3352c and Ox. ed.

4 *Millesies morimur ipso metu qui*, ib.

5 *Ipso metu qui posset*, ibid.

6 *Super omnia*, ibid.

7 *Subalternatorum*, ibid.

8 *Quia*, ms. 797.

9 *Victritiorum*, ms. 797 and Ox. ed. That edition gives the variation *auctorum*.

all to come, they being deputed to us for their service, and thus the common provision for their maintenance ought forever to be derived from us.[a]

"Again: we complain of another kind of calamity that is very often unjustly imposed upon our persons; for we are sold like slaves and female captives, or left as pledges in taverns without redemption.[b] We are given to cruel butchers to be cut up like sheep and cattle; we do not behold this without pious tears,[c] and where there is death in a thousand forms, we die of fear itself.

a This translation differs decidedly from our text, which we confess is not very intelligible to us. M. Cocheris's version of the passage I have translated into English as follows: They even go so far as to remove the cushions placed under the gospels, to which the clergy ought especially to give aid from their revenues, thus furnishing the necessaries of life to those who were charged with their own maintenance. —*Ed.*

b I have thought the following note appended by M Cocheris to his French translation, worth translating and preserving in this edition:

The fable, *Departement des Livres* (see Critical Preface), is vividly recalled by this passage, but there are two poems which describe still better the joyous lives led by the clergy. The first is by Walter Maps, the jolly archdeacon of Oxford, the prototype, not to say father, of the *Goliardi.*

Tales versus facio, quale vinum bibo.
Nihil possum scribere, nisi sumpto cibo.
Nihil valet penitus, quod jejunus scribo:
Nasonem, post calices, carmine præibo.

Mihi nunquam spiritus pœtriæ datur,
Nisi tunc cum fuerit venter bene satur;
Cum in arce cerebri Bacchus dominatur,
In me Phœbus irruit, et miranda fatur.

The following, entitled: *Des Fames, des Dez, et de la Taverne*, has been published by Meon (*Fabliaux*, vol. IV, p. 48), and it is even gayer than the preceding:

I live a pretty godly life *semper quantum possum*,
But when the landlord calls on me, I answer: *Ecce assum.*
To spend and scatter all my cash *semper paratus sum*,
For in my heart, I've often thought, *et meditatus sum*,
Aeger dives habet nummos, se non habet ipsum.

Women and wine and play too *libenter colo*,
A little game after supper *cum deciis volo*,
Though well I know the dice *non sunt sine dolo:*
Una vice I lose, I win on another throw;
Omnia sunt hominum tenui pendentia filo.

They even went so far as to parody the most sacred things; and in England, the native country of *Dame Drunkenness*, according to the minstrel Robert de Houdan, they composed a mass for drunkards; in Germany, for gamesters. There was a credo for drinkers, another for usurers, and a confiteor of Bacchus. "Our Father" was parodied as follows: "*Pater noster, qui es in scyphis, sanctificetur vinum istud. Adveniat Bacchi potus; fiat tempestas tua, sicut in vino et in taberna. Panem nostrum ad devorandum da nobis hodie, et dimittis nobis pocula magna, sicut et nos dimittimus potatoribus nostris, et ne nos inducas in vini tentationem, sed libera nos a vestimento.*"

The clergy were then for nothing but women, wine and gaming; and reading over these buffooneries, we may say with the author of the following couplets:

Je ne voi abe, ne moine,
Ne clerc, ne prestre ne chanoine
Frere menor, ne Jacobin
Qui tuit ne s' accordent au vin.

The reader desirous of becoming more thoroughly acquainted with this little reverential, not to say blasphemous literature of an age reputed religious, can consult the spicy article devoted to it by M. Victor Leclerc, in the 22d volume of the *Hist. Litt. de France.*—*Ed.*

c The text is: Where we do not see without pious tears sheep and cattle butchered, etc.—*Ed.*

dem superstitibus nos, recenter editos rapere moliantur. Ah, quoties nos antiquos fingitis nuper natos, et qui patres sumus, filios nominare conamini. Quique vos ad esse clericale creavimus, studiorum vestrorum fabricas appellatis. Revera de Athenis exstitimus oriundi, qui fingimur nunc Romani,[1] semper namque Carmentis latruncula fuit Cadmi, et qui nuper nascebamur in Anglia, cras Parisiis renascemur : et inde delati Bononiam, Italicam sortiemur originem nulla consanguinitate suffultam. Heu ! quam falsis scriptoribus nos exarandos committitis, quam corrupte[a] nos legitis et medicando[2] necatis, quos[3] pio zelo corrigere debebatis ![4] Interpretes barbaros sustinemus multoties, et qui linguarum idiomata nesciunt, nos de lingua ad linguam transferre præsumunt: sicque proprietate sermonis ablata, fit sententia contra sensum auctoris turpiter maculata ![5] Bone generosa[6] fuisset librorum conditio, si turris Babelonis[7] nullatenus obfuisset præsumptio, si totius humani generis unica descendisset sermonis species propagata !

a Notwithstanding all the warnings the author has given to transcribers, his own book has probably suffered more from them than any other work of so little importance. There is not a single page of the Oxford text that agrees with the first or Cologne edition of 1473, from which the present translation is made, with only such corrections of evident errors as were necessary. Some omissions are also supplied, but there are some in all the editions. The translator accidentally discovered from another work of Mr. James's, that he was not a man to be satisfied with correcting errors or supplying omissions of transcribers and printers; he even doubts his having collated various ancient manuscripts, but has no doubt of his having preferred his own words to those of the author. He may or may not have been a better Latinist than the Bishop: but he was not better versed in the dialect used by him and others of his time and country, who spoke it fluently, and wrote as they were accustomed to speak. It would be as great an absurdity to modernize every other line of Chaucer, as to reduce every other line of monkish Latin to the best ancient standard. This translation would not have appeared if there had been any other, good or bad. It is the work of one whom the Bishop would have debarred from the use of any book but a ledger. The translator has no quarrel with him on that account, and has nowhere willfully misrepresented him; on the contrary, he holds him in great respect, believing him to have been a lover of truth, and an exception to his order; he has therefore endeavored to give his meaning literally and correctly. It was curiosity to find out what manner of people lived, and how they acted and thought in the middle ages of our era, that induced the translator to read the language they usually wrote in, and to translate this book, which was done some years ago as an exercise: the regular bred scholar may find blunders in it, but it is hoped not such as to alter the meaning of the author. Many readers will be pleased to see it in any form, for the Latin editions are not easily to be found.—*Inglis.*

1 *Nunc de Roma*, mss. 797, 3352c, and Ox. ed.

2 *Et quoties meditando*, ibid.

3 *Quod*, Ox. ed.

4 *Credebatis*, mss. 797, 3352c, and Ox. ed.

5 *Mutilata*, ibid.

6 *Gratiosa*, ibid.

7 *Babel*, Ox. ed.

which is able to overthrow irresolute man. We are turned over to Jews, Saracens, heretics and pagans, whose poison we dread above all things, and by whose pestiferous venom it is evident some of our forefathers have been corrupted.

Truly, we who ought to be considered as the master builders in science, who give orders to our subject mechanics, are on the contrary subjected to the government of subalterns: as if a most noble monarch should be trampled upon by rustic heels. Every botcher, cobbler, and tailor whatever, or any artificer of whatever trade, keeps us shut up in prison, for the superfluous and lascivious pleasures of the clergy.

We will now proceed to a new sort of insult by which we are injured both in our persons and in our fame, than which we possess nothing dearer to us. Our genuineness is every day detracted from, for new names of authors are imposed upon us by worthless compilers, translators, and transformers; being reproduced in multiplied regeneration, our ancient nobility is changed, and we become altogether degenerate: and thus the names of vile authors are fixed upon us against our will, and the words of the true fathers are filched from them by the sons. A certain pseudo-versifier usurped the verses of Virgil while he was yet living; and one Fidentinus falsely arrogated to himself the books of Martial the cook, upon whom the said Martial justly retorted in these words:

> The book thou recitest, Fidentinus, is mine,
> Though from vile recitation it passeth for thine.

What wonder is it then if clerical apes magnify their margins from the works of authors who are dead; as while they are yet living they endeavor to seize upon their recent editions? Ah, how often do you pretend that we who are old are but just born, and attempt to call us sons, who are fathers? and to call that which brought you into clerical existence, the fabric of your own studies? In truth, we who now pretend to be

Ultimam prolixæ nostræ querelæ, sed pro materia quam habemus brevissimæ,[a] clausulam subjungimus. In nobis etenim commutatur naturalis usus in eum usum, qui est contra naturam, dum passim pictoribus subdimur literarum ignaris et aurifabris, proh dolor! commendamur nos, qui sumus lumen fidelium animarum, ut fiamus ac si non essemus sapientiæ sacræ vasa, repositoria bractearum: devolvimur indebite, in laicorum dominium, quod est nobis amarius omni morte, quoniam hi vendiderunt populum nostrum sine pretio, et inimici nostri judices nostri sunt.

Liquet omnibus ex præmissis,[1] quod infinita possemus in clericos invectiva convitiari,[2] si non honestati proprie parceremus. Nam miles emeritus clypeum veneratur et arma, gratusque Coridon aratro tepescenti[3] bigæ, trahæ, tribulæ ac ligoni: et omnis artifex manualis hypoduliam[4] propriam suis exhibet instrumentis: solus ingratus clericus parvipendit, et negligit ea, per[5] quæ sui honoris auspicia semper sumit.

a Quere, *brevissime?—Ed.*

1 *Prædictis*, mss. 797, 3352c, and Ox. ed.

2 *Commiscere*, ibid.

3 *Tabescente*, Ox. ed.

4 *Hyperdouliam*, Ox. ed.

5 *Negligit per*, Ox. ed.; *Negligit ea quæ*, ms. 3352c.

Romans, are evidently sprung from the Athenians; for Carmentis was ever a pillager of Cadmus: and we who are just born in England shall be born again to-morrow in Paris, and being thence carried on to Bononia, shall be allotted an Italian origin, unsupported by any consanguinity. Alas, to how many false transcribers have you committed us to be copied; how corruptly do you read us, and by amending, destroy what in pious zeal you intend to correct. In how many ways do we suffer from barbarous interpreters, who presume to translate us from one language to another, though ignorant of the idioms of either. The propriety of speech being thus taken away, its sense is basely mutilated, and contrary to the meaning of the author. The condition of books would have been right genuine, if the presumption of the Tower of Babel had not come in its way, and the only preserved form of speech of the whole human race had descended to us.

We will now subjoin the last of our prolix complaints, but most briefly, in proportion to the matter we have to complain of; for indeed natural use in us is converted into that which is contrary to nature: as, for instance, we are given up to painters ignorant of letters; and we who are the light of faithful souls are shamefully consigned to goldsmiths, that we may become repositories for gold leaf, as if we were not the sacred vessels of science. We fall unduly into the power of laymen, which to us is more bitter than any death; for they sell our people without a price, and our enemies become our judges. It is clear from all these premises, what infinite invectives we could have thrown out against the clergy if we had not spared them for our own credit. For the pensioned soldier venerates his shield and arms. Carts, harrows, flails, and spades are grateful to the worn-out plowman Coridon; and every manual artificer exhibits extraordinary care for his own tools.[18] The ungrateful clerk alone undervalues and neglects those things from which he must ever take the prognostics of his future honor.

CAPITULUM V.

QUOD BONI RELIGIOSI LIBROS SCRIBUNT, MALI ALIIS OCCUPANTUR.[1]

RELIGIONUM veneranda devotio in librorum cultu solet esse sollicita et in eorum colloquiis[2] sicut in omnibus divitiis delectari. Scribunt[3] namque nonnulli propriis manibus inter horas canonicas, intervallis captatis et tempora pro quiete corporis accommodata[4] fabricandis codicibus concesserunt. De quorum laboribus hodie, in plerisque splendent monasteriis, illa sacra gazophylacia, cherubicis literis[5] plena, ad dandam scientiam salutis studentibus, atque lumen delectabile semitis laicorum. O labor manualis felicior omni cura georgica! O devota sollicitudo, qua[6] nec meretur Martha corrumpi[7] nec Maria! O domus jucunda, in qua Racheli formosæ Lya non invidet fæcunda, sed contemplatio cum activa gaudia sua miscet. Felix providentia pro futuro infinitis posteris valitura, cui nulla virgultorum plantatio, nulla seminum statio comparatur,[8] nulla castrorum constructio munitorum! Quamobrem immortalis debet esse patrum illorum memoria, quos solius sapientiæ delectabat thesaurus. Qui contra futuras caligines, luminosas lucernas artificiosissime providerunt, et contra famem audiendi verbum Dei, panes non subcinericeos, neque hordeaceos, nec muscidos, sed panes azymos de purissima simila sacræ Sophiæ confectos accuratissime parant, quibus esurientes feliciter cibantur.[9] Hi fuerunt autem probissimi pugiles Christianiæ militiæ, qui nostram infirmitatem

1 *Querimonia librorum contra religiosos possessionatos*, mss. 797, 3352c and Ox. ed.
2 *Eloquiis*, ibid.
3 *Scribebant*, ibid.
4 *Commodata*, ibid.
5 *Libris*, ibid.
6 *Sollicitudo ubi*, ms. 797 and Ox. ed.
7 *Corripi*, Ox. ed. This sentence, *O devota*, etc., is omitted in ms. 3352c.
8 *Comparatur, nulla bucolica curiositas quorum libet armentorum*, mss. 797, 3352c and Ox. ed.
9 *Paraverunt quibus esurientes animæ feliciter cibarentur*, ibid.

CHAPTER V.

GOOD PROFESSORS OF RELIGION WRITE BOOKS; BAD ONES ARE OCCUPIED WITH OTHER THINGS.

THERE used to be an anxious and reverential devotion in the culture of books of religious offices, and the clergy delighted in communing with them as their whole wealth; for many wrote them out with their own hands in the intervals of the canonical hours, and gave up the time appointed for bodily rest to the fabrication of volumes: those sacred treasuries of whose labors, filled with cherubic letters, are at this day resplendent in most monasteries, to give the knowledge of salvation to students, and a delectable light to the paths of the laity. Oh happy manual labor above all agricultural cares! Oh devout solicitude, from which neither Martha nor Mary would have earned the wages of corruption! Oh joyful house, in which the fair Rachael envieth not the prolific Lya, but where contemplation mingles with its own active pleasures! Happy provision for the future, available to infinite posterity; to which no planting of trees, no sowing of seeds, no pastoral curiosity about any sort of cattle,[a] no building of fortified castles is to be compared. Wherefore the memory of those fathers ought to be immortal, whom the treasure of wisdom alone delighted, who most artificially provided luminous lanterns against future darkness, and prepared, against a dearth of hearing the word of God, bread not baked in ashes, nor musty, nor of barley, but unleavened loaves most carefully composed of the purest flour of holy wisdom, with which they fed the souls of the hungry. But these were the most virtuous com-

[a] This sentence is wanting in our text. It appears in the Oxford edition. See note 8, on the opposite page. —*Ed.*

armis fortissimis munierunt. Hi fuerunt suis temporibus vulpium veneratores[1] cautissimi, qui nobis jam sua retia reliquerunt, ut parvulas caperemus vulpeculas, quæ non cessant florentes vineas demoliri. Vere patres egregii benedictione perpetua recolendi, felices merito fuissetis, si vobis similem sobolem genuisse, si prolem[2] degenerem nec æquivocam reliquisse in[3] sequentis temporis subsidium licuisset.

Sed, quod dolentes referimus, jam Thersites ignavus arma contrectat Achillis et dextrariorum phaleræ electæ[4] pigritantibus asinis substernuntur, aquilarum nidis cæcutientes noctuæ dominantur, et in accipitris pertica residet vecors milvus. Liber Bacchus respicitur, et in ventrem projicitur[5] nocte dieque, liber codex despicitur,[6] et a manu rejicitur longe lateque, atque[7] si cujusdam æquivocationis multiplicitate fallatur simplex plebs[8] moderna, dum Liber potationum[9] præponitur libro patrum, calicibus epotandis non codicibus emendandis indulget hodie:[10] quibus lascivam Timothei musicam pudicis moribus æmulam non verentur adjungere, sicque cantus ludentis non planctus lugentis officium efficitur monachale. Greges et valera, fruges et horrea, porri et holera, potus et patera, lectiones sunt hodie et studia monachorum, exceptis quibusdam paucis electis, in quibus patrum præcedentium non imago, sed vestigium remanet aliquale. Rursus nulla nobis materia ministratur omnino, qua de[11] nostro cultu vel studio commendentur hodie canonici regulares, qui licet a geminata regula nomen portant eximium, Augustini tamen regulæ notabilem neglexere versiculum, quo sub his verbis clericis suis commendamur: *Codices certa hora singulis diebus petantur: extra horam qui petierit, non accipiet.* Hunc devotum studii canonem vix observat aliquis post ecclesiastica cantica repetita, sed sapere quæ sunt sæculi et

1 This should certainly be *venatores*.
2 *Prolum non*, mss. 797, 3352c and Ox. ed.
3 *Ad*, ibid.
4 *Præelectæ*, ibid.
5 *Trajicitur*, mss. 797 and Ox. ed.
6 *Aquilarum nidis cæcutientes nocte dieque liber codex despicitur*, ms. 3352c.
7 *Tanquam*, mss. 797, 3352c and Ox. ed.
8 *Simplex monachica proles*, ibid.
9 *Liber pater*, mss. and Ox. ed.
10 *Hodie studium monachorum*, mss. 797, 3352c and Ox. ed.
11 *Quam ut de*, Ox. ed.

batants of the Christian militia, who fortified our infirmity with most powerful arms. They were the most cunning fox hunters of their times, who have yet left us their snares, that we may catch the little foxes which never cease to demolish the flourishing vines. Truly these mighty fathers are to be remembered with perpetual benedictions. Deservedly happy would you be, if a similar progeny were begotten by you, if it were permitted to you to leave an heir neither degenerate nor doubtful, to be a help in times to come. But now (we say it with sorrow) base Thersites handles the arms of Achilles; the choicest trappings are thrown away upon lazy asses; blinking night-birds lord it in the nests of eagles, and the silly kite sits on the perch of the hawk. *Liber Bacchus* is respected, and passes daily and nightly into the belly: *Liber Codex* is rejected far and wide out of reach; so that the simple modern people are deceived by a multiplicity of equivocations of every kind; *Liber Patera* takes precedence of *Liber Patrum* (libations, of the lives of the fathers).[a] The study of the monks [b] nowadays dispenses with emptying bowls, not emending books, to which they neither scruple to add the lascivious music of Timotheus,[c] nor to emulate his shameless manners; and thus the song of merriment, not the plaint of mournfulness, is become the monasterial duty.[d] Flocks and fleeces, crops and barns, gardens and olive yards, drink and cups, are now the lessons and studies of monks; excepting, of some chosen few, in whom not the image but a slight vestige of their forefathers remains.[e]

a This translation seems to us senseless; *libro patrum* simply means, the book of the fathers: *liber potationum*, the god of drink.—*Ed.*

b *Studium monachorum* omitted in our text.—*Ed.*

c A musician born in 446 A. D., author of *Semele*, a licentious poem. This passage, according to our text, should be: A lascivious music, rivaling that of Timotheus.—*Ed.*

d The drunkenness and gluttony of the lower clergy, says M. Cocheris, of which we have already spoken, caused the invention of the *pays de la cuisine*, otherwise called Cocaigne, stories concerning which, both French and English, have been published by Meon and by Ellis, the former in his *Recueil de fabliaux* (IV, 175), the latter in his *Specimens of the Early English Poetry* (I, 66). Warton has inserted in his *History of English Poetry* (I, 49), an interesting document entitled *L'ordre du bel eyse*, which contains curious details of the jolly life led by the monks in the counties of York and Lincolnshire.—*Ed.*

e This whole paragraph is in the

relictum aratrum intueri summa prudentia reputatur. Tollunt pharetram et arcum, apprehendunt arma et scutum, eleemosynarum tributum canibus tribuunt, non egenis, inserviunt aleis et taxillis, et his, quæ nos sæcularibus inhibere solebamus. Ut non quidem miremur, si nos non dignemur[1] respicere, quot sic suis moribus cernunt[2] contraire.

Patres igitur[3] reverendi, patrum vestrorum dignemini vos reminisci et librorum sacrorum propensius indulgere[4] studio, sine quibus quælibet vacillabit religio,[5] et sine quibus nullum præberi poterit[6] lumen mundo.

1 *Solemus; ut non miremur si nos non dignentur*, mss. 797, 3352c and Ox. ed.

2 *Cernerent*, ibid.

3 *Ergo*, ms. 797 and Ox. ed.

4 *Et librorum propensius indulgete*, mss. and Ox. ed.

5 *Vacillabit religio; sine quibus ut testa, virtus devotionis arescet; sine*, mss. 797, 3352c and Ox. ed.

6 *Lumen poteritis mundo præbere*, Ox. ed.

Again: none whatever of that matter is administered to us, touching our culture and study, for which the regular canons can at this day be commended; who, though they bear the great name of Augustine from the double rule, yet neglect the notable little verse by which we are recommended to his clergy in these words: "Books are to be asked for at certain hours every day; "he who demands them out of hours shall not receive "them." This devout canon of study scarcely any one observes after repeating the church service or Horæ; [a] but to be knowing in secular affairs, and to look after the neglected plough, is held to be the height of prudence. They carry bows and arrows; assume arms and bucklers; distribute the tribute of alms amongst their dogs, not amongst the necessitous; use dice and draughts, and such things as we are accustomed to forbid to secular men; so that indeed we wonder not that they never deign to look upon us, whom they thus perceive to oppose their immoral practices.

Condescend therefore, reverend fathers, to remember your predecessors, and to indulge more freely in the study of the sacred books; without which, all religion whatever will vacillate; without which, as a watering pot, the virtue of devotion will dry up; [b] and without which, no light will be held up to the world.

original extremely neat, forcible and epigrammatic. The author puns very aptly. He even breaks into rhyme in the following sentence, though perhaps unconsciously:

Liber Bacchus respicitur,
Et in ventrem projicitur,
Nocte dieque,
Liber codex despicitur,
Et a manu rejicitur
Longe lateque.

It is of course impossible to give a perfect translation of such a passage, but this one seems to us particularly clumsy, and entirely lacking in spirit and judgment. What sense is there in this sentence, for example? "The study of the monks dispenses with emptying bowls, not emending books." We confess that the only meaning we can extract from it is exactly the r-verse of that of the text.—*Ed.*

a Horæ. This word is inserted because it was the daily service of the monks, invented to help them to pass their time. The nuns also used the *Horæ Beati Virginis*, and many a deep drawn sigh have the words *ecce concipies* forced from the bottom of their hearts.—*Inglis.*

b Ut testa virtus devotionis arescet, wanting in our text, is here translated.—*Ed.*

CAPITULUM VI.

DE LAUDE RELIGIOSORUM MENDICANTIUM PRIORUM CUM REPREHENSIONE MODERNORUM.[1]

PAUPERES spiritu, sed fide ditissimi, mundi peripsema et sal terræ, sæculi contemptores, et hominum piscatores, quam beati estis, si penuriam patientes pro Christo, animas vestras scitis in patientia possidere. Non enim vos ultrix iniquitatis inopia, nec parentum adversa fortuna, nec violenta necessitas sic[2] oppressit inedia, sed devota voluntas et electio Christi formis, qua vitam illam optimam prædicavit.[3] Sane vos estis semper post parentes novi fœtus,[4] pro patribus et prophetis noviter substituti divinitus, ut in omnem terram exeat sonus vester, ut nostris salutaribus instituti doctrinis, cunctis regibus[5] et gentibus, promulgetis inexpugnabilem fidem Christi. Porro fidem patrum potissime libris esse inclusam secundum capitulum supra satis asseruit, quo constat luce clarius, quod librorum debetis esse zelotypi, qui præ ceteris Christianis seminare jubemini super omnes aquas, quia[6] non est personarum acceptor Altissimus, nec vult mortem peccatorum piissimus, qui occidi voluit pro eisdem: sed contritos corde mederi desiderat atque lapsos erigi et perversos corrigi spiritu lenitatis. Ad quem effectum saluberrimum, alma mater ecclesia vos plantavit gratuitos, plantatosque rigavit favoribus et rigatos privilegiis suffulcivit,[a] ut cum pastoribus et curatis coadjutores essetis ad procurandam salutem fidelium animarum.[7]

1 *Querimonia librorum contra religiosos mendicantes*, mss. 797, 3352c, Ox. ed.
2 *Nec ulla violenta sic*, Ox. ed.
3 *Æstimastis, quam Deus omnipotens factus homo, tam verbo quam exemplo, optimam prædicavit*, mss. 797, 3352c and Ox. ed.
4 *Semper parientis ecclesiæ novus fœtus*, mss. 797, 3352c and Ox. ed.
5 *Coram regibus*, ibid.
6 *Quoniam*, ibid.
7 *Salutem animarum*, Ox. ed.
a *Suffulsit* is the ordinary form of the preterit.—*Ed.*

CHAPTER VI.

IN PRAISE OF THE ANCIENT, AND REPREHENSION OF THE MODERN RELIGIOUS MENDICANTS.

POOR in spirit, but most rich in faith, the offscourings of the world,[19] the salt of the earth, despisers of worldly affairs, and fishers of men! how happy are you if, suffering penury for Christ, you know you possess your souls in suffering![20] For thus neither the revenger, from lack of injury, nor the adverse fortune of relations, nor any violent necessity, nor hunger oppresses you; if the will is devout and the election Christiform, by which you have chosen that best life, which God Almighty made man set forth both by word and example.[a] Truly you are the new birth of the ever procreating church,[b] recently and divinely substituted for the fathers and prophets, that the sound of your voice may go forth over all the earth; for being instructed in our salutary doctrines, you can promulgate the unassailable doctrine of the faith of Christ to all kings and people. Moreover, our second chapter superabundantly proves the faith of the fathers to be most amply contained in books; wherefore it most clearly appears that you ought to be zealous lovers of books, who above all other Christians are commanded to sow upon all waters. For the Most High is no respecter of persons; nor doth the most pious, who was willing to be slain for sinners, wish for the death of sinners, but he desires the broken-hearted to be healed, the fallen

a This is not found in our text, but is in the Oxford edition; see note 3 of the opposite page. The translation of the whole sentence varies from the text, of which the literal version is more like the following: For neither misery the punisher of crime, nor the misfortunes of your family, nor a violent necessity, forces you to this abstinence, but a devout desire, a free choice of that life of Christ which he has taught you to be the best.—*Ed.*

b Differing from the text, but conforming to that of the Ox. ed. See note 4 opposite page.—*Ed.*

Unde et Prædicatorum ordinem, propter sacræ scripturæ studium, et proximorum salutem principaliter institutum, constitutiones pronunciant eorumdem : ut non solum ex regula[1] præsulis Augustini, qui codices singulis diebus jubet esse petendos ; verum mox cum earumdem constitutionum prologum legerint, ex ipsius libri capite, ad amorem librorum se noverint obligatos.

Sed, proh dolor! quod tam hos quam alios istorum sectantes effigiem a paterna cura[2] librorum et studio subtraxit triplex cura superflua, ventris videlicet vestium et domorum. Sunt enim (neglecta Salvatoris providentia, quem Psalmista circa pauperem et mendicum promittit esse sollicitum) circa labentas corporis indigentias occupati, ut sint epulæ splendidæ, vestesque contra regulam delicatæ : nec non et ædificiorum fabricæ, ut castrorum propugnacula tali proceritate, quæ paupertati non conveniat exaltatæ.

Propter hæc tria, nos libri qui semper eos proveximus ad perfectum,[3] et inter potentes et nobiles sedes honoris concessimus, elongati a cordis affectibus quasi inter supervacua reputamur : excepto quod quibusdam quaternis parvi valoris insistunt, de quibus nænias[4] et apocrypha deliramenta producunt, non ad refocillativum[5] animorum edulium, sed potius ad pruritum aurium auditorum. Sacra scriptura non exponitur sed seponitur[6] quasi trita per vicos et omnibus divulgata supponitur ; cujus tamen fimbrias paucissimi tetigerunt, cujus etiam tanta est[7] profunditas, ut ab humano intellectu, quantumcunque vigilet,[8] summo otio et maximo studio nequeat comprehendi, sicut sanctus asserit Augustinus. De hac mille moralis disciplinæ sententias enucleare poterit, qui indulget assidue, si tamen[9] ostium aperire dignetur ille qui condidit spiritum pietatis, quæ et recentissima novitate pollebunt, et sapientissima[10] suavitate auditorum

1 *Regula reverendi*, ms. 797 and Ox. ed.; *Ex regula præsulis Beatissimi Augustini*, ms. 3352c.
2 *Cultura*, mss. 797, 3352c and Ox. [ed.
3 *Profectum*, ibid.
4 *Quibus venias hiberas*, ibid.
5 *Refocillationem*, ms. 797 and Ox. ed.
6 *Sed omnino deponitur*, Ox. ed.
7 *Est litterarum*, mss. 797, 3352c and Ox. ed.
8 *Invigilet*, ms. 797.
9 *Tum*, Ox. ed.
10 *Sapidissima*, ms. 797 and Ox. ed.

to be raised up, and the perverse to be corrected in the spirit of lenity.[21] For which most salutary purpose, our fostering mother church gratuitously planted you; being planted, she watered you with favors; and being watered, propped you with privileges that you might be coadjutors to pastors and curates in procuring the salvation of faithful souls. Whence also, as their constitutions declare, the order of preachers[22] was principally instituted for the study of holy writ[23] and for the salvation of their neighbors; as not only from the rule of their founder Augustine, who ordered books to be sought for every day, but immediately upon reading the preface of the said constitutions, at the beginning of his own volume, they know the love of books to be an obligation imposed upon them. But, to their shame,[a] both these and others following their example are withdrawn from the study and paternal care of books by a threefold superfluous care; namely, of their bellies, clothing and houses.[b] For, neglecting the providence of our Saviour, whom the psalmist premises to be solicitous about the poor and mendicant, they are occupied about the wants of their perishable bodies—such as splendid banquets, delicate garments contrary to their rule, and even piles of buildings like the bulwarks of fortifications, raised to a height little consistent with the profession of poverty. For the sake of these three things, we their books, who have ever advanced them to preferment[c] and conceded the seat of honor to them amongst the powerful and noble, are estranged from the affections of their hearts and looked upon as useless lumber, excepting that they make some account of certain tracts[24] of little value, from which they produce mongrel[d] trifles and

a The text is *dolor*, not *pudor*.—*Ed.*

b Guiot de Provins, says M. Cocheris in a note to his translation of this passage, reproaches the monks of the order of Grand Mont with taking too much care of their beards:

La nuit (dit il) quand ils doivent couchier,
Se font bien laver et pinguier
Les barbes et enveloper,
Et en trois parties bender
Por estre beles et luisans.

c This is the translation of the *profectum* of the Oxford edition.—*Ed.*

d Not in our text.—*Ed.*

intelligentias removebunt.[1] Quamobrem paupertatis evangelicæ professores primarii post utrumque[2] salutatas scientias sæculares, toto mentis ingenio recollecto, hujus se sacræ scripturæ laboribus, devenerunt[3] nocte dieque in lege Domini meditantes. Quicquid vero poterant a famescente ventre furari vel corpori semitecto surripere, illud lucrum præcipuum arbitrantes[4] codicibus adscripserunt. Quorum contemporanei sæculares tam officium intuentes quam studium libros eos,[5] quos in diversis hinc inde mundi partibus sumptuose collegerant, ad totius ecclesiæ ædificationem contulerunt.

Sane diebus istis cum sint[6] tota diligentia circa quæstus intenti, præsumptione probabili credi potest, si per antropospathos sermo fiat, Deum[7] circa eos[8] minorem sollicitudinem gerere, quos de sua promissione perpendit diffidere, in humanis providentiis, spem habentes, corvum non considerantes[9] nec lilia, quos pascit et vestit Altissimus.

Danielem et Habacuc cocti pulmenti discophorum non pensatis, nec Eliam recolitis nunc in deserto per angelos, nunc in torrente per corvos, nunc in Sarepta per viduam, largitate divina, quæ dat escam omni carni tempore opportuno, a famis inedia liberatum. Climate miserabili[10] (ut timetur) descenditis, cum divinæ pietatis diffidentia prudentiæ sollicitudinem generat terrenorum;[11] sollicitudo quoque nimia terrenorum amorem adimit tam librorum quam studiorum:[12] et sic cedit paupertas hodie per abusum in verbi[13] Dei dispendium, quod solum propter ipsius adminiculum elegistis.

1 *Refovebunt*, mss. 797, 3352c and Ox. ed.

2 *Utcunque*, Ox. ed.

3 *Hujus se scripturæ laboribus devoverunt*, mss. 797, 3352c and Ox. ed.

4 *Arbitrantes vel emendis vel edendis*, ibid.

5 *Libris eis*, Ox. ed.

6 *Sitis*, mss. 797, 3352c and Ox. ed.

7 Ανθρωποπάθειαν *sermo fiat Dei*, Ox. ed.; *Domini*, ms. 797.

8 *Vos*, mss. and Ox. ed,

9 *Consideratis*, Ox. ed.

10 *Mirabili*, ms. 3352c.

11 *Climate miserabili (ut timetur) descenditis, dum divinæ pietatis diffidentia, prudentiæ propriæ producit invisum. Invisus vero prudentiæ propriæ sollicitudinem generat terrenorum.* Mss. and Ox. ed. Apropos of the word *invisum*. James, in his Ox. ed., makes this remark: "Locus satis obscurus, legendum arbitror innisum."

12 *Studium*, mss. 797, 3352c; Ox. ed.

13 *Paupertas homini per abusum hodie verbi*, Ox. ed.

apocryphal ravings, not for the refreshment of hungry souls, but rather to tickle the ears of their auditors.

The holy scriptures are not expounded, but exploded as trite sayings supposed to be already divulged in the streets and to all men, whose margins however very few have touched, whose profundity is even so great that it cannot be comprehended by human intellect, however vigilant it may be, at its utmost leisure and with the greatest study. He who constantly studies these, will be able to pick out the thousand maxims of moral discipline which they enforce with the most perfect novelty, refreshing the understandings of their hearers with the most soothing[a] suavity, if he who founded the spirit of piety will only deign to open the door. For which reason the first professors of evangelical poverty, taking leave of every secular science whatever, gathering together the whole force of their minds, devoted themselves to the labors of these holy writings, meditating daily and nightly on the law of the Lord. Whatsoever they could steal from their famishing stomachs or tear from their half-covered bodies, they applied to emending or editing books,[b] esteeming them their greatest gain; their secular contemporaries, holding both their office and studies in respect, having conferred such books upon them as they had collected at great cost, here and there in divers parts of the world, to the edification of the whole church.

Truly in these days, when with all diligence you are intent upon lucre, it might be believed with probable presumption, according to *anthropospathos* (if the word may be allowed) or human feeling, that God entertains little anxiety about those whom he considers to distrust his promises, placing their hopes upon human foresight, neither considering the crow nor the lily which the

a *Sapientissima* in the text.—*Ed.*

b This follows the text of the Oxford edition. See note 4 opposite page.—*Ed.*

c This passage is difficult, and the translation is certainly not very clear, but I think it comes nearer the original than does M. Cocheris, who renders the passage thus: Thus poverty now comes upon the man who loses the word of God, which you have chosen on account of its support alone.—*Ed.*

Uncinis pomorum, ut populus fabulatur, puerulos ad religionem attrahitis, quos professos doctrinis non instruitis: vi et metu, sicut exigit ætas illa, mendicativis[1] discursibus sustinetis intendere, atque tempus, in quo possent addiscere in captandis favoribus amicorum, consumere sinitis in offensam parentum, puerorum[2] periculum et ordinis detrimentum. Sicque nimirum contingit, quod qui parvuli discere minime cogebantur inviti, grandiores effecti docere præsumant indigni penitus et indocti, et parvus error in principio, maximus fit in fine. Est sic namque[3] in grege vestro promiscuo, laicorum quædam multitudo plurimis[4] onerosa, qui tamen se ad prædicationis officium tanto improbius ingerunt, quanto minus ea, quæ loquuntur, intelligunt in contemptum sermonis Domini[5] et in perniciem animarum. Sane contra legem in bove et asino aratis, cum doctis et indoctis culturam agri Dominici committitis. Pari passu, scriptum est, boves arabant et asinæ pascebantur juxta eos. Quanquam discretorum est[6] prædicare, simplicium vero per auditum sacri eloquii sub silentio se cibare. Quot lapides mittitis in acervum Mercurii[a] his diebus? Quot eunuchis sapientiæ nuptias procuratis? Quot cœcos speculatores super[7] ecclesiæ muros circumire præcipitis? O piscatores inertes solis retibus alienis utentes, qui rupta vix empirice reficitis:[8] nova vero nullatenus commodatis,[9] aliorum studia recitatis, aliorum sapientiam superficialiter repetitis,[10] theatrali strepitu labiatis. Quemadmodum psittacus idiota auditas voces effigiat, sic tales

a M. Cocheris explains this by the following note: An allusion to the words of the Bible, "Celui qui eleve en honneur un homme qui n'est pas sage, est comme celui qui jette une pierre dans le monceau de Mercure." *Proverbs*, xxvi, 8.

This verse in our English version is: "As he that bindeth a stone in a sling, so is he that giveth honor to a fool."

The vulgate is thus: Sicut qui mittit lapidem in acervum Mercurii: ita qui tribuit insipienti honorum.

The septuagint has the Greek like our English version. The original Hebrew seems to be literally: Who bindeth a stone upon a heap of stones.—*Ed.*

1 *Sed menducaturis*, Ox. ed.
2 *Parvorum*, ibid.
3 *Succrescit namque*, mss. 797 and 3352c, and Ox. ed.
4 *Plurimum*, Ox. ed.
5 *Divini*, mss. 797, 3352c, and Ox.ed.
6 *Quoniam discretorum interest*, ibid.
7 *Quot cœcos super*, Ox. ed.
8 *Imperite resuitis*, ibid.
9 *Commodatis aliorum labores intratis, aliorum*, etc., ms. 797 and Ox. ed.
10 *Repetitam*, mss. 797, 3352c, and Ox. ed.

Most High feeds and clothes. You ponder not upon Daniel, nor Habakkuk the bearer of the dish of boiled pottage, nor remember Elijah fed by angels in the desert, again by crows at the brook, and, lastly, by the widow at Zarepta, relieved from the cravings of hunger by the divine bounty, which gives food to all flesh in due season. You are descending, we fear, by a wretched ladder, while a reliance upon self-sufficiency produces distrust of divine piety, but reliance upon self-sufficiency begets solicitude about worldly affairs, and too much solicitude about worldly affairs takes away the love of books and study, and thus poverty now gives way through abuse, at the expense of the word of God, though you chose it only for its support.[a] You draw boys into your religion with hooks of apples as the people commonly report, whom having professed, you do not instruct in doctrines by compulsion and fear as their age requires, but maintain them to go upon beggarly excursions, and suffer them to consume the time in which they might learn, in catching at the favors of their friends, to the offence of their parents, the danger of the boys, and the detriment of the order. And thus without doubt it happens that unwilling boys, in no way compelled to learn, when grown up presume to teach, being altogether worthless and ignorant. A small error in the beginning becomes a very great one in the end; for thus also a certain and generally burthensome multitude of laymen grows up in your promiscuous flock, who however thrust themselves into the office of preaching the more impudently the less they understand what they talk about, in contempt of the word of the Lord and to the ruin of souls. Verily you plough with the ox and the ass contrary to the law, when you commit the culture of the Lord's field to the learned and unlearned without distinction. It is written, oxen plough and asses feed by them; because it is the business of the discreet to preach, but of the simple to feed themselves in silence by hearing sa-

a See note *c*, p. 95.

recitatores fiunt omnium,[1] sed nullius auditores;[2] asinam Balaam imitantes, quæ licet[3] intrinsecus insensata, lingua tamen diserta facta est tam Domini, quam[4] prophetæ magistra. Resipiscite[5] pauperes Christi, et nos libros inspicite studiose, sine quibus in præparatione[a] evangelii pacis nunquam poteritis debite calciari.

Paulus apostolus, prædicator veritatis et doctor eximius gentium, ista sibi per Timotheum, pro omni supellectili, tria jussit afferri, penulam, libros et membranas, *secunda Timothei, capitulo ultimo.*[6] Viris evangelicis[7] formam præbens, ut habitum deferant ordinatum, libros habeant ad studendi subsidium, et membranas, quas apostolus maxime ponderat ad scribendum, *maxime*, inquit, et *membranas.* Revera mancus est clericus[8] et ad multarum rerum jacturam, turpiter quidem mutilatus,[9] qui artis scribendi totaliter est ignarus. Aërem vocibus verberat, et præsentes tantum ædificat, absentibus et posteris nihil parat. Atramentarium scriptoris gestabat vir in renibus, qui frontes gementium Tau[b] signabat, *Ezech.* ix. Insinuans figurate, quia[10] si quis scribendi peritia careat, prædicandi pœnitentiam[11][c] officium non præsumat.

Tandem in præsentis calce capituli supplicant vobis libri, juvenes nescios ingenio[12] aptos studiis applicare,[13] necessaria ministrantes, quos non solum modo veritatem[14] verum et disciplinam et sententiam[15] doceatis, verberibus terreatis, attrahatis blanditiis, molliatis munusculis, et pœnosis rigoribus, ut et Socratici[16] moribus et doc-

a *Properationem—præperationem*—Ox. ed., in advancement.—*Inglis.*

b *Tau*, *Ezek.* ix, 3. The T, is not in the text, nor in our translation; but it is in the older English Bibles, and in the Latin and Hebrew, if we are to believe Jerome and Pagninus.—*Inglis.*

c *Prædicandi pœnitentiam*, preach penitence; the church of Rome preaches nothing else, it is a profitable doctrine.—*Inglis.*

1 *Omnino*, ms. 797 and Ox. ed.

2 *Auctores*, mss. 797, 3352c; Ox. ed.

3 *Licet esset*, ibid.

4 *Facta est tam diu, quam*, Ox. ed.

5 *Respicite*, ibid.

6 *Secundo ad Timothæum ult*, ms. 797 and Ox. ed. *Secunda ad Thunum ultimo*, ms. 3352c.

7 *Ecclesiasticis*, Ox. ed.

8 *Est ille clericus*, ibid.

9 *Ad multorum jacturam turpiter mutilatus*, mss. 797, 3352c, and Ox. ed.

10 *Quod*, ibid.

11 *Provinciam*, Ox. ed.

12 *Ingenio vestros*, mss. 797, 3352c, and Ox. ed.

13 *Applicate*, ibid.

14 *Bonitatem*, ms. 797 and Ox. ed. *Bonitatem verum etiam*, ms. 3352c.

15 *Scientiam*, Ox. ed.

16 *Rigoribus urgeatis, ut Socratici*, Ox. ed.

cred eloquence. How many stones do you throw upon the heap of Mercury in these days? how many marriages do you procure for the eunuchs of wisdom? how many blind speculators do you teach to go about upon the walls of the church?

Oh slothful fishermen, who only use other men's nets, which you have hardly skill to mend if broken, and none whatever to weave anew! you intrude upon the labors of others, recite their compositions, repeat their wisdom by rote, and mouth it with theatrical rant. As the stupid parrot imitates the words it hears, so such as you become reciters of everything, authors[a] of nothing, imitating Balaam's ass, which though naturally insensible of language, yet by her eloquent tongue was made the schoolmistress both of a master and a prophet.

Repent, ye paupers of Christ, and studiously revert to us your books, without whom you will never be able to put on your shoes in advancement of the gospel of peace. Paul the apostle, preacher of the truth and first teacher of the Gentiles, ordered these three things to be brought to him by Timothy instead of all his furniture—his cloak, books and parchment (2 *Tim.*); exhibiting a formulary to evangelical men, that they may wear the habit ordained, have books to aid them in studying, and parchment for writing, which the apostle lays most stress upon, saying, "but especially the "parchments." Truly that clergyman is maimed, and indeed basely mutilated, to the wreck of many things, who is totally ignorant of the art of writing: he beats the air with his voice; he edifies only the present, and provides nothing for the absent or for posterity. "A man "carried the inkhorn of a writer at his loins, who set "the mark T upon the foreheads of those who sighed," figuratively insinuating that if any man is deficient in the skill of writing he must not take upon himself the office of preaching penitence.

Finally, in closing the present chapter, your books,

a Hearers in the text (*auditores*), but see note 2, p. 98.—*Ed.*

trinis Peripatetici simul fiant. Heri quasi[1] undecima vos discretus pater familias introduxit in vineam, ante sero penitus pigeat otiari. Utinam cum prudenti villico mendicandi tam improbe verecundiam haberetis, tunc enim proculdubio, nobis libris[2] et studio propensius vacaretis.

1 *Quasi hora*, mss. 797, 3352c, and Ox. ed.

2 *Tunc proculdubio libris*, Ox. ed.

administering the needful, supplicate you to turn the attention of ignorant youths of apt wit to their studies, that you may not only truly teach them truth, discipline and knowledge, but terrify them with the rod, attract them with blandishments, soothe them with presents, and urge them with penal severities, that they may at once be made Socratics in morals and Peripatetics in doctrine.

Yesterday, as it were at the eleventh hour, the discreet landlord introduced you into the vineyard; repent therefore of being idle before it is altogether too late. Would that with the prudent steward you would be ashamed of begging so dishonorably! for then without doubt you would have leisure for us your books, and for study.

CAPITULUM VII.

DEPLORATIO DESTRUCTIONIS LIBRORUM PER BELLA ET INCENDIA.[1]

PACIS auctor et amator altissime, dissipa gentes bella volentes, quæ[2] super omnes pestilentias libris nocent. Bella namque carentia rationis judicio, furiosos efficiunt impetus in adversa: et dum rationis moderamine non utuntur, sine differentia discretionis progressa, vasa destruunt rationis. Tunc prudens Apollo Plutoni[3] subjicitur: et tunc Phronesis[a] pariens mater fit phrenesis, et in phrenesis redigitur potestatem.[4] Tunc pennatus Pegasus stabulo Coridonis includitur, et facundus Mercurius suffocatur. Tunc Pallas prudens erroris mucrone tunditur,[5] et jucundæ Pierides truculenta furoris tyrannide supprimuntur. O crudele spectaculum, ubi Phœbum philosophorum[6] Aristotelem, cui omni dominii Dominus ipse[7] commisit dominium, scelerosis manibus vinculatum, ferramentis infamibus compeditum, lanistarum humeris a Socratis[8] ædibus cernitur asportari, et qui in mundi magistratu magisterium atque super imperatorem imperium meruit obtinere, injustissimo jure belli videres subjici vili scurræ! O potestas iniquissima tenebrarum, quæ Platonis[b] non veretur pessumdare divinitatem probatam,[9] qui solus, aspectui[10] creatoris,

a The three daughters of Phronesis are, Philosophy, Philology, and Philocalia. In the contemplation of divine things Phronesis is called Sophia.—*Inglis.*

b Plato, says M. Cocheris, was placed by some authorities of the church of Rome among the saints.—*Ed.*

1 *Querimonia librorum contra bella*, mss. 797, 3352c and Ox. ed.

2 *Quia*, Ox. ed.

3 *Pytoni*, mss. and Ox. ed. *Phitoni*, ms. 3352c.

4 *Et tunc Phronesis pia mater in frenesis redigitur potestatem*, mss. and Ox. ed.

5 *Conciditur*, ibid.

6 *Philosophorum archisophum*, ibid.

7 *Cui orbis Dominium Deus ipse*, mss. and Ox. ed. *Cui in omnibus Dominii*, edition 1610.

8 *Socratis ædibus asportari*, mss. and Ox. ed.

9 *Deitatem approbatam*, ms. 797 and Ox. ed. *Deitatem probatam*, ms. 3352c.

10 *Conspectui*, mss. and Ox. ed.

CHAPTER VII.

DEPLORING THE DESTRUCTION OF BOOKS BY WARS AND FIRE.

OH most high author and lover of peace! scatter the nations that are desirous of war, more injurious to books than all other plagues; for war, wanting the discretion of reason, furiously attacks whatever falls in its way, and, not being under the guidance of reason, it destroys the vessels of reason, having no scale of discretion. Then the wise Apollo is subjected to Pluto, the prolific mother Phronesis becomes *phrenesis*, and is submitted to the power of frenzy. Then the winged Pegasus is shut up in the stable of Corydon, and the eloquent Mercury is choked. The prudent Pallas is pierced by the dart of error, and the jocund Pierides are suppressed by the truculent tyranny of fury. Oh cruel sight! where Aristotle the Phœbus of philosophers, to whom the lord of the domain himself committed the dominion over all things, is seen bound by impious hands, fettered with infamous chains, and carried off from the house of Socrates upon the shoulders of gladiators; and him who deserved to obtain the magistracy in the government of the world, and the empire over its emperor, you may see subjected to a vile scoffer, by the most unjust rights of war.

Oh most iniquitous power of darkness! that feared not to trample upon the approved divinity of Plato, who alone in the sight of the Creator was worthy to interpose ideal forms, before he could appease the strife of jarring chaos, and before he could invest matter with permanent form;[25] that he might demonstrate the archetype world from its author, and that the sensible world might be deduced from its supernal prototype.

priusquam bellantis chaos placaret litigium, et antequam hylen entelechiam induisset, species ideales objicere dignus fuit, ut[1] mundum archetypum demonstraret auctori, et[2] de superno exemplo mundus sensibilis duceretur. O lacrymosus intuitus! quo moralis Socrates, cujus actus, virtus et sermo doctrinæ, qui de naturæ principiis politiæ produxit justitiam vitiosi vespillonis addictus videtur[3] servituti! Pythagoram plangimus harmoniæ parentem cum cantricibus furiis[4] flagellatum atrociter, vice cantus gemitus edere columbinos. Miseremur Zenonis[a] principis stoicorum, qui ne consilium proderet,[5] linguam morsu secuit et exspuit in tyrannum intrepide. Heu jam rursus Adiomerita tritus in mortario[6] pistillatur.

Certe non sufficimus singulos libros luctu lamentari condigno, qui in diversis mundi partibus bellorum discrimine perierunt. Horribilem tamen stragem, quæ per auxiliares milites secundo bello Alexandrino contigit in Ægypto, stylo flebili memoramus, ubi decem[7] millia voluminum[b] ignibus conflagrarunt, quæ sub regibus Ptolomæis per multa curricula temporum sunt collecta, sicut recitat Aulus Gellius *Noctium Atticarum, lib.* VI, *cap.* XVI.[8] Quanta proles Atlantica tunc occubuisse putabitur, orbium motus, omnes conjunctiones planetarum, galaxiæ natura, et generationes prognosticæ cometarum, et quæcumque in cœlo fiunt vel athere comprehenduntur?[9] Quis tam infaustum holocaustum, ubi loco cruoris incaustum offertur, non exhorreat?

Pruinæ[10] candentes pergameni crepitantis sanguine vernabantur, ubi tot innocentium millia, in quorum ore non inventum est mendacium, flamma vorax consumpsit:

a Zeno the Stoic died a natural death, at an advanced age. Probably the author has confounded him with a Zeno of Elis mentioned by Plutarch. —*Cocheris.*

b 700,000 is the ordinary account, not 70,000 as in the text.—*Cocheris.*

1 *Nec*, Oxford edition.

2 *Quo*, mss. 797, 3352c, and Ox. ed.

3 *Cernitur*, ibid.

4 *Parentem, bellorum incentricibus furiis*, ms. 797 and Ox. ed. *Parentem, bellorum cum cantatricibus furiis*, ms. 2454. *Parentem; libellorum incentricibus furiis*, ms. 3352c.

5 *Perderet*, ms. 797 and Ox. ed.

6 *Rursus adiometonta tritus in tortario*, ms. 797. *Rursus a Dyomedonta tritus in mortario*, mss. 2454 and 3352c. *Nam rursus Anaxarchus tritus in mortario*, Ox. ed.

7 *Septuaginta*, mss. and Ox. ed.

8 *Cap.* xvii, Ox. ed. *Cap.* xvi, ms. 2454.

9 *Comprehendens*, mss. *Comprehendentes*, edition 1702.

10 *Ubi pruinæ*, Ox. ed.

Oh sorrowful sight! where the moral Socrates, whose acts are virtue, and whose words are doctrine, who produced justness of policy from the principles of nature, is seen devoted to the service of a depraved undertaker.[a] We lament Pythagoras[26] the parent of harmony, atrociously scourged by furious female singers, uttering plaintive groans instead of songs. We pity Zeno[27] the chief of the Stoics, who rather than divulge a secret, bit off his tongue, and boldly spat it in the face of a tyrant. Alas, now again, for the bruised Anaxarchus[b] pounded in a mortar by Nicrocreon. Certainly, we are not competent to lament with befitting sorrow each of the books which has perished in various parts of the world by the hazards of war. We may however record with a tearful pen the horrible havoc that happened through the auxiliary soldiers in the second Alexandrine war in Egypt, where 700,000[c] volumes, collected by the Ptolemies kings of Egypt during a long course of time, were consumed by fire, as Aulus Gellius relates, *Attic Nights*, book VI, c. xvii. What an Atlantic progeny is supposed to have then perished! comprehending the motions of the spheres, all the conjunctions of the planets, the nature and generation of the galaxy, the prognostications of comets, and whatsoever things are done in heaven or in the air. Who is not horrified by such an evil-omened holocaust, in which ink is offered up instead of blood, where glowing sparks spring from the blood of crackling parchment? where voracious flames consume so many thousands of innocents in whose mouths no falsehood is found; where fire that knows not when to spare, converts so many shrines of eternal truth into fetid ashes. The pious virgin daughters of Jephthah and Agamemnon, murdered for the glory of their fathers, may be thought victims of a minor

a *Vespillonis.* Among the classics this word means one who carries out the corpse by night. It was applied to the undertakers of the poor, who could not afford the pomp necessary to a funeral in the day time.—*Ed.*

b *Adiomerita* in the text.—*Ed.*

c Ten thousand in the text Seven hundred thousand is the ordinary account. This was the first Alexandrine war, not the second.—*Ed.*

ubi tot scrinia veritatis æternæ ignis parcere nesciens in fœtentem cinerem commutavit. Minoris facinoris æstimatur tam Jeptæ quam Agamemnonis victima, ubi pia filia virgo, patris gloria[1] jugulatur. Quot labores celebris Herculis tunc periisse putamus, qui ob astronomiæ peritiam, collo flexo,[2] cœlum describitur sustulisse, cum jam secundo Hercules flammis sit injectus.

Arcana cœlorum, quæ Jonanchus[3] non ab homine neque per hominem didicit, sed divinitus inspiratus accepit; quæcunque[4] Zoroastes germanus ejusdem immundorum servitor spirituum[5] deseruit;[6] quæ etiam sacratus Enneck[7] Paradisi[8] præfectus, priusquam deferretur[9] de sæculo, prophetavit; imo, quæ primus Adam filios docuit, ut raptus in exstasi in libro æternitatis præviderat, flammis illis nefandis probabiliter æstimantur esse destructa.[10]

Ægyptiorum religio, quam liber *Logostaliosiæ*[11] commendat egregie polios[12] veterum Athenarum: quæ cum millibus[13] annorum Athenis Græciæ præcesserunt carmina, Chaldæorum considerationes, Arabum et Indorum ceremoniæ, Judæorum architecta,[14] Babyloniorum Noe georgica, Mosis præsagia[15] Josuæ planimetria, Samsonis ænigmata, Salomonis problemata a cedro Libani usque ad hyssopum planissime disputata, Æsculapii antidota, Cadmi grammatica, Parnassi poëmata, Apollinis oracula, argonautica Jasonis, stratagemata Palamedis, et alia infinita scientiarum secreta, hujusmodi incendiis creduntur[16] sublata.

Numquid Aristotelem de circuli quadratura syllogis-

1 *Si pia filia, virgo, patris gladio,* mss. and Ox. ed.

2 *Irreflexo*. mss. 797, 3352c, Ox. ed.

3 *Jonathas*. Ox. ed.; *Jovi et thus*, ms. 797; *Joinchus*, mss. 2454 and 3352c.

4 *Quæque*, ms. 2454 and ed 1610; *Quem Rosoastes*, ms. 3352c; *Quem Zoroastres*, Ox. ed.

5 *Spirituum Bacteranis*, ms. 2454; *Spirituum Brachmannis*, Ox. ed.; *Bachianis*. ms 3352c.

6 *Accepit servitor spirituum Bactrianis disseruit*. ms. 797.

7 *Sanctus Enoch*, mss. and Ox. ed.

8 *Prothi*, ed. 1500. 1610 and 1702.

9 *Transferretur*, Ox. ed.

10 *Æstimantur destructa*, mss. and Ox. ed.

11 *Logostilius*, *sic*, Ox. ed.

12 *Egregie politia*. mss. 797, 3352c, and Ox. ed.; *Egregie eliopoleos*. ms. 2454.

13 *Quæ novem millibus*, mss. 797, 3352c and Ox. ed.

14 *Architectura*, mss. and Ox. ed.

15 *Præstigia*, ibid.

16 *Hujus incendii tempestate creduntur*, ibid.

crime. How many labors of the celebrated Hercules, who, for his skill in astronomy, is described as having supported the heavens upon his shoulders, may we imagine to have perished, when he was now for the second time thrown into the flames! The secrets of heaven, that Inachus[a] neither learned from man nor by human means, but received by divime inspiration; whatsoever his half-brother Zoroaster, the servant of unclean spirits, disseminated amongst the Bramins;[b] whatsoever holy Enoch, the governor of Paradise, prophesied before he was transferred from the world; yea, whatsoever the first Adam taught his sons, as he had previously seen it in the book of eternity, when rapt in an ecstasy—may with probability be thought to have been destroyed by those impious flames. The religion of the Egyptians, which the book called *Logistoricus*[c] so highly commends; the polity of the ancient Athenians, who preceded the Athenians of Greece 9000 years;[d] the verses of the Chaldeans; the astronomy of the Arabs and Indians; the ceremonies of the Jews; the architecture of the Babylonians; the georgics of Noah; the divinations of Moses; the trigonometry of Joshua; the enigmas of Samson; the problems of Solomon, most clearly argued from the cedar of Lebanon to the hyssop:[e]

a Jonanchus, an apocryphal son of Noah. The author makes Zoroaster his brother, on what authority I do not know. M. Cocheris says that Abraham and Zoroaster are according to the Persian magi the same, and Abraham was of course not the brother of the son of Noah.—*Ed.*

b This varies slightly from the text and is wrong in fact; but see note 5, opposite page.—*Ed.*

c Logostoricus, a sort of note book, written by Varro, in which the subjects were arranged under different heads: it is not extant.—*Inglis.*

The text has *Logostuliosiæ*. M. Cocheris conjectures that this is *Logos Tales* (λογος θαλετις) that is, the treatise of Thales: and he supports this opinion by citing the belief, prevailing among the learned in the middle ages, that Thales first communicated the wisdom of the Egyptians to the Greeks. Thales, however, was of Miletus, and not an Athenian.—*Ed.*

d See Plato's *Critias*. The bishop may have given a latitude to his fancy in this enumeration of lost books. Some of the authors can be traced, if other names may be given to them, according to the chronicles of various countries. The subject is too complicated for this place.—*Inglis.*

e This chapter alludes to many traditions and works now regarded as apocryphal. The punctuation of the text is such, that the translation varies from it considerably. The text is thus: The religion of the Egyptians, which the book *Logostalios* taught to the excellent republic of old Athens; the songs of Greece which were composed thousands of years before Athens existed; the observations of the Chaldeans; the ceremonies of the Arabs and

mus apodicticus latuisset, si libros veterum, methodos naturæ totius habentium, permisissent nefanda prælia superesse. Nec[1] de mundi æternitate problema neutrum fecisset, nec de intellectuum humanorum pluralitate eorumque perpetuitate, ut verisimiliter creditur, dubitasset ullatenus, si perfectæ scientiæ veterum invisorum bellorum pressuris obnoxiæ non fuissent.

Per bella namque ad patrias peregrinas dissipamur[2] obtruncamur, vulneramur, et enormiter mutilamur, sub terra fodimur, in mari submergimur, flammis exurimur, et omni necis genere trucidamur. Quantum sanguinis nostri effudit[3] Scipio bellicosus cum eversioni Carthaginis Romani imperii impugnatricis et æmulæ anxius incumbebat! Quot millia millium prælium decennale Trojanum ab hac luce transmisit! Quot per Antonium, Tullio jam occiso, externarum provinciarum latebras adierunt! Quot de nobis per Theodoricum, exsulante Boëthio, in diversa mundi climata, sicut oves percusso pastore sunt dispersi! Quot Seneca succumbente Neronis malitiæ, cum et nolens et volens portas mortis adiret, ab eo divisi retrocessimus lacrymantes, et in quibus partibus hospitari deberemus ignorantes![4]

Felix fuit illa librorum translatio, quam in Persas de Athenis Xerxes fecisse describitur, quos rursus de Persis in Athenas Seleucus reduxit. O gaudium gratiosum,[5] o mira lætitia, quam tunc cerneres in Athenis cum proli suæ genetrix obviaret tripudians, matrisque thalamum senescenti jam soboli denuo demonstraret, reassignatis hospitiis veteribus inquilinis. Mox tabulata cedrina cum lignis et trabibus lævigatis aptissime complanantur auro et ebore, epigrammata designantur camerulis,[6] quibus ipsa volumina reverenter illata suavissime collocantur, sic ut nullum alterius ingressum impediat vel propinquitate vero nimia fratrem suum lædat.[7]

1 *Nec enim*, mss. and Ox. ed.
2 *Distrahimur*, ibid.
3 *Fudit*, ibid.
4 *Hospitari possemus penitus ignorantes*, ibid.
5 *O post liminum gratiosum*, mss.; *O post liminium salutare et gratiosum?* Ox. ed.
6 *Camerulis singulis*, mss. and Ox. edition.
7 *Propinquitate nimia fratrem lædat*, ibid.

the antidotes of Esculapius; the grammatics of Cadmus; the poems of Parnassus; the oracles of Apollo; the argonautics of Jason; the stratagems of Palamedes;[a] and an infinity of other secrets of science—are believed to have been lost in like manner by fires.

Would the demonstrative syllogism[b] of the quadrature of the circle have been concealed from Aristotle, if wicked wars had permitted the books of the ancients, containing the methods of the whole of nature, to be forthcoming? or would he have left the problem of the eternity of the world undecided, or have at all doubted about the plurality of human intellects, and of their perpetuity, as he is with some reason believed to have done, if the perfect sciences of the ancients had not been exposed to the pressure of odious wars? For by wars we are dispersed in foreign countries, dismembered, wounded, and enormously mutilated, buried in the earth, drowned in the sea, burned in the fire, and slain by every species of violent slaughter. How much of our blood did the warlike Scipio shed, when earnestly bent upon the overthrow of Carthage, the emulous assailant of the Roman empire! How many thousands of thousands did the ten years Trojan war send out of the world! How many, upon the murder of Tully by Anthony, went into the recesses of remote provinces! How many of us, when Boëtius was banished by Theodorick, were dispersed into the various regions of the world like sheep whose shepherd is slain! How many, when Seneca fell by the malice of Nero, and willingly or unwillingly went towards the gates of death, withdrew weeping, and not knowing where we ought to take

Indians; the architecture of the Jews; the agriculture taught by Noah to the Babylonians; the prophecies of Moses, &c.

The prophecies of Enoch, the teachings of Noah, and the presages of Moses, here mentioned, are apocryphal books, now little known. The treatise of Solomon upon trees is mentioned in 1 Kings, chap. iv.—*Ed.*

a An allusion to the game of chess, supposed to have been invented by Palamedes at the siege of Troy.—*Ed.*

b No positive proof of the practicability or impracticability of the solution of this problem has yet been produced. When it appears, it will be most remarkable for its simplicity.—*Inglis.*

Ceterum quidem infinita sunt dispendia, quæ per seditiones bellorum, librorum generi illata. Et quoniam quidem infinita nullatenus transgredi atque pertransire[1] contingit. Hic familiariter[2] statuemus querimoniæ nostræ Gades et ad preces, quibus incepimus, regyramus habenas, rogantes suppliciter, ut rector Olympi ac mundi totius dispensator Altissimus firmet pacem, et bella removeat, ac tempora faciat sua protectione tranquilla.

1 *Et quoniam infinita nullatenus pertransire*, mss. and Ox. ed.

2 *Finaliter*, Ox. ed.

up our abode, when separated from him. Fortunate was that transfer of books which Xerxes is described to have made from the Athenians to the Persians, and which Zeleucus [a] brought back from the Persians to Athens. Oh, what becoming pride, what admirable exultation might you behold, when the mother, leaping for joy, met her children, and the bride-chamber of the now aged parent was once more pointed out to her offspring as the lodging assigned to its former tenants! Now cedar shelves with light beams and supporters are most neatly planed, labels are designed in gold and ivory for each partition, in which the volumes themselves are reverently deposited and most nicely arranged, so that no one can impede the entrance of another, or injure its brother by over pressure.

In all other respects indeed, the damages which are brought on by the tumults of war, especially upon the race of books, are infinite; and forasmuch also as it is a property of the infinite, that it can neither be stepped over nor passed through, we will here finally [b] set up the pillars of our complaints, and, drawing in our reins, return to the prayers with which we set out, suppliantly beseeching the ruler of Olympus and the most high Dispenser of all the world, that he may abolish war, establish peace, and bring about tranquil times under his own special protection.

a Should be Seleucus.—*Ed.*

b *Familiariter*, in the text.—*Ed.*

CAPITULUM VIII.

DE MULTIPLICI OPPORTUNITATE AUCTORIS IN COLLIGENDIS LIBRIS CIRCUMQUAQUE.[1]

CUM omni negotio tempus sit et[2] opportunitas, ut testatur *Ecclesiastes*, *cap.* viii,[3] jam progredimur enarrare multiplices opportunitates, quibus in acquisitione librorum, proposita[4] divinitate propitia, juvabamur. Quamvis enim ab adolescentia nostra semper specialem socialemque communionem[5] cum viris literatis et librorum dilectoribus delectaremur habere, succedentibus[6] prosperis regiæ majestatis consecuti notitiam, et in ipsius acceptati familia, facultatem suscepimus[7] ampliorem ubilibet visitandi pro libito, et venandi quasi saltus[8] quosdam delicatissimos, tum privatas, tum communes, tum regularium, tum sæcularium librarias.

Sane dum invictissimi principis ac semper magnifice triumphantis regis[9] Angliæ Eduardi III post conquæstum, cujus tempora conservare[10] dignetur Altissimus, diutine et tranquille, primo quidem suam concernentibus curam,[11] deinde vero rempublicam regni sui cancellarii scilicet ac thesaurarii fungeremur officiis, præstabatur[12] nobis aditus facilis, regalis favoris intuitu, ad librorum latebras libere perscrutandas.

Amoris quippe nostri fama volatilis jam ubique percrebuit, tantumque librorum et maxime veterum ferebamur cupiditate languescere; posse vero quem libet nostrum per quaternos facilius quam per pecuniam adi-

1 *De multiplici opportunitate quam habuimus librorum copiam conquirendi*, mss. 797, 3352c and Ox. ed.

2 *Ut*, ms. 3352c.

3 *Sapiens Ecclesiastis*, iii, Ox. ed.; *Sapiens Ecclesiastes*, viii, mss.

4 *Nostris propositis*, mss. and Ox. ed.

5 *Semper socialem communionem*, ib.

6 *Succedentibus tamen*, ibid.

7 *Accepimus*, ibid.

8 *Venandi saltus*, Ox. ed.

9 *Sane dum invictissimi regis*, Ox. ed.

10 *Servare*, mss. 797, 3352c; *Serenare*, Ox. ed.

11 *Curiam*, mss. 797, 3352c, Ox. ed.

12 *Patescebat*, ibid.

CHAPTER VIII.

OF THE NUMEROUS OPPORTUNITIES OF THE AUTHOR OF COLLECTING BOOKS FROM ALL QUARTERS.

AS there is a time and opportunity for every purpose, as Ecclesiastes witnesseth (ch. iii), we will now proceed to particularize the numerous opportunities we have enjoyed, under divine propitiation, in our proposed acquisition of books. For, although from our youth we have ever been delighted to hold special and social communion with literary men and lovers of books, yet prosperity attending us, having obtained the notice of his majesty the king, and being received into his own family, we acquired a most ample facility of visiting at pleasure and of hunting as it were some of the most delightful covers, the public and private libraries both of the regulars and seculars. Indeed, while we performed the duties of chancellor and treasurer of the most invincible and ever magnificently triumphant king of England, Edward III (of that name) after the conquest, whose days may the Most High long and tranquilly deign to preserve! after first inquiring into the things that concerned his court, and then the public affairs of his kingdom, an easy opening was afforded us, under the countenance of royal favor, for freely searching the hiding places of books. For the flying flame of our love had already spread in all directions, and it was reported not only that we had a longing desire for books, and especially for old ones, but that any body could more easily obtain our favor by quartos than by money. Wherefore when supported by the bounty of the aforesaid prince of worthy memory, we were enabled to oppose or advance, to appoint or discharge; crazy quartos and tottering folios, precious however in our sight as

pisci favorem: quamobrem cum supra dicti Principis recolendæ memoriæ bonitatis suffulti possemus obesse et prodesse, proficere et officere vehementer tam majoribus quam pusillis, affluxerunt loco encœniorum[1] et munerum, locoque donorum et jocalium, cænulenti quaterni ac decrepiti codices, nostris tam aspectibus quam affectibus pretiosi.

Tunc nobilissimorum monasteriorum aperiebantur armaria, referebantur scrinia et cistulæ solvebantur, et per longa sæcula in sepulchris soporata volumina expergiscuntur attomata,[2] quæque in locis tenebrosis latuerant, novæ lucis radiis perfunduntur. Delicatissimi quondam libri corrupti et abominabiles jam effecti murium quidem fœtibus cooperti, et vermium morsibus terebrati, jacebant exanimes. Et qui olim purpura vestiebantur et bysso, nunc in cinere et cilicio recubantes, oblivioni traditi videbantur domicilia tinearum.

Inter hæc nihilominus captatis temporibus magis voluptuose concedimus, quem fecisset medicus delicatus inter aromatum apothecas, ubi amoris[3] objectum reperimus et fomentum. Sic sacra vasa scientiæ ad nostræ dispensationis pervenerunt[4] arbitrium; quædam data, quædam vendita, et nonnulla pro tempore accommodata.

Nimirum cum nos plerique de hujusmodi donariis cernerent contentatos, ea sponte nostris usibus studuerunt tribuere quibus ipsi libentius caruerunt, quam ea, quæ nostris assistentes servitiis abstulerunt. Quorum[5] tamen negotia sic expedire curavimus gratiose, ut eisdem emolumentum accresceret, nullum tamen justitia detrimentum sentiret.

Porro si scyphos aureos et argenteos, si equos egregios, si nummorum summas non modicas amassemus, tunc temporis dives nobis ærarium instaurasse potuissemus.[6] Sed revera libros non libras maluimus codicesque plus diligimus, quam[7] florenos ac panfletos exiguos phale-

1 *Xeniorum*, mss. 797, 2454, and Ox. ed.

2 *Expergiscunt attonita*, mss. 797, 3352c, and Ox. ed.

3 *Amoris nostri*, mss. and Ox. ed.

4 *Provenerunt*, ms. 797 and Ox. ed.

5 *Libentius caruerunt: quorum*, Ox. ed.

6 *Possemus*, mss. and Ox. ed.

7 *Codicesque plus quam*, Ox. ed.

well as in our affections, flowed in most rapidly from the great and the small, instead of new year's gifts and remunerations, and instead of presents and jewels. Then the cabinets of the most noble monasteries were opened; cases were unlocked; caskets were unclasped, and astonished volumes which had slumbered for long ages in their sepulchres were roused up, and those that lay hid in dark places were overwhelmed with the rays of a new light. Books heretofore most delicate, now become corrupted and abominable, lay lifeless, covered indeed with the excrements of mice and pierced through with the gnawing of worms; and those that were formerly clothed with purple and fine linen, were now seen reposing in dust and ashes, given over to oblivion, the abodes of moths. Amongst these nevertheless, as time served, we sat down more voluptuously than the delicate physician could do amidst his stores of aromatics; and where we found an object of love, we found also an assuagement. Thus the sacred vessels of science came into the power of our disposal—some being given, some sold, and not a few lent for a time. Without doubt, many who perceived us to be contented with gifts of this kind, studied to contribute those things freely to our use, which they could most willingly do without themselves. We took care, however, to conduct the business of such so favorably, that the profit might accrue to them; justice therefore suffered no detriment.

Moreover, if we would have amassed cups of gold and silver, excellent horses, or no mean sums of money, we could in those days have laid up abundance of wealth for ourselves; but indeed we wished for books, not bags; we delighted more in folios than florins, and preferred paltry pamphlets to pampered palfreys. In addition to this, we were charged with the frequent embassies of the said prince of everlasting memory, and, owing to the multiplicity of state affairs, were sent first to the Roman chair, then to the court of France, then to various other kingdoms of the world, on tedious embassies,

ratis[1] prætulimus palfridis. Ad hæc ejus Principis[2] sempiternæ memoriæ legationibus crebris functi, et ob multiplicia regni negotia, nunc ad sedem Romæ, nunc ad curiam Franciæ, nunc ad mundi diversa dominia tædiosis ambassiatibus et periculosis temporibus mittebamur, circumferentes tamen[3] illam quam aquæ plurimæ nequiverunt exstinguere, charitatem librorum. Hæc enim peregrinationum[4] absinthia quasi quadam pigmenta[5] dulcoravit. Hæc post perplexas intricationes et scrupulosis causarum anfractus, et vix egressibiles reipublicæ labyrinthos ad respirandum parumper temperiem auræ lenis aperiunt.

O beate Deus Deorum in Sion, quantus fluminis impetus voluptatis lætificavit cor nostrum, quoties paradysum mundi Parisiis visitare vacavimus[6] moraturi: ubi nobis semper dies pauci præ amoris magnitudine videbantur. Ibi bibliothecæ jucundæ super cellas aromatum redolentes: ibi virens viridarium universorum voluminum: ibi prata[7] academica terræ motum trementia, Athenarum Peripateticorum diverticula,[8] Parnassi promunctoria, et porticus Stoicorum: ibi cernitur tam artis quam scientiæ mensurator Aristoteles, cujus est totum, quod est optimum in doctrinis, in regione duntaxat transmutabili sublunari: ibi Ptolemæus epicyclos et eccentricos auges, atque Genzachar planetarum figuris et numeris emetitur: ibi Paulus arcana revelat: ibi Dionysius[9] hierarchias coordinat et distinguit: ibi quicquid[10] Cadmus grammatice recollegit, et Phænices, totum virgo Carmentis charactere repræsentat Latino: ibi revera thesauris apertis et sacculorum corrigiis resolutis, pecuniam læto corde dispersimus, atque libros impreciabiles luto redemimus et arena.

Nequaquam malum est, insonuit omnis emptor. Sed

1 *Incrassatis*, Ox. ed.

2 *Adhæc ejus illustrissimi principis*, ms. 797; *Adhæc, ejusdem illustrissimi sempiternæ*, Ox. ed.; *Ad hæc ejusdem illustrissimi principis*, ms. 3352c.

3 *Tum ubique*, Ox. ed.; *Tamen ubique*, mss.

4 *Hæc omnia peregrinarum nationum*, Ox. ed.

5 *Pigmentaria potio*, mss. and Ox. ed.

6 *Vacavimus ibi*, Ox. ed.

7 *Porta*, ibid.

8 *Athenarum diverticula*, *Peripateticorum itinera*, mss. and Ox. ed.

9 *Dionysius convicinus*, mss. 797, 3352c and Ox. ed.; *Dionysius Corinthius*, ms. 24. 4.

10 *Quoque quod*, Ox. ed.

and in perilous times, carrying about with us, however, that fondness for books which many waters could not extinguish; for this, like a certain drug, sweetened the wormwood of peregrination; this, after the perplexing intricacies, scrupulous circumlocutions of debate, and almost inextricable labyrinths of public business, left an opening for a little while to breathe the temperature of a milder atmosphere. Oh blessed God of gods in Sion! what a rush of the flood of pleasure rejoiced our heart as often as we visited Paris, the paradise of the world! There we longed to remain, where, on account of the greatness of our love, the days ever appeared to us to be few. There are delightful libraries in cells redolent of aromatics; there flourishing greenhouses of all sorts of volumes; there academic meads trembling with the earthquake of Athenian Peripatetics pacing up and down; there the promontories of Parnassus, and the porticos of the Stoics. There is to be seen Aristotle the surveyor of arts and sciences, to whom alone belongs all that is most excellent in doctrine in this transitory world. There Ptolemy extends cycles and eccentrics; and Gensachar plans out the figures and numbers of the planets. There Paul reveals his arcana; and Dionysius arranges and distinguishes the hierarchies. There whatsoever Cadmus the Phœnician collected of grammatics, the virgin Carmentis represents entire in the Latin character. There in very deed, with an open treasury and untied purse strings, we scattered money with a light heart, and redeemed inestimable books with dirt and dust. Every buyer is apt to boast of his great bargains; but consider, how good, how agreeable it is to collect the arms of the clerical militia into one pile, that it may afford us the means of resisting the attacks of heretics if they rise against us. Furthermore, we are conscious of having seized the greatest opportunity in this—namely, that from an early age, bound by no matter what partial favor, we attached ourselves with most exquisite solicitude to the society of masters, scholars and professors of various

ecce quam bonum et quam jucundum, arma clericalis militiæ congregare in unum, ut suppetat nobis unde hæreticorum bella conterere,[1] si insurgant. Amplius opportunitatem maximam nos captasse cognoscimus per hoc, quod ab ætate tenera, magistrorum et scholarium ac diversorum artium professorum,[2] quos ingenii perspicacitas ac doctrinæ celebritas clariores effecerant, relegato quolibet partiali favore, exquisitissima sollicitudine, nostræ comitivæ conjunximus;[3] quorum consolativis colloquiis confortati, nunc argumentorum ostensivis investigationibus, nunc physicorum[4] processuum ac catholicorum doctorum tractatuum recitationibus,[5] velut multiplicatis et alternatis ingenii ferculis, dulcius fovebamur. Tales in nostro tirocinio commilitones elegimus; tales in thalamo collaterales habuimus; tales in itinere comites; tales in hospitio commensales; et tales penitus in omni fortuna sodales. Verum quia nulla felicitas diu durare permittitur, privabamus non nunquam luminum aliquorum præsentia corporali, cum eisdem promotiones ecclesiasticæ ac dignitates debitæ, prospiciente justitia de cœlo, provenerunt. Quo fiebat, ut incumbentes, sicut oportuit, curæ propriæ, se a nostris cogerentur obsequiis absentare.

Rursus compendiosissimam semitam subjungemus, per quam ad manus nostras pervenit librorum tam veterum quam novorum plurima multitudo. Religiosorum[6] siquidem paupertatem susceptam pro Christo nunquam indignantes horruimus: verum ipsos ubique terrarum in nostræ compassionis ulnas admisimus mansuetas, affabilitate familiarissima in personæ nostræ devotionem alleximus, allectosque beneficiorum liberalitate munifica fovimus propter Deum; quorum sic eramus omnium benefactores communes, ut nihilominus videremur quadam paternitatis proprietate singulos adoptasse. Istis in statu quodlibet facti sumus refugium, istis nunquam clausimus gratiæ nostræ sinum, quamobrem istos

1 *Conteramus*, Ox. ed.
2 *Professores*, ed. 1500, 1610, & 1702.
3 *Nostra semper conjunximus commercia*, Ox. ed.
4 *Philosophicorum*, ms. 2454; Ox.ed.
5 *Recitationibus, nunc moralitatum excitattivis collationibus*, mss. & Ox. ed.
6 *Religiosorum mendicantium*, ibid.

arts, whom perspicacity of wit and celebrity in learning had rendered most conspicuous; encouraged by whose consolatory conversation, we were most deliciously nourished, sometimes with explanatory investigation of arguments, at others with recitations of treatises on the progress of physics, and of the Catholic doctors, as it were with multiplied and successive dishes of learning. Such were the comrades we chose in our boyhood; such we entertained as the inmates of our chambers; such the companions of our journeys; such the messmates of our board and such entirely our associates in all our fortunes. But as no happiness is permitted to be of long duration, we were sometimes deprived of the personal presence of some of these luminaries, when, Justice looking down upon them from heaven, well earned ecclesiastical promotions and dignities fell in their way; whence it came to pass, as it should do, that, being incumbents of their own cures, they were compelled to absent themselves from our courtesies.

Again. We will add a most compendious way by which a great multitude of books, as well old as new, came into our hands. Never indeed having disdained[28] the poverty of religious devotees, assumed for Christ, we never held them in abhorrence, but admitted them from all parts of the world in the kindly embraces of our compassion; we allured them with most familiar affability into a devotion to our person, and, having allured, cherished them for the love of God with munificent liberality, as if we were the common benefactor of them all, but nevertheless with a certain propriety of patronage, that we might not appear to have given preference to any; to these under all circumstances we became a refuge; to these we never closed the bosom of our favor. Wherefore we deserved to have those as the most peculiar and zealous promoters of our wishes, as well by their personal as their mental labors, who, going about by sea and land, surveying the whole compass of the earth, and also inquiring into the general studies of the universities of

votorum nostrorum peculiarissimos zelatores meruimus habere et tam opere quam opera promotores. Qui circumeuntes mare et aridam, orbis ambitum perlustrantes, universitatum quoque diversarum[1] provinciarum generalia studia perscrutantes, nostris desideriis militare studebant, certissima spe mercedis.

Quis inter tot argutissimos venatores lepusculus delitesceret? Quis pisciculus istorum nunc hamos, nunc retia, nunc sagenas evaderet?

A corpore legis divinæ[2] usque ad quaternum sophismatum externorum, nihil istos præterire potuit scrutatores. Si in fonte fidei Christianæ, Curia sacrosancta Romana, sermo devotus insonuit, vel si pro novis causis quæstio ventilabatur extranea; si Parisiensis soliditas, quæ plus antiquitati discendæ, quam veritati subtiliter producendæ jam studet: si Anglicana perspicacitas, quæ antiquis perfusa luminaribus novos semper radios veritatis emittit, quicquid ad augmentum scientiæ vel declarationem fidei promulgavit; hoc statim nostris recens infundebatur auribus,[3] nullo denigratum semi verbio, nulla nugacitate[4] corruptum, sed de prælo purissimi torcularis in nostræ memoriæ dolia deferendum[5] transibat.

Cum vero nos ad civitates et loca contingeret declinare, ubi præfati pauperes conventus habebant, eorum armaria ac quæcunque librorum repositoria visitare non piguit: imo ibi in altissima paupertate, altissimas divitias[6] thesaurizatas invenimus: non solum in eorum sarniculis et sportellis, micas de mensa dominorum cadentes reperimus pro catellis, verum etiam panes popositionis absque fermento, panemque angelorum omne in se delectamentum habentem : imo horrea Joseph plena frumentis, totamque Ægypti supellectilem, atque dona ditissima,[7] quæ regina Saba detulit Salomoni.

Hi sunt formicæ continue[8] congregantes in messe et

1 *Qui circuentes mare et aridam, ac orbis ambitum perlustrantes, universitates, diversarumque*, mss. 797, 3352c, 2454, and Ox. ed.

2 *Sanctæ legis dominicæ*, Ox. ed.; *Sacræ legis divinæ*, ms. 3352c.

3 *Auditibas*, mss. and Ox. ed.

4 *Semini verbo nulloque nugace*, ibid.

5 *Torcularis, nostræ memoriæ dolium defæcandum*, Ox. ed.

6 *Divitias sapientiæ*, mss. 797, 3352c, and Ox. ed.

7 *Altissima*, Ox. ed.

8 *Quetidio*, ibid.

the various provinces, were anxious to administer to our wants, under a most certain hope of reward.

Amongst so many of the keenest hunters, what leveret could lie hid? What fry could evade the hook, the net, or the trawl of these men? From the body of divine law, down to the latest controversial tract of the day, nothing could escape the notice of these scrutinizers. If a devout sermon resounded at the fount of Christian faith, the most holy Roman court, or if an extraneous question were to be sifted on account of some new pretext; if the dullness of Paris, which now attends more to studying antiquities than to subtly producing truth; if English perspicacity overspread with ancient lights always emitted new rays of truth—whatsoever it promulgated, either for the increase of knowledge or in declaration of the faith—this, while recent, was poured into our ears, not mystified by imperfect narration nor corrupted by absurdity, but from the press of the purest presser it passed, dregless, into the vat of our memory. When indeed we happened to turn aside to the towns and places where the aforesaid paupers[29] had convents, we were not slack in visiting their chests and other repositories of books; for there, amidst the deepest poverty, we found the most exalted riches treasured up; there, in their satchels and baskets, we discovered not only the crumbs that fell from the master's table for the little dogs, but indeed the show bread without leaven, the bread of angels, containing in itself all that is delectable—yea the granaries of Joseph full of corn and all the furniture of Egypt, and the richest gifts that the queen of Sheba brought to Solomon. These are the ants that lay up in harvest, the laborious bees that are continually fabricating cells of honey; the successors of Belzaleel, in devising whatsoever can be made by the workman in gold, silver and precious stones, with which the temple of the church may be decorated; these, the ingenious embroiderers who make the ephod and breastplate of the pontiff, as also the various garments of the

apes argumentosæ fabricantes jugiter cellas mellis. Hi successores Bezeleel ad excogitandum quicquid fabrefieri poterit[1] in argento et auro et gemmis, quibus templum ecclesiæ decoretur. Hi prudentes polymitarii, qui superhumerale ac rationale pontificis, sed et vestes varias efficiunt sacerdotum. Hi cortinas, saga, pellesque arietum rubricatas resarciunt, quibus ecclesiæ militantis tabernaculum contegatur. Hi sunt agricolæ[2] seminantes, boves triturantes, tubæ buccinantes, Pleiades emicantes et stellæ manentes in ordine suo, quæ Sysaram expugnare non cessant. Et ut veritas honoretur, salvo judicio cujuscunque, licet, hi nuper hora undecima, vineam sint ingressi Dominicam, sicut amantissimi nobis libri cap. vi supra anxius allegabant, plus tamen in hac hora brevissima sacratorum librorum adjecerunt propagini[3] quam omnes residui vinitores. Pauli sectantes vestigia, qui vocatione novissimus, prædicatione primus, multo latius[4] evangelium Christi sparsit. De istis ad statum pontificalem assumptis, nonnullos habuimus de duobus ordinibus, Prædicatorum videlicet et Minorum, nostris assistentes lateribus, nostræ quoque familiæ commensales, viros utique tam moribus quam litteris insignitos: qui diversorum voluminum correctionibus, expositionibus, tabulationibus, ac compilationibus, indefessis studiis incumbebant.

Sane quamvis omnium religiosorum communicatione multiplici, plurimorum operum copiam tam novorum quam veterum assecuti fuerimus, Prædicatores tamen extollimus merito speciali præconio in hac parte, quod eos præ cunctis religiosis, suorum sine invidia gratissimæ communicationis invenimus, ac divina quadam liberalitate perfusos, sapientiæ luminosæ probavimus non avaros sed idoneos possessores.[5]

Præter has opportunitates omnes prætactas, stationariorum ac librariorum notitiam non solum intra natalis soli[6] provinciam, sed per regnum Franciæ, Teutoniæ et Italiæ comparavimus dispersorum, faciliter pecunia præ-

1 *A fabre fieri potest*, Ox. ed.
2 *Contegatur*, *Agricolæ*, ibid.
3 *Paginæ*, ibid.
4 *Latius aliis*, mss. and Ox. ed.
5 *Professores*, ed. 1500, 1610, & 1702.
6 *Sui*, ed. 1702.

priests. These keep in repair the curtains, cloths, and red ram skins with which the tabernacle of the church militant is covered over. These are the husbandmen that sow; the oxen that tread out the corn; the blowers of the trumpets; the twinkling Pleiades, and the stars remaining in their order, which cease not to fight against Sisera. And that truth may be honored (saving the opinion of any man), although these may have lately entered the Lord's vineyard at the eleventh hour, as our most beloved books anxiously alleged in the sixth chapter, they have nevertheless in that shortest hour trained more layers of the sacred books, than all the rest of the vinedressers, following the footsteps of Paul, who, being the last in vocation but the first in preaching, most widely spread the gospel of Christ. Amongst these we had some of two of the orders, namely, Preachers and Minors,[22] who were raised to the pontifical state, who had stood at our elbows, and been the guests of our family; men in every way distinguished as well by their morals as by their learning, and who had applied themselves with unwearied industry to the correction, explanation, indexing and compilation of various volumes.

Indeed, although we had obtained abundance both of old and new works through an extensive communication with all the religious orders, yet we must in justice extol the Preachers with a special commendation in this respect; for we found them above all other religious devotees ungrudging of their most acceptable communications, and overflowing with a certain divine liberality; we experienced them, not to be selfish hoarders, but meet professors of enlightened knowledge. Besides all the opportunities already touched upon, we easily acquired the notice of the stationers and librarians, not only within the provinces of our native soil, but of those dispersed over the kingdoms of France, Germany, and Italy, by the prevailing power of money; no distance whatever impeded, no fury of the sea deterred them; nor was cash wanting for their expenses when they sent

volante: nec eos ullatenus impedivit distantia, neque furor maris absterruit, nec eis æs pro[1] expensa deficit, quin ad nos optatos libros transmitterent vel afferrent. Sciebant enim pro certo, quod[2] spes eorum in sinu nostro reposita defraudari non poterat, sed restabat apud nos copiosa redemptio cum usuris.

Denique nec rectores scholarium[3] puerorumque rudium pædagogos, nostra neglexit communio[4] singulorum captatrix amoris. Sed potius cum vacaret eorum hortulos et allegos ingressi, flores superficietenus redolentes collegimus, ac radices effodimus obsoletas, studiosis tamen accommodatas, et quæ possent, digesta barbarie rancida, pectorales arterias eloquentiæ munere medicare.[5] Inter hujusmodi pleraque, comperimus renovari dignissima, quæ solerter elimata, turpi[6] larva vetustatis deposita, merebantur venustis vultibus denuo reformari. Quæ nos adhibita necessariorum sufficentia, in futuræ resurrectionis exemplum, resuscitata quodam modo, redivivæ reddidimus sospitati. Ceterum apud nos, in nostris atriis[7] multitudo non modica semper erat, antiquariorum, scriptorum, colligatorum, correctorum, illuminatorum et generaliter omnium, qui poterant librorum servitiis utiliter insudare.

Postremo omnes utriusque sexus, omnisque status vel dignitatis conditio, cujus erat cum libris aliquale commercium, cordis nostri januas pulsu poterant aperire facillime, et in nostro gremio[8] commodosum reperire cubile. Sic omnes admisimus codices afferentes, ut nec[9] præcedentum multitudo fastidium posteriorum efficeret vel hesternum beneficium præcollatum, præjudicium pareret hodierno. Quapropter cum omnibus memoratis personis, quasi quibusdam adamantibus attractivis librorum, jugiter uteremur, fiebat ad nos desideratus accessus vasorum scientiæ, et multifarius volatus voluminum optimorum.

Et hoc est, quod præsenti capitulo sumpsimus enarrare.

1 *Nec eis pro*, Ox. ed.
2 *Sciebant profecto quod*, ibid.
3 *Scholarum ruralium*, ibid.
4 *Communes*, ed. 1500, 1610, & 1702.
5 *Meditari*, mss. and Ox. ed.
6 *Rubigine turpi*, ibid.
7 *Maneriis*, ibid.
8 *Nostræ gratiæ gremio*, mss. 797, 3352c, and Ox. ed.
9 *Nunquam*, mss. and Ox. ed.

or brought us the wished for books; for they knew to a certainty that their hopes reposed in our bosom could not be disappointed, but ample redemption with interest was secure with us. Lastly, our common captivatrix of the love of all men (money) did not neglect the rectors of country schools nor the pedagogues of clownish boys; but rather, when we had leisure to enter their little gardens and paddocks, we culled redolent flowers upon the surface, and dug up neglected roots (not however useless to the studious), and such coarse digests of barbarism as with the gift of eloquence might be made sanative to the pectoral arteries. Amongst productions of this kind we found many most worthy of renovation, which when the foul rust was skillfully polished off and the mask of old age removed, deserved to be once more remodelled into comely countenances, and which, we having applied a sufficiency of the needful means, resuscitated for an examplar of future resurrection, having in some measure restored them to renewed soundness. Moreover, there was always about us in our halls no small assemblage of antiquaries, scribes, bookbinders, correctors, illuminators, and generally of all such persons as were qualified to labor advantageously in the service of books.

To conclude. All of either sex of every degree, estate or dignity, whose pursuits were in any way connected with books, could with a knock most easily open the door of our heart, and find a convenient reposing place in our bosom. We so admitted all who brought books, that neither the multitude of first-comers could produce a fastidiousness of the last, nor the benefit conferred yesterday be prejudicial to that of to-day. Wherefore, as we were continually resorted to by all the aforesaid persons as to a sort of adamant attractive of books, the desired accession of the vessels of science, and a multifarious flight of the best volumes were made to us. And this is what we undertook to relate at large in the present chapter.

CAPITULUM IX.

QUOD ANTIQUI STUDENTES PRÆCEDUNT MODERNOS FERVORE DISCENDI.[1]

LICET nostris desideriis novitas modernorum nunquam fuerit onerosa,[2] qui vacantes studiis, ac primorum[3] patrum sententiis[4] quicquid vel subtiliter vel utiliter adjicientes, grata semper affectione coluimus, antiquorum tamen examinatos[5] labores, securiori cupiditate cupivimus perscrutari. Sive enim naturaliter viguerunt perspicaciori mentis ingenio, sive instantiori studio forsitan indulserunt, sive utriusque suffulti[6] subsidio profecerunt,[7] hoc unum comperimus evidenter, quod vix sufficiunt successores priorum comperta discutere, atque ea per doctrinæ captare compendium,[8] quæ antiqui anfractuosis adinventionibus effoderunt. Sicut enim corporis probitate præstantiores legimus præcessisse, quam moderna tempora exhibere noscantur, ita luculentioribus sensibus præfulsisse, plerosque nitimur opinari,[9] nullatenus est absurdum, cum utrosque opera quæ fecerunt,[10] inattingibiles posteris æque præbent. Unde Focas in prologo grammaticæ suæ scribit.

> Omnia cum veterum sint explorata libellis,
> Multa loqui breviter sit novitatis opus.

Nempe si de fervore discendi ac diligentia studii fiat sermo, ille philosophiæ vitam totam integre devoverunt. Nostri vero sæculi contemporanei, paucos annos fervidæ juventutis æstuantes, vicissim incendiis vitiorum segniter

1 *Quod licet opera veterum amplius amaremus, non tamen dampnamus studia modernorum*, mss. 797, 3352c, and Ox. ed.
2 *Odiosa*, mss. and Ox. ed.
3 *Priorum*, ibid.
4 *Semitis*, Ox. ed.
5 *Examinatos libros vel*, ibid.
6 *Mentis ingenio, sive utriusque suffulti*, ibid.
7 *Perfecerunt*, ibid.
8 *Dispendium*, ibid.
9 *Plerosque veterum opinari*, mss. 797, 3352c, and Ox. ed.; *Plerosque opinari*, ms. 2454, and ed. 1702.
10 *Gesserunt*, Ox. ed.

CHAPTER IX.

THE ANCIENT STUDENTS SURPASSED THE MODERN IN FERVENCY OF LEARNING.

ALTHOUGH the novelties of the moderns were never the burthen of our desires, we have always with grateful affection honored those who found leisure for the studies and opinions of the primitive fathers, and ingeniously or usefully added anything to them. We have nevertheless coveted with a more undisturbed desire, the well digested labors of the ancients. Whether they were naturally invigorated with the capacity of a more perspicacious mind, whether they addicted themselves perhaps to more intense study, or whether they succeeded by the support of both these aids, we have clearly discovered this one thing—that their successors are scarcely competent to discuss the discoveries of those who preceded them, or to comprehend those things by the shorter way of instruction which the ancients quarried up by their own roundabout contrivances.

For as we read that they possessed a more excellent proportion of body than what modern times are known to exhibit, so there is no absurdity in believing that most of the ancients were more refulgent in the clearness of their understandings, as the works they performed, by both appear alike unattainable by their successors. Whence Phocas in the prologue of his grammar writes :

As in the books of the ancients all things have been explored,
Novelty is requisite much in few words to afford.

For certainly if the question is about ardor in learning and diligence in study, these devoted their whole life entirely to philosophy ; but the contemporaries of our age negligently apply a few years of ardent youth, burn-

applicant, et cum sedatis passionibus, discernendæ ambiguæ veritatis acumen attigerint, externis[1] implicati negotiis retrocedunt, et philosophiæ gymnasiis valedicunt. Mustum fumosum juvenilis ingenii philosophiæ difficultati delibant, vinumque maturius defæcatum æconomicæ sollicitudini largiuntur. Amplius sicut Ovidius, primo *De Vetula*, merito lamentatur:

Omnes declinant ad eas, quæ lucra ministrant.
Utque sciant discunt pauci, plures ut abundent.
Sic te prostituunt, O virgo scientia! sic te
Venalem faciunt castis amplexibus aptam,
Non te propter te quærentes, sed lucra per te.
Ditarique volunt potius, quam philosophari.

Et infra[2] sic:

. . . Sed Philosophia
Exilium patitur, et Philopecunia regnat.

Quam constat esse violentissimum toxicum disciplinæ.

Qualiter vero non alium terminum studio posuerunt antiqui quam vitæ, declarat Valerius ad Tiberium lib. VIII, cap. vii, per exempla multorum. Carneades, inquit, laboriosus ac diutinus scientiæ[3] miles fuit. Siquidem expletis nonaginta annis idem illi vivendi ac philosophandi finis fuit. Et Socrates[4] xciv agens, nobilissimum librum scripsit. Sophocles prope centesimum annum agens *Œdipodeon*, id est, librum de gestis Œdipodis, scripsit. Simonides[5] lxxx anno carmina scripsit. A. Gellius non effectavit diutius vivere, quam esset idoneus ad scribendum, teste se ipso in prologo *Noctium Atticarum*. Fervorem vero studii, quem habebat Euclides Socraticus, recitare solebat Taurus philosophus, ut juvenes ad studium animaret, sicut refert A. Gellius lib VI, cap. x voluminis memorati. Athenienses namque cum Megarenses odirent, decreverunt, quod si quis de Megarensibus Athenas intraret, capite plecteretur. Tunc Euclides, qui Megarensis erat, et ante illud decre-

1 *Mox externis*, mss. and Ox. ed.
2 *Infra*, ms. 3352c.; *Ita sicut philosophia*, Ox. ed.
3 *Sapientiæ*, mss. and Ox. ed.
4 *Fuit consocrates*, ms. 3352c.
5 *Annum agens; Simonides*, etc., mss. and Ox. ed.

ing by turns with the fire of vice; and when they have attained the acumen of discerning a doubtful truth, they immediately become involved in extraneous business, retire, and say farewell to the schools of philosophy; they sip the frothy must of juvenile wit over the difficulties of philosophy, and pour out the purified old wine with economical care.

Further, as Ovid justly laments, *De Vetula:*[30]

> All men incline to things affording gain;
> Few study wisdom, more for riches strain;
> Thee they prostitute, oh virgin Science;
> Thee venal make, whose chaste compliance
> None for thy own sake ask. Man rather tries
> Through thee to thrive, than to philosophize.

And thus as the love of wisdom is doomed to exile, the love of money rules, which is evidently the most violent poison of discipline. In what manner indeed the ancients set no other limit to their studies than that of their life, Valerius Maximus shows to Tiberius by the examples of many: book VIII, chap. vii. Carneades (he says) was a laborious and constant soldier of science; for having completed his ninetieth year, that same was the end of his living and philosophizing. Socrates during his ninety-fourth year wrote a most noble book. Sophocles being nearly one hundred years old wrote his *Œdipodeon*, that is the book of the acts of Œdipus. Simonides wrote verses in his eightieth year. Aulus Gellius wished to live no longer than while he was competent to write, as he testifies in the prologue of his *Attic Nights*. But the philosopher Taurus, in order to excite young people to study, used to adduce the fervor of study that possessed Euclid the Socratic, as Aulus Gellius relates in his aforesaid volume, book VI, chap. x. For as the Athenians hated the Megarenses, they decreed that if any one of them should enter Athens he should be beheaded; but Euclid,[31] who was a Megarensian, and had heard Socrates before that decree, went afterwards to hear him in the night disguised as a woman and returned, the distance from Megara to Athens

tum Socratem audierat, muliebri ornamento contectus,[1] de nocte ad Socratem, ut eum audiret, ibat de Megaris ad Athenas viginti millia passuum et redibat. Imprudens et nimius fuit fervor Archimedis, qui geometriæ facultatis amator nomen edicere[2] noluit, nec a figura protracta caput erigere, quo vitæ mortalis fatum prolongasset;[3] sed indulgens studio plus quam vitæ, studiosam figuram vitali sanguine cruentavit. Quam plurima hujusmodi nostri propositi sunt exempla, nec ea quidem transcurrere brevitas effectata permittit. Sed quod dolentes referimus, iter prorsus diversum incedunt clerici celebres his diebus. Ambitione siquidem in ætate tenera laborantes, ac præsumptionis pennas Icareas ineptis et inexpertis[4] lacertis fragiliter coaptantes, pileum magistralem immaturi præripiunt; fiuntque pueruli facultatum plurimum[5] professores immeriti, quas nequaquam pedetentim pertranseunt, sed ad instar caprearum saltatim ascendunt. Cumque parum de grandi torrente gustaverint, arbitrantur se totum funditus sorbuisse, vix faucibus humectatis. Et quia in primis rudimentis tempore congruo non fundantur super instabile[6] fundamentum, opus ædificant ruinosum. Jamque profectos[7] pudet addiscere, quæ tenellos decuerat didicisse, et sic profecto coguntur perpetuo luere quod ad fasces indebitos præpropere salierunt. Propter hæc et his[8] similia, tyrones scholastici soliditatem doctrinæ quam veteres habuerunt, eam paucis lucubratiunculis non attingunt, quantumque[9] fungantur honoribus, censeantur nominibus, auctorizentur habitibus, locenturque solemniter in cathedris seniorum. Prisciani regulas et Donati statim de cunis erepti, et sic celeriter ablactati perlingunt *Categorias*[10] *Perihermenias*, in cujus scriptura summus Aristoteles calamum in corde tinxit,[11] infantuli balbutie resonant impubes

1 *Contentus est*, Ox. ed.
2 *Edisserere*, mss. 797, 2454; Ox. ed.
3 *Fata poterat prolongasse*, ms. 797 and Ox. ed.; *Fatum poterat prolongasse*, ms. 3352c.
4 *Icarias inexpertis*, mss. 797, 3352c and Ox. ed.
5 *Proripiunt. fiuntque parvuli facultatum plurium*, Ox. ed.
6 *Debile*, mss. and Ox. ed.
7 *Provectos*, Ox. ed.
8 *Et alia*, ibid.
9 *Quantumcunque*, ibid.
10 *Categorias et perihermenias*, ibid.
11 *Tinxisse confingitur*, ms. 3352c and Ox. ed.; *Calamum balbutie resonant*, ms. 797; *Calamum in corde configitur*, ms. 2454.

being twenty miles. Imprudent and excessive was the fervor of Archimedes, a lover of the geometric art, who would neither tell his name, nor raise his head from a figure he had drawn, by doing which he might have prolonged the fate of his mortal life; but thinking more of his study than his life, he imbrued his favorite figure with his vital blood. There are many more examples of the same sort to our purpose, which the brevity we affect does not permit us to detail. But with sorrow we say, that the celebrated clerks of these days fall into a very different course. Laboring, indeed, under ambition at an early age, fitting Icarian wings upon their feeble and untried arms, they immaturely seize upon the magisterial cap, and become worthless puerile professors of many faculties, which they by no means pass through step by step, but ascend to by leaps, after the manner of goats; and when they have tasted a little of the great stream, they think they have drunk it to the bottom, their mouths being scarcely wetted. They raise up a ruinous edifice upon an unstable foundation, because they were not founded in the first rudiments at the proper time: being now promoted, they are ashamed to learn what it would have become them to have learnt when younger, and thus in effect they are perpetually compelled to pay the penalty of having too hastily leaped into undue authority. For these and other similar causes scholastic tyros do not obtain, by their scanty lucubrations, that soundness of learning that the ancients possessed, inasmuch as they can now be endowed with honors, distinguished by names, authorized by the garb of office, and solemnly placed in the chairs of their seniors, as soon as they have crept out of their cradles, been hastily weaned, and can repeat the rules of Priscian and Donatus by rote. In their teens and beardless, they reëcho with infantine prattle the *Categories* and *Perihermenias*,[32] in the writing of which the great Aristotle is feigned to have dipped his pen in his heart's blood. Passing the routine of which faculties, with dangerous brevity and a baneful diploma,[33] they lay violent hands

et imberbes. Quarum facultatum itinera dispendioso compendio, damnosoque diplomate transmeantes, in S. Moisem manus injiciunt violentas, ac se tenebrosis aquis in nubibus aeris faciliter[1] aspergentes, ad pontificatus infulam caput parant, nulla decoratum canicie senectutis. Promovent plurimum istam pestem juvantque ad istum phantasticum clericatum tam[2] pernicibus passibus attingendum; papalis provisio seductivis[3] precibus impetrata, nec non et preces, quæ repelli non possunt, cardinalium et potentium, amicorum cupiditas et parentum, qui ædificantes Sion in sanguinibus prius suis nepotibus et alumnis ecclesiasticas dignitates aucupant,[4] quam naturæ successu, vel doctrinæ tempore[5] maturescant.

Ideo[6] proh dolor paroxismo quem plangimus, Parisiense palladium nostris mœstis temporibus cernimus jam sublatum, ubi tepuit imo, ubi fere friguit zelus scholæ tam nobilis, cujus olim radii lucem dabant universis angulis orbis terræ. Quiescit ibidem jam calamus omnis scribæ, nec librorum generatio propagatur ulterius, nec est, qui

Incipiat novus auctor haberi.

Involvunt sententias sermonibus imperitis, et omnis logicæ proprietate privantur; nisi quod Anglicanas subtilitates, quibus palam detrahunt, vigiliis furtivis addiscunt.

Minerva mirabiles[7] nationes hominum circuire videtur et a fine usque ad finem attingit fortiter, ut se ipsam communicet universis. Indos, Babylonios, Ægyptios atque Græcos, Arabes et Latinos eam jam pertransisse[8] cernimus, jam Athenas deseruit, jam a Roma recessit, jam Parisios præterivit, jam ad Britanniam insularum insignissimam, quin potius microcosmum, accessit feliciter, ut se Græcis et Barbaris debitricem ostendat. Quo miraculo[9] conjicitur a plerisque, quod sicut Galliæ jam Sophia tepescit, sic ejusdem militia penitus evirata languescit.

1 *Feraliter*, Ox. ed.; *Facialiter*, mss. 797 and 3352c.
2 *Cum*, Ox. ed.
3 *Seductoris*, ibid.
4 *Anticipant*, mss. and Ox. ed.
5 *Temperie*, ibid.
6 *Isto*, mss. 797, 3352c and Ox. ed.
7 *Mirabilis*, Ox. ed.
8 *Prætermisisse*, ibid.
9 *Miraculo perfecto*, ibid.

upon holy Moses; and sprinkling their faces with the dark waters[34] of the clouds of the air, they prepare their heads, unadorned by any of the greyness of old age, for the mitre of the pontificate. By such pernicious steps are these pests put forward, and aided in attaining to that fantastical clerkship. The papal provision is importuned by the seductive entreaties, or rather prayers of cardinals and powerful friends which cannot be rejected, and the cupidity of relations, who, building up Sion upon their own blood, watch for ecclesiastical dignities for their nephews and wards before they are matured by the course of nature or sufficient instruction. Hence not without shame we observe the Parisian palladium in our woeful times, suffering under the paroxysm we are deploring. There, where zeal was lately hot, it now almost freezes: where the rays of so noble a school formerly gave light to every corner of the earth, there the pen of every scribe is now at rest, the generation of books is no longer propagated, nor is there any one who can attempt to be considered as a new author. They involve their opinions in unskillful language, and are destitute of all logical propriety, excepting, that with furtive vigilance they find out English subtleties, which they manifestly carry off.

The admirable Minerva seems to have made the tour of the nations of mankind, and casually come in contact with them all, from one end of the world to the other, that she might communicate herself to each. We perceive her to have passed through the Indians, Babylonians, Egyptians, Greeks, Arabians, and Latins. She next deserted Athens, and then retired from Rome: and having already given the slip to the Parisians, she has at last happily reached Britain, the most renowned of islands, or rather the microcosm, that she may show herself indebted[35] to Greeks and barbarians. From the accomplishment of which miracle it is conjectured by many, that as the Sophia of Gaul has now become lukewarm, so her emasculated militia is become altogether languid.

CAPITULUM X.

QUOD SUCCESSIVE SCIENTIA AD PERFECTIONEM CREVIT ET QUOD AUCTOR GRAMMATICAM GRÆCAM ET HEBRÆAM PROCURAVIT.[1]

SAPIENTIAM veterum exquirentes assidue, juxta sapientis consilium *Ecclesiast.* xxxix,[2] "Sapientiam" inquit, "omnium antiquorum exquirit sapiens;" non in illam opinionem dignum duximus declinandum, ut primos artium fundatores omnem ruditatem elimasse dicamus, scientes ad inventionem cujusque fidelium conamine[3] ponderatam, pusillam efficere scientiæ portionem; sed[4] plurimorum investigationes sollicitas, quasi datis symbolis singulatim, scientiarum ingentia corpora, ad immensas quas cernimus copias,[5] successivis augmentationibus succreverunt. Semper namque discipuli, magistrorum sententias, iterata fornace liquantes, præneglectam scoriam excoxerunt, donec fieret aurum electum, probatum,[6] terræ purgatum, septuplum, et[7] nullius erronei vel dubii admixtione fucatum. Neque enim Aristoteles, quamvis ingenio giganter floreret, in quo naturæ complacuit experiri, quantum mortalitati,[8] rationis posset admittere,[9] quemque paulo minus ab angelis minoravit Altissimus, illa mira volumina, quæ totus vix capit orbis, ex digitis suis suxit. Quin imo[10] Babyloniorum, Ægyptiorum, Chaldæorum, Persarum, et Medorum, quos omnes diserta Græcia in thesauros suos transtulerat, sacros libros oculis lynceis penetrando perviderat. Quorum recte dicta rccipiens, aspera complanavit, superflua resecuit,

1 *De successiva librorum perfectione*, Ox. ed.
2 *xxx*, ibid.
3 *Fideli canone*, mss. 797, 2454, and Ox. ed.; *Canonio*, ms. 3352c.
4 *Sed per*, Ox ed.
5 *Quantitates*, mss. and Ox. ed.
6 *Electum purgatum*, Ox. ed.
7 *Et perfectæ*, mss. 797, 3352c, and Ox. ed.
8 *Immortalitati*, Ox. ed.
9 *Committere*, ibid.
10 *Imo Hebræorum*, mss. 797, 3352c, and Ox. ed.

CHAPTER X.

SCIENCE GREW TO PERFECTION BY DEGREES. THE AUTHOR PROVIDED A GREEK AND A HEBREW GRAMMAR.

ASSIDUOUSLY searching out the wisdom of the ancients according to the advice of the wise man (*Ecc.* xxxix), who says: "A wise man searches out all "the wisdom of the ancients;" we have not led ourselves into that opinion for the purpose of saying that the first founders cleared away all the rudeness of the arts, knowing that the invention of every one has been weighed, in the faithful endeavor to make a small portion of science efficient. But through the careful investigations of many, the symbols being given as it were one by one, the vigorous bodies of the sciences grew up by successive augmentations into the immense copiousness we now behold: for scholars ever melted down the opinions of their masters in renewed furnaces, running off the previously neglected dross till they became choice gold, proved, seven times purged of earth, and unalloyed by any admixture of error or doubt. Even Aristotle, although of gigantic mind, in whom it pleased nature to try how great a portion of reason she could admit into mortality, and whom the Most High made but little inferior to the angels, who sucked those wonderful volumes out of his own fingers which the whole world scarcely comprehends, would not have flourished if he had not, with the penetrating eyes of a lynx, looked through the sacred books of the Babylonians, Egyptians, Chaldeans, Persians, and Medes, all which he transferred into his own treasuries in eloquent Greek. Receiving their correct assertions, he polished their asperities, cut off their superfluities, supplied their deficiencies, expunged their

diminuta supplevit et erronea[1] delevit. Ac non solum sincere docentibus, sed etiam oberrantibus regratiandum censuit, quasi viam præbentibus, veritatem facilius inquirendi, sicut ipsemet in secundo *Metaphysicæ* clare docet. Sic multi jurisperiti condidere *Pandectam*, sic medici multi *Tegni*, sic et Avicenna *Canonem*, sic Plinius molem illam *Historiæ Naturalis*, sic Ptolemæus edidit *Almagestum*. Quemadmodum namque in scriptoribus annalium considerare non est difficile, quod semper posterior præsupponit priorem, sine quo prælapsa tempora nullatenus enarrare valeret: sic est in scientiarum auctoribus æstimandum. Nemo namque solus quamcunque scientiam generavit. cum inter veterrimos[2] et novellos, intermedios reperimus; antiquos quidem si nostris ætatibus[3] comparentur, novos vero, si ad[4] fundamina referantur, et istos doctissimos arbitramur.

Quid fecisset Virgilius Latinorum poeta præcipuus, si Theocritum, Lucretium, et Homerum minime spoliasset, et in eorum vitula non errasset?[5] Quid nisi Parthenium Pindarumque, cujus eloquentiam non modo potuit imitari, aliquatenus lectitasset? Quid Sallustius, Tullius, Boethius, Macrobius, Lactantius, Martianus, imo tota cohors generaliter Latinorum, si Athenarum studia vel Græcorum volumina non vidissent? Parum certe Hieronymus trium linguarum peritus in scripturæ gazophylacium, Ambrosius, Augustinus, qui tamen literas Græcas se fatetur odisse, imo Gregorius, qui prorsus eas nescisse describitur,[6] ad doctrinam ecclesiæ contulissent, si nihil eisdem doctior Græcia commodasset. Cujus rivulis Roma rigata, sicut prius generavit philosophos ad Græcorum effigiem, pari forma postea protulit orthodoxæ fidei tractatores. Sudores sunt Græcorum, symbola quæ cantamus, eorumdem declarata conciliis, et multorum martyrio confirmata. Cedit tamen, ad gloriam Latinorum per accidens hebetudo[7] nativa, quoniam sicut fuerunt in

1 *Errata*, mss. and Ox. ed.
2 *Tamen inter vetustissimos*, ibid.
3 *Temporibus*, Ox. ed,
4 *Ad studiorum fundamina*, ms. 797, and Ox. ed.; *Ad fundamenta*, ms. 3352c.
5 *Arasset*, mss. and Ox. ed.
6 *Eas se nescire describit*, ibid.
7 *Habitudo*, Ox. ed.

errors, and thought it right to return thanks, not only to those who taught truly, but also to those who erred, as their errors point out a way of more easily investigating truth, as he himself clearly shows (2 *Metaph.*). Thus many lawyers compiled the *Pandect*, many physicians the *Tegni*,[36] and Avicenna the *Canon*. Thus Pliny edited that mass of *Natural History*, and Ptolemy the *Almagest:* for after this manner it is not difficult to perceive in writers of annals that the last always presupposes a prior, without whom he would in no way have been competent to detail past events. The same thing holds good amongst the authors of science, as no man produced any science whatever alone; for between the more ancient and the more recent we find intermediates, old, indeed, if compared with our times, but new, if referred to the ground-work of science; and these are held to be the most learned. What would Virgil, the greatest poet of the Latins, have done, if he had not at all plundered Theocritus, Lucretius, and Homer, or ploughed with their heifer? What could Horace[37] anyhow have pored over, but Parthenius and Pindar, whose eloquence he could in no way imitate? What Sallust, Tully, Boëtius, Macrobius, Lactantius, Martianus, nay, the whole cohort of the Latins in general, if they had not seen the labors of the Athenians or volumes of the Greeks? Jerome, skilled in the treasures of the three languages of scripture; Ambrose; Augustine, who, however, confessed that he hated Greek literature; and still more, Gregory, who is described as altogether ignorant of it—would certainly have contributed little to the doctrines of the church, if they had borrowed nothing from the more learned Greeks; watered by whose rivulets, Rome, as she first generated philosophers after the image of the Greeks, so afterwards in like form she brought forth treatisers[38] of the orthodox faith. The creeds we chant are the sweat of the Greeks, declared in their councils and confirmed by the martyrdom of many. Native dullness, however, as it falls out

studiis minus docti, sic et in erroribus minus mali. Ariana nempe malitia fere totam eclipsavit[1] ecclesiam. Nestoriana nequitia,[2] blasphema[3] rabie debacchari præsumpsit in virginem, nam tam nomen quam definitionem θεοτόχος abstulisset reginæ,[4] nisi miles invictus Cyrillus monomachiæ congressum paratus exsufflasset.[5] Innumerabiles nobis sunt Græcarum hæresium tam species quam auctores; nam sicut fuerunt sacrosanctæ fidei primitivi cultores, ita primi zizaniorum satores, prout dicitur et producuntur historiis[6] fide dignis. Sicque posterius profecerunt in pejus, quod dum inconsutilem Domini tunicam scindere niterentur, claritatem doctrinæ philosophicæ perdiderunt totaliter,[7] ac novis tenebris excæcati, decidunt in abyssum, nisi ille sua occulta dispenset potentia, cujus sapientiam numerus non metitur. Hæc hactenus, nam hic nobis subducitur judicandi facultas.

Unum tamen elicimus ex prædictis, quod damnosa hodie nimis est studio Latinorum Græci sermonis inscitia,[8] sine quo scriptorum veterum dogmata, sive Christianorum sive gentilium nequeunt comprehendi.[9] Idemque de Arabico in plerisque tractatibus astronomicis, ac de Hebraico textu[10] *Sacræ Bibliæ* versimiliter est censendum, quibus defectibus proinde Clemens quintus occurrit, si tamen prælati, quæ faciliter statuunt, fideliter observarent. Quamobrem grammaticam tam Græcam quam Hebræam nostris scolaribus providere curavimus, cum quibusdam adjunctis, quorum adminiculo, studiosi lectores in dictarum linguarum scriptura, lectura, necnon intellectu poterunt[11] informari, licet proprietatem idiomatis solus auditus auris animo[12] repræsentet.

1 *Eclipsarat*, mss. 797, 3352c, and Ox. ed.

2 *Nequitia quæ*, ibid.

3 *Malitia que blasphema*, ms. 2454.

4 *Reginæ; non pugnando, sed disputando, nisi*, ms. 3352c and Ox. ed.

5 *Cyrillus, ad monomachiæ congressum paratus, eam (favente consilio Ephesino) in spiritu vehementi penitus exsuflasset*, mss. 797, 3352c and Ox. ed.

6 *Satores, produntur historiis*, ibid; *Satores, pro ut dicitur historiis, sicque*, ms. 2454.

7 *Inconsutilem tunicam scindere molirentur, claritatem doctrinæ prohibitam prodiderunt totaliter*, Ox. ed. and ms. 2454; *Quod dum luentur claritatem doctrinæ philosophicam perdiderunt totaliter*, ms. 797; *Inconsubilem tunicam scindere molirentur, claritatem doctrinæ præhabitam perdiderunt totaliter*, ms. 3352c.

8 *Inscientia*, Ox. ed.; *Ignorantia*, ms. 2454.

9 *Apprehendi*, Ox. ed.

10 *Et Hebraico pro textu*, mss. and [Ox. ed.

11 *Scriptura, imo et intellectu plurimum poterunt*, Ox. ed.; *Nec non etiam intellectu plurimum poterunt*. ms. 3352c.

12 *Auditus aurium animæ*, Ox. ed.

gives way to the glory of the Latins; inasmuch as, if they were less learned in their studies, so they were less wicked in their errors. For instance, the Arian malice nearly eclipsed the whole church. The Nestorian profligacy presumed to rave against the Virgin with blasphemous madness; for it would have taken from her the name of queen as well as the definition *theotocos*,[39] θεοτοκος (divine genetrix), had not the invincible soldier, Cyril, been prepared to attack and extinguish it in a single combat. We can neither enumerate the various kinds nor the authors of the heresies of the Greeks; for as they were the primitive cultivators of the most holy faith, so they were also the first sowers of darnel, as already said, and as they are declared to have been in histories worthy of credit. From this they afterwards proceeded to worse; for while they endeavored to rend the seamless garment of the Lord, they entirely lost the light of philosophical doctrine; and being blind, they will fall into the abyss of new darknesses, unless He, by his hidden power, shall take care of them, whose wisdom numbers cannot measure. But enough of this, for here the power of judging is taken from us. We draw this one conclusion, however, from what has been said; namely, that ignorance of the Greek language is at this day highly injurious to the study of the Latins, without which the dogmas either of the ancient Christians or Gentiles cannot be comprehended. The same may credibly be supposed of the Arabic in many astronomical treatises, and of the Hebrew in reading the *Holy Bible*. Clement the Vth providently meets these defects, if prelates would only faithfully observe what is easily ordained. Wherefore we have taken care to provide for our scholars a Hebrew as well as a Greek grammar, with certain adjuncts, by the help of which studious readers may be instructed in writing, reading and understanding the said languages, although the hearing alone with the ears can represent propriety of idiom to the mind.

CAPITULUM XI.

QUOD LEGES PROPRIE NON SUNT SCIENTIÆ NEC LIBRI.[1]

IN libris juris positivi,[2] lucrativa peritia dispensandis terrenis accommoda, quanto hujus sæculi filiis famulatur utilius, tanto minus, ad capescenda sacræ scripturæ mysteria et arcana fidei sacramenta, filiis lucis confert: utpote quæ disponit peculiariter ad amicitiam hujus mundi, per quam homo, Jacobo testante, Dei constituitur inimicus. Hæc[3] nimirum lites humanas, quas infinita producit cupiditas,[4] intricatis legibus, quæ ad utrumque duci possunt,[5] extendit crebrius quam exstinguit: ad quas tamen sedandas, a jurisconsultis et piis[6] principibus dignoscitur[7] emanasse. Sane cum contrariorum sit eadem disciplina, potentiaque rationalis ad opposita valeat, simulque[8] sensus humanus proclivior sit ad malum, hujus facultatis exercitatoribus accidit, ut plerumque litibus extendendis[9] indulgeant plusquam paci, et jura non secundum legislatoris[10] intentum referant, sed ad suæ machinationis effectum verba retorqueant violenter.

Quamobrem licet mentem nostram librorum amor hæres possideret[11] a puero, quorum zelo languore vitæ[12] voluptatis accepimus, minus tamen librorum civilium appetitus nostris adhæsit affectibus, minusque hujusmodi voluminibus acquirendis concessimus tam operæ quam

1 *Quare libros liberalium artium prætulimus libris juris*, ms. 797 and Ox ed.; *Quare libros liberalium litterarum*, etc., ms. 3352c.
2 *Juris positivi*, mss. 797, 3352c. and Ox. ed.; *In libris positivis*, ms. 2454.
3 *Hinc*, Ox. ed.
4 *Tepiditas*, ibid.
5 *Ad utrumlibet dici possunt*, ibid.
6 *Propriis*, ibid.
7 *Noscitur*, mss. and Ox. ed.; *Et principibus noscitur*, ms. 2454.
8 *Similisque*, Ox. ed.
9 *Intendendis*, mss. 797, 3352c. and Ox ed.
10 *Non ad legislatoris*, mss. and Ox.ed.
11 *Amor possideret*, ed. 1702.
12 *Zelo languescere vice*, Ox. ed.

CHAPTER XI.

LAWS ARE, PROPERLY SPEAKING, NEITHER SCIENCES NOR BOOKS.

THE lucrative skill adapted to worldly dispensations in the books of positive law, is the more usefully serviceable to the sons of the world, the less it contributes to the sons of light, towards comprehending the mysteries of holy scripture and the arcane sacraments of the faith, inasmuch as it peculiarly disposes to the friendship of this world, by which man is made the enemy of God, as James witnesseth (iv, 4). Hence, without doubt, human cupidity produces infinite contentions, which it extends oftener than it extinguishes, by intricate laws that can be turned to either side. Positive law, however, is distinguished as having emanated from lawyers and pious princes to appease such contentions.[a] Because the discipline of contraries is one and the same, and the reasoning power is available to opposites, and at the same time human feelings are most prone to mischief, it happens, that the practitioners of this faculty indulge more in protracting litigation than in peace; and quote the law, not according to the intention of the legislator, but violently twist his words to the purpose of their own machinations.[b]

a This sentence is not a translation of our text, though no different reading is mentioned in the notes.—*Ed.*

b Of this chapter, it may be said generally, that the church and the law were never on good terms, because lawyers were often obliged to defend themselves and others against the rapacity of the church: if they were also rapacious, the dislike between the parties would be the more confirmed. The lawyers were perhaps too prudent to write much against the church; but the church did not spare them, as may be seen in the legends and collections of miracles. "A lawyer had often sold his tongue "when living; when he opened his "mouth to take his last gasp, it dis-"appeared." It is to be hoped he had redeemed the rest of his body. The following ditty was found in a breviary, apparently of the 13th century, set to music so as to resemble the hymns:

Venditores labiorum,
 Fleant advocati,
Qui plus student premiorum,
 Dande quantitati.
Quam causæ qualitati,
Ad consulta prelatorum,
 Multi sunt vocati.

expensæ.[1] Sunt enim utilia, sicut scorpio in Tyriaca,[2] quemadmodum libro *De Pomo et Morte* [a] Aristoteles,[3] sol doctrinæ, de logica diffinivit. Cernebamus inter[4] leges et scientias quamdam naturæ differentiam[5] manifestam, dum omnis scientia jucundatur et appetit, quod suorum principiorum præcordia, introspectis visceribus pateant, et radices suæ pullulationis emineant, suæque scaturiginis emanatio luceat evidenter; sic enim ex cognato et consono lumine veritatis conclusionis ad principia, ipsum corpus scientiæ lucidum fiet totum, non habens partem aliquam tenebrarum. At vero leges, cum sint quædam pacta humana, statuta ad civiliter vivendum vel juga principum superjecta cornibus[6] subditorum, recusant reduci ad ipsam synderisim[7] veritatis ac æquitatis originem, eo quod[8] plus habere se timeant, de voluntatis imperio, quam de rationis arbitrio. Quapropter causas

a This tract describes Aristotle as patiently awaiting the approach of death, and refreshing himself with the smell of an apple or some other fruit. His friends or disciples lamented his situation, but expressed their surprise at his cheerfulness and resignation. He smiled and said: "Think not that "I am cheerful because I am about to "escape the smallest of my infirmities "(disease). I well know that I must "die, and cannot evade death; its "pains increase, and I might already "have been dead but for the refresh-"ment I receive from this apple, which "may have prolonged my life for a "few moments." He continued philosophizing till he expired. Hence the substance of his discourse, which was afterwards put in writing, was called *De Pomo et Morte*. Speaking of those rhetoricians who make a bad use of their powers, to mislead others, he says: "Disputations are necessary, as "the scorpion is useful in treacle, it "diminishes pain, but affords a reme-"dy." The treacle of the old physicians was a mixture: they pretended it was made of scorpions and serpents in some remote country; it came from Egypt, where sugar was made. Venice treacle is a remnant of the ancient quackery. The numerous panegyrics upon Aristotle in this tract arise from his authority having been considered as infallible, in the middle ages, in all things that did not interfere with the church: even that, was dependent on him and other ancients for all its knowledge, and for the little it wrote well, as the 10th chapter admits. It would be a tedious task to point out how many of the dogmas of the church were taken from the ancients, and how often they were quoted and misquoted in support of some they never heard of—auricular confession for instance: "Sane est nocturna vigilia et "oris apertio" "Sed tunc per oris aper-"tionem confessio designatur." Aristot. *De Regimine Principum*. Hippocrates is also quoted to the same effect. In the *Metalogicon* of John of Salisbury we are told why Aristotle was distinguished by the name of philosopher above all other men: "because he "settled the demonstrative discipline, "a science of the greatest authority "amongst the Peripatetics." Pythagoras, however, was the first to whom the name was given. Thomas Aquinas labors hard to prove Aristotle's orthodoxy, against those who doubt his belief in the immortality of the soul See p. 109." with some reason."—*Inglis*.

1 *Tam opera quam impensis*, Ox. ed. *Tum opere quam impense*, ms. 3352c.

2 *Scorpio et Theriaca*, Ox. ed.

3 *Pomo. Aristoteles*, mss. 797, 3352c, and Ox. ed.

4 *Etiam inter se*, mss. and Ox. ed.

5 *Habere*, Ox. ed.

6 *Cervicibus*, mss. and Ox. ed.

7 *Ad ipsam synteresim, æquitatis*, mss. and Ox. ed.

8 *Eoque*, Ox. ed.

Wherefore although the master love of books possessed our mind from childhood, a longing for which we took to instead of a desire for pleasure, yet an appetite for the books of civilians took little hold of our affections, and we bestowed but little labor and expense on acquiring volumes of that sort. They are nevertheless useful things, like the scorpion in treacle, as Aristotle the sun of doctrine said of logic in the book *De Pomo et Morte*. We have even perceived a certain manifest difference of nature between laws and sciences; as every science is delightful, and desires that, its bowels being inspected, the vitals of its principles may be laid open, the roots of its germination appear, and the emanation of its spring come to light; for thus, from the connate and consistent light of the truth of conclusion from principles, the body itself of science will become entirely lucid without any particle of obscurity. But laws, indeed, as they are certain covenants and human enactments for regulating civil life, or yokes of princes thrown over the horns of their subjects, they refuse to be reduced to the very *synderesis* of truth and origin of equity, and on that account may be feared to have more of the empire of will in them than of the judgment of reason: for the same reason it is the opinion of wise men that the causes of laws are for the most part not to be discussed. For many laws acquire strength by custom alone, not from syllogistic necessity, like the arts, as Aristotle, the Phœbus of the school, affirms in the 2d book of his *Politics*, where he argues against the policy of Hippodamus, which promised to bestow rewards upon the inventors of new laws, because to abolish old laws and decree new, is to weaken the validity of those that exist; for things which receive stability from custom alone, must necessarily go to ruin by disuse.

Sed electi pauci quorum,
Adquiescat animorum,
Virtus equitati.
Parcunt veritati,
Stantes causis pro reorum.
Jus pervertunt decretorum,
Sanctas leges antiquorum,
Nummis obligati.
Duplices probati,
Mala fovent perversorum,
Scelus operati,
Quod attentat occultorum.
Judex Chrite non eorum,
Parcat falsitati.—*Inglis.*

legum discutiendas non esse, suadet in pluribus sententia sapientum. Nempe consuetudine sola, leges multæ vigorem acquirunt, non necessitate syllogistica, sicut artes, prout secundo[1] *Politicæ* adstruit Aristoteles, Phœbus scholæ, ubi politiam redarguit Hypodami, quæ novarum legum inventoribus præmia largiri pollicetur,[2] quia leges veteres abrogare et novas statuere, est ipsarum quæ sunt valetudinem infirmare. Quæ enim sola consuetudine stabilitatem accipiunt, hæc necesse est dissuetudine dirimantur.[3]

Ex quibus liquide satis constat, quod sicut leges nec artes sunt, nec scientiæ, sic nec libri legum, libri scientiarum vel artium proprie dici possunt. Nec est hæc facultas inter scientias recensenda, quam licet geologiam[a] appropriato vocabulo nominare. Libri vero liberalium literarum tam utiles sunt scripturæ divinæ, quod sine ipsorum subsidio frustra ad ipsius notitiam intellectus aspiret.

a *Geology.* The earliest authority I have met with for this word; and here it is but a poor joke—an earthly science.—*Inglis.*

1 *Artes provenire secundo,* Ox. ed.
2 *Præmia pollicetur,* mss. and Ox. ed.
3 *Dimittantur,* Ox. ed.

From all which it appears sufficiently clear, that as laws are neither arts nor sciences, so neither can law books be properly called books of science or art; nor is this faculty to be numbered amongst the sciences, though by an appropriate word it may be called geology; but books of liberal literature are so useful to divine scripture, that the understanding may in vain aspire to a knowledge of it, without their aid.[a]

a I have thought the following note appended by M. Cocheris in his French translation, at the end of the 11th chapter, worth translating and printing in this edition:

At the beginning of the 13th century, scholars began to abandon the study of the liberal arts for that of sciences more lucrative, such as jurisprudence and medicine. Matthew Paris, in 1250, writes that this was the reason of the neglect of grammar. In truth, after the close of the 12th century, the desire of gain induced students to learn law. Even the monks became advocates, and it was only by the authority of the bishops and the prohibition of the councils that they were prevented from devoting themselves to that pursuit. Peter of Blois recounts a bibliophilistic anecdote which proves that at that time treatises upon jurisprudence were held in the highest estimation. Being at Paris in 1170, to negotiate there concerning certain important affairs in the name of the king of England, he entered one day a bookseller's shop, in which he found a collection of law books, which he hastened to purchase. Unfortunately when he returned to take them away, they had disappeared. Another book lover, the provost of Sexeburgh, had passed by, and finding them to his taste, carried them off with him, paying a much larger price. (See *Bibl. Vetr. Patr.* XXIV; Petri Blesei, *Epistol.* lxxi, 990.)

Theological studies were so entirely abandoned that Pope Honorius III, to revive a taste for that science, thought it proper, in 1218, to prohibit lectures upon law.

Richard de Bury upon this subject agrees with John of Salisbury, the learned author of *Policraticon*, who advised St. Thomas of Canterbury to apply himself as little as possible to the study of the law.—*Ed.*

CAPITULUM XII.

DE UTILITATE ET NECESSITATE GRAMMATICÆ.[1]

CUM librorum lectionibus foveremur assidue, quos moris erat quotidie legere vel audire, perpendimus evidenter, quantum impediat intellectus officium vel unius vocabuli semi plena notitia, dum nullius enunciationis sententia capitur, cujus pars quantalibet ignoratur. Quapropter exarticorum[2] verborum interpretationes mira sedulitate[3] jussimus annotari, antiquorum grammaticorum orthographiam, prosodyam, etymologiam et diasynthesim,[4] inconcussa curiositate consideravimus, terminosque vetustate nimia caligantes, descriptionibus congruis delucidare[5] curavimus, quatenus iter planum nostris studentibus pararemus. Hæc est sane sententia[6] totalis, quare tot grammaticorum antiqua volumina, emendatis codicibus, renovare studuimus, ut stratas regias sterneremus, quibus ad artes quascunque, nostri futuri scolares incederent inoffense.

1 *Quare libros grammaticales tanta diligentia curavimus renovare*, mss 797 3352c and Ox. ed.
2 *Exoticorum*, Ox. ed.
3 *Mira subtilitate*, ibid.
4 *Ac syntaxin*, ms. 797 and Ox. ed.; *Dyasenteticam*, ms. 3352c.
5 *Lucidare*, mss. 797, 3352c, and Ox. ed.
6 *Summa*, ibid.

CHAPTER XII.

OF THE UTILITY AND NECESSITY OF GRAMMAR.

AS we were carefully nurtured in the reading of books, which it was our custom to read or hear daily, we duly considered how much an imperfect knowledge even of a single word may impede the business of the understanding, as the meaning of a proposition, of which any part whatever is unknown, cannot be comprehended. Wherefore, with wonderful perseverance, we ordered the interpretation of exotic words to be noted down.[40] We considered the orthography, prosody, etymology, and diasynthesis, of the ancient grammarians[a] with unyielding curiosity, and we took care to elucidate terms becoming obscure from too great age with suitable descriptions, so that we might prepare a level way for our students. And this is really the whole reason why we have labored to renovate so many ancient volumes of the grammarians in emended editions; that we might so pave the king's highway with them, that our future scholars might walk towards any of the arts whatever without stumbling.

a The grammarians were very numerous in the middle ages. Under Charlemagne, a period when this study was in great favor, the systems of Donati, of Nicomachus, of Dositheus, of Priscian, of Smaragdos, and above all, of Alcuin, were used. In the 11th century, Papias composed his *Elements* and Remi of Auxerre his *Commentaries* upon Priscian. In the 12th century, the small and large Priscian, and the work of Petit Helie were studied. In the 13th appeared the celebrated *Græcismus* of Eberhard de Bethune, the *Doctrinal* of Alexander of Ville-Dieu, the *Exposition* upon Priscian of Albert Magnus; the Grammar of Vincent de Beauvais, which forms the second book of his *Speculum Doctrinale*, and which is taken in great part from Priscian, Isidore of Seville and Pierre Helie; and lastly the treatise of William of Tournay, entitled *De Modo Docendi Pueros*. But after the 13th century, this study fell into entire neglect, and logic took the first place. Henry d'Andeli, in a very curious work entitled *Bataille des Sept Arts*, shows this decline of grammar, and the importance which logic immediately attained. (*Extract translated from a note of M. Cocheris.*)—*Ed.*

CAPITULUM XIII.

DE EXCUSATIONE POESIS ET UTILITATE EJUSDEM.[1]

OMNIA genera machinarum, quibus contra poetas solius nudæ veritatis amatores objiciunt, duplici refelluntur umbone; quia vel in obscena materia, gratus[2] cultus sermonis addiscitur, vel ubi ficta sed honesta sententia tractatur, naturalis vel histiorialis veritas indagatur sub eloquio typicæ fictionis.

Quamvis nimirum omnes homines natura[3] scire desiderent, non tamen omnes delectantur equaliter addiscere, quinimo studii labore gustato, et sensuum fatigatione percepta, plerique nucem[4] abjiciunt inconsulte, priusquam testa soluta, nucleus attingatur. Innatus est homini duplex amor, videlicet propriæ libertatis[5] in regimine et aliquantæ voluptatis in opere; unde nullus sine causa alieno se subdit imperio vel opus quodcunque exercet cum tædio sua sponte. Delectatio namque perficit operationem, sicut pulchritudo juventutem, sicut Aristoteles verissime dogmatizat x *Ethicorum*. Idcirco prudentia veterum adinvenit remedium quo lascivum genus[6] humanum caperetur, quodammodo pio dolo, dum sub voluptatis iconio delicata Minerva[7] delitesceret in occulto. Muneribus parvulos solemus allicere, ut illa gratis velint addiscere, quibus eos vel invitos intendimus applicare. Non enim natura corrupta eo impetitur,[8] quo prona se pellit ad vitia, transmigrat ad virtutes. Hoc enim brevi versiculo nobis declarat Horatius, ubi artem poeticam tradit dicens:

Aut prodesse volunt, aut delectare poetæ.

1 *Quare non omnino neglegimus fabulas poetarum*, Ox. ed.
2 *In obscena ingratus*, ibid.
3 *Naturaliter*, ibid.
4 *Invicem*, ibid.
5 *Innatus est enim hominum 24 annorum, amor propriæ libertatis*, ibid.
6 *Ingenium*, mss. and Ox. ed.
7 *Munera*, Ox. ed.
8 *Eo impetu*, ibid.

CHAPTER XIII.

A VINDICATION OF POETRY AND ITS UTILITY.

THE missiles of all sorts, which lovers of naked truth only, cast at poets, may be warded off by a twofold shield; because either a graceful turn of language is to be learned, where the subject is impure, or natural or historical truth may be traced where feigned but honest sentiments are treated of under the eloquence of typical fiction. Although all men certainly desire to know, yet all do not equally like to learn. Wherefore, feeling the labor of study, and finding it to fatigue the senses, most of them inconsiderately throw away the nut before they have broken the shell and got at the kernel: for there is a twofold innate love in mankind; namely, of self-liberty in conduct, and of a certain portion of pleasure in labor; whence no man submits himself to the rule of another without cause, or undertakes any labor whatever, that is tiresome, of his own free will; for cheerfulness perfects labor as beauty does youth,[41] as Aristotle most truly affirms (10 *Nic. Eth.*). Wherefore the prudence of the ancients discovered a remedy by which the wanton part of mankind might, in a manner, be taken in by a pious fraud, and the delicate Minerva lie hid under the dissembling mask of pleasure.

We are accustomed to allure children[42] with gifts, to make them willing to learn those things freely which we mean them to apply to, even if unwilling; for does not corrupt nature impel itself by the same instinct by which, being prone to vice, it transmigrates to virtue? This, Horace declares to us in a short verse, where he treats of the art of poetry, saying:

> Poets would improve or delight mankind.

Hoc idem alio versu ejusdem libri potenter insinuavit, ita dicens :[1]

Omne tulit punctum, qui miscuit utile dulci.

Quot Euclidis discipulos rejecit Ellefuga[2] quasi scopulus eminens et abruptus, qui nullo scholarium suffragio[3] scandi posset. Durus est, inquiunt, hic sermo et quis potest eum audire. Filius inconstantiæ, qui tandem in asinum transformari volebat, philosophiæ nullatenus forsitan studium dimisisset, si eidem contecta voluptatis velamine familiariter occurrisset; sed mox Cratonis cathedra stupefactus et quæstionibus infinitis quasi quodam fulmine subito repercussus, nullum prorsus videbat refugium nisi fugam.

Hæc in excusationem adduximus poetarum, jamque studentes intentione debita in eisdem ostendimus inculpandos. Ignorantia quidem solius unius vocabuli, prægrandis sententiæ impedit intellectum, sicut proximo capitulo est assumptum. Cum ergo dicta sanctorum, poetarum figmentis frequenter alludant, evenit, necesse est, ut nescio[4] poemate introducto, tota ipsius auctoris intentio penitus obstruatur; et certe sicut dicit Cassiodorus libro suo de *Institutione Divinarum Litterarum*, non sunt parva censenda sine quibus magna constare non possunt. Restat ergo[5] ut ignoratis poesibus ignoretur Hieronimus, Augustinus, Boethius, Lactantius, Sidonius, et plerique alii, quorum litaniam prolixum capitulum non teneret.

Venerabilis Beda vero hujusmodi dubitationis articulum discussione[6] declaravit dilucida, sicut recitat compilator egregius Gratianus, plurium repetitor auctorum, qui sicut fuit avarus in compilationis[7] materia, sic confusus reperitur in forma, scribens[8] distinctione tricesima septima. Turbat acumen, sæculares litteras quidam le-

1 *In alio versu ejusdem libri, patenter insinuat ita scribens*, mss. and Ox. ed.

2 *Retrojecit Eleqfuga*, ibid.

3 *Nullo scalarum suffragio*, Ox. ed.

4 *Alludant; evenire necesse est, ut nescito*, mss. and Ox. ed.

5 *Igitur*, ibid.

6 *Distinctione*, mss. 797, 3352c, and Ox. ed.

7 *Avarior, in compilationibus*, Ox. ed.

8 *Scribit tamen sic*, mss. 797, 3352c, and Ox. ed.

And the same thing in another of his verses, writing,

> He carries every point who mixes the useful with the delightful.

How many scholars has the Helleflight[43] of Euclid repelled, as if it were a high and steep cliff that could not be scaled by the help of any ladder! [a] This is crabbed language, say they, and who can listen to it? That son of inconstancy,[44] who at last wished to be transformed into an ass, would perhaps never have rejected the study of philosophy if it had familiarly fallen in his way, covered with this same veil of pleasure; but being suddenly stupified at the chair of Crato, and thunderstruck as it were by his infinite questions, he saw no safety whatever but in flight. We have adduced this much in exculpation of poets, and will now show, that those who study them with a proper intention are blameless. Ignorance indeed of a single word impedes the understanding of the most important sentences, as assumed in the preceding chapter. As the sayings therefore of the sacred poets frequently allude to fictions, [b] it necessarily follows, that the poem introduced being unknown, the whole meaning of the author is entirely obstructed; and certainly, as Cassiodorus says, in his book upon the institution of divine literature, those things are not to be thought small, without which great ones cannot subsist. It holds good, therefore, that, being ignorant of poetry, we cannot understand Jerome, Augustine, Boëtius, Lactantius, Sidonius, and many others, whose joyful songs a long chapter would not contain. But venerable Bede has in a lucid discussion settled the point of this sort of doubtfulness, as the great compiler Gratian, the repeater of many authors, recites, who, as he was niggardly in the matter, so he is found to be confused in the manner of his compilation. He writes, in distinction 37, beginning, Turbat acumen:[45] "Some "read secular literature for pleasure, being delighted

a *Nullo scholarium suffragio* in the text; the meaning is, by no labor of the scholars.—*Ed.*

b In the text: as the sayings of the saints frequently allude to the fictions of the poets.—*Ed.*

gunt[1] ad voluptatem, poetarum figmentis et verborum ornatu[2] delectati; quidam vero ad eruditionem eas addiscunt, ut errores gentilium legendo detestentur, et utilia quæ in eis invenerint,[3] ad usum sacræ eruditionis devoti innectant.[4] Tales laudabiliter sæculares litteras addiscunt. Hæc Beda.

Hac institutione salutifera moniti, sileant detrahentes studentibus in poetis ad tempus, nec ignorantes hujusmodi connescientes[5] desiderent, quia hoc simile est solatio miserorum.

Statuat sibi[6] quisque piæ intentionis affectum, et de quacunque materia, observatis virtutis circumstantiis, faciat studium Deo gratum. Et si in poeta profecerit, quemadmodum magnus Maro[7] de se fatetur in Ennio, non amisit.

1 *Sæculares quidem nostros legunt*, ed. 1702.
2 *Ordinatu*, Ox. ed.
3 *Inveniuntur*, ibid.
4 *Convertant*, ms. 797, and Ox. ed.
5 *Hujusmodi quæstiones*, Ox. ed.
6 *Statuat igitur*, ibid.
7 *Varro*, differs from the Ox. ed.

" with the fictions of poets, and the ornament of their " words; but others study them for erudition, that, by " reading the errors of the gentiles, they may detest " them, and that they may devoutly carry off what they " find in them useful for the service of sacred erudition; " such as these, study secular literature laudably." Thus far Bede.[46]

Admonished by this salutary instruction, let the detractors of poetical students be silent for the present; nor should ignorant people of this sort wish for fellow-ignoramuses, for this is like the solace of the miserable. Let every man therefore confine himself to the feelings of a pious intention; he may thus make his study grateful to God from any materials whatever, the circumstances of virtue being observed. And if he should become a poet, as the great Maro[47] confesses himself to have done by the help of Ennius, he has not lost his labor.[a]

a The author, in this chapter, touches upon a question which has been often since discussed. Whether it is wise or prudent to put into the hands of youth the lying, impure, and even in many instances obscene literature of the ancients, some of the works of Horace, Juvenal, Martial, Propertius, Anacreon and Aristophanes, for example. The argument in favor of the practice, occurring to our worthy bishop, we regard as rather an unfortunate one. He seems to advocate it on the ground, that it is necessary to entice students by means of such allurements to the acquisition of knowledge. The man, at the present day, who should, with however good an intent, supply such seasoning to books prepared for the use of the young, would bring upon himself universal execration. It is perhaps fair to say however that Bury may refer rather to the beauties of thought and diction to be found in the classics than to their falsehoods and impurities.

In truth it has always seemed to us that the danger to morals arising from the study of the Greek and Roman poetical literature, has been often greatly overrated. We doubt whether in any case vicious inclinations or conduct have ever been traced, or could ever be fairly attributed to it as a cause, though I am aware that Burton has in his *Anatomy of Melancholy* expressed himself to the contrary. Besides the same objection can be raised to almost every great literary production of former times, to Shakespeare, Spencer and Chaucer. Even the *Old Testament* is liable to the same criticism.

The expurgated editions of classic authors to which resort has been had to avoid the fancied evil, have, in our opinion, been far from effecting their purpose. They even have the effect to inflame the curiosity and lead the mind to conjectures worse than the reality.—*Ed.*

CAPITULUM XIV.

DE ILLIS QUI PRÆCIPUE DEBERENT LIBROS DILIGERE.[1]

RECOLLIGENTI prædicta palam est perspicuum, qui deberent esse librorum præcipui dilectores. Qui namque sapientia magis egent, ad sui status officium utiliter exsequendum, hi potissime sacris vasis sapientiæ, propensiorem procul dubio exhibere tenentur sollicitum grati cordis affectum. Est autem sapientis officium bene ordinare et alios et se ipsum secundum Phœbum philosophorum Aristotelem, prooemio *Metaphysicæ*, qui nec fallit nec fallitur in humanis. Quapropter principes et prælati judices et doctores et quicumque reipublicæ directores, sicut præ aliis, sapientia opus habent, ita præ aliis, vasorum[2] sapientiæ zelum debent habere. Philosophiam nimirum confinxit[3] Boethius, in sinistra quidem sceptrum et in dextra libros gestantem, per quod universis evidenter ostenditur, nullam posse rempublicam debite regere sine libris. Tu, inquit Boethius, loquens philosophiæ, hanc sententiam Platonis ore sanxisti, beatas fore respublicas, si eas vel studiosi sapientiæ regerent, vel earum rectores studere sapientiæ contigisset. Rursus hoc nobis insinuat ipse gestus imaginis, quod quanto dextra sinistram præcellit, tanto contemplativa vita dignior[4] est activa, simulque sapientis[5] interesse monstratur, nunc studio veritatis, nunc dispensationi temporalium indulgere vicissim.

Philippum legimus Diis regratiatum devote, quod Alexandrum concesserant temporibus Aristotelis esse

1 *Quinam deberent esse librorum potissimi dilectores*, mss. 797, 3352c, and Ox. ed.

2 *Vasis*, mss.

3 *Ita præ aliis vasis sapientiæ zelum debent, philosophiam nimirum conspexit*, mss. 797 and 3352c; *Ita præ aliis, vasis sapientiæ opus habent. Philosophiam nimirum respexit*, Ox. ed.

4 *Contemplativa dignior*, mss. and Ox. ed.

5 *Sapientissime*, Ox. ed.

CHAPTER XIV.

OF THOSE WHO OUGHT MOST PARTICULARLY TO LOVE BOOKS.

TO him who recollects what has been said, it is evident and perspicuous who ought to be the greatest lovers of books. For who stand most in need of wisdom, in fulfilling the duties of their calling usefully? Those, without doubt, who are most firmly bound to exhibit the most ready and anxious affection of a grateful heart for the sacred vessels of wisdom. But as Aristotle, the Phœbus of philosophers, who is neither mistaken nor to be mistaken in human affairs, says in the proem of his *Metaphysics:* "It is the business of a wise man to re- "gulate both himself and others properly." Wherefore princes and prelates, judges and teachers, and all other directors of public affairs whatever, as they have need of wisdom beyond other men, so they ought to be zealous beyond other men about the vessels of wisdom. Boëtius indeed emblematically represented Philosophy holding a sceptre in her left hand, and a book in her right; by which it is evidently shown to all men, that no one can duly govern a state without books. You, says Boëtius, addressing himself to Philosophy, sanctioned this axiom by the mouth of Plato, "That states "would be happy, if those who studied wisdom ruled "them, or if it could happen that wisdom had the ap- "pointment of their rulers." Again, the bearing of the emblem itself insinuates this to us—that in as much as the right hand excels the left, in so much a contemplative life is more worthy than an active; and at the same time it is shown to be the business of a wise man, first to employ himself in the study of truth, and then in the dispensation of temporal affairs, each in its turn.

natum, cujus instructione[1] educatus, regni paterni moderamine dignus esset. Dum Phaëton ignarus regiminis, fit currus auriga paterni; nunc vicinitate nimia, nunc remota distantia, mortalibus æstum Phœbus[2] infeliciter administrat, ac[3] ne omnes periclitarentur subjecti, pro iniquo regimine juste meruit[4] fulminari. Referunt tam Græcorum quam Latinorum historiæ, quod nobiles inter eos principes non fuerunt, qui litterarum peritia caruerunt. Sacra lex Moysaica præscribens regi regulam per quam regat, librum legis divinæ sibi præcipit habere descriptum, *Deuteronomi* xvii; secundum exemplar a sacerdotibus exhibendum, in quo sibi legendum esset omnibus diebus vitæ suæ. Sane labilitatem humanæ memoriæ et instabilitatem virtuosæ voluntatis in homine, satis noverat Deus ipse, qui condidit, qui et fingit quotidie corda hominum singillatim. Quamobrem quasi omnium malorum antidotum voluit esse librum, cujus lectionem et usum tanquam saluberrimum spiritus alimentum quotidianum jugiter esse jussit. Quo refocillatus intellectus, nec enervis nec dubius trepidaret ullatenus in agendis. Istud[5] eleganter Johannes Saresburiensis[6] pertractat in suo *Policraticon*, libro quarto. Ceterum omne genus hominum qui tonsura vel nomine clericali præfulgent, contra quos libri quarto, quinto et sexto capitulis querebantur, libris tenentur veneratione perpetua[7] famulari.

1 *Tempore Aristotelis concesserant esse natum; cujus instructionibus*, Ox. ed.
2 *Æstum Phœbi*, ms. 3352c.
3 *At*, Ox. ed.
4 *Metuit*, ed. 1702.
5 *Illud*, Ox. ed.
6 *Salisberiensis*, ms. 3352c.
7 *Papæ*, ed. 1500, 1610, and 1702.

We read that Philip devoutly returned thanks to the gods, because they had granted to Alexander to be born in the days of Aristotle, educated under whose tuition he might be worthy to govern his paternal kingdom. As Phæton, become the driver of his father's chariot, was ignorant of its management, and unfortunately administered the heat of Phœbus sometimes at too near and sometimes at too remote a distance, he justly deserved to be struck with thunder for his unsteady driving, and that all below might not be put in peril. The histories both of the Greeks and Latins relate that there were no noble princes amongst them, who were unskilled in literature. The sacred Mosaic law, prescribing a rule for a king by which he must reign, commands him to have the book of divine law written out for himself, [a] according to the copy set forth by the priests, in which he is to read all the days of his life. Truly God himself, who made, and daily and individually fashions the hearts of men, had sufficiently known the slipperiness of human memory, and the instability of virtuous intentions in mankind. For which reason it was his will that there should be a book, an antidote as it were to all evil, of which he ordered the continued reading and use, as the most wholesome daily food of the spirit; by which the understanding, being refreshed and neither enervated nor doubtful, might be altogether fearless in action. This, John of Salisbury elegantly touches upon in his *Policraticon*, book IV. To conclude: [b] All sorts of men who are distinguished by the tonsure or clerical name, against whom the 4th, 5th and 6th chapters of this book complained, are bound to render service to books with perpetual veneration.

a The reference to the chapter in Deuteronomy, made in the text, seems to be omitted here.—*Ed.*

b Wanting in the text.—*Ed.*

CAPITULUM XV.

DE MULTIPLICI EFFECTU SCIENTIÆ QUÆ IN LIBRIS CONTINETUR.[1]

HUMANUM excedit[2] ingenium, quantumcunque[3] de fonte Pægaseo potatum, instantis capituli titulum explicare perfecte, si linguis[4] hominum et angelorum quis loquatur, si in Mercurium transformaretur aut Tullium, si dulcescat Titi Livii eloquentia lactea, si Demosthenis suavitate peroret, aut Moysi balbutiem allegabit, vel cum Jeremia se puerum nescientem confitebitur,[5] adhuc loqui, vel imitabitur resonantem in montibus altis echo. Amorem namque librorum, amorem sapientiæ constat esse, sicut secundo capitulo est probatum;[6] hic autem amor *philosophia* Græco vocabulo nuncupatur,[7] cujus virtutem nulla comprehendit creata[8] intelligentia, quoniam creditur[9] omnium bonorum mater esse, *Sapientiæ* septimo. Æstus quippe carnalium vitiorum quasi cœlicus ros exstinguit, dum motus incensus virtutum animalium, vires naturalium virtutum remittit, otio penitus effugato. Quo sublato

> . . . . periere Cupidinis arcus [a]
> Omnes.[10]

Hinc Plato in *Phedone*. In hoc, inquit, manifestus est philosophus, si absolvit animam a corporis differentis[11] aliis hominibus. "Ama, inquit Hieronimus, scien-

1 *Quot commoda confert amor librorum*, mss. 797, 3352c and Ox. ed.
2 *Transcendit*, mss. and Ox. ed.
3 *Quodcunque fuerit*, Ox. ed.
4 *Perf·cte, linguis*, ed. 1702.
5 *Futebitur*, Ox. ed.
6 *Compertum*, ibid.
7 *Appellatur*, ms. 3352c.
8 *Creatura*, Ox. ed.
9 *Vere creditur*, mss. and Ox. ed.
10 *Cupidinis artes omnes*, ms. 797; *Arcus omnes*, mss. 2454 and 3352c; *Cupidinis arcus*, Ox. ed.
11 *A corporis communione differentius*, mss. and Ox. ed.

a *Periere Cupidinis arcus*. The Oxford edition makes a quotation of this. It may be an allusion in the original, but quotation appears to have been purposely avoided—"perierunt Cupidinis arcus omnes."—*Inglis*.

CHAPTER XV.

OF THE MANIFOLD EFFECTS OF THE SCIENCES WHICH ARE CONTAINED IN BOOKS.

IT is beyond the wit of man, however deeply he may have drunk of the Pegasean fountain, perfectly to unfold the title of this present chapter. If any one can speak with the tongues of men and angels; if he can be transformed into Mercury or Tully; if he can charm with the creamy eloquence of Livy; if he can plead with the suavity of Demosthenes—even he, will allege the hesitation of Moses, or confess with Jeremiah that he is a child, not yet knowing how to speak, or will imitate the echo resounding in the lofty mountains: for the love of books is evidently the love of wisdom, which has been proved to be ineffable. *a* This love is also called by a Greek word, philosophy, whose virtue no created intelligence comprehends, wherefore it is believed to be the mother of everything that is good (*Wisd.* vii), for like a heavenly dew it extinguishes the heat of carnal vices, when the intense commotion of the animal powers abates the force of natural virtue; by entirely expelling idleness, which being removed, every particle of concupiscence will perish.[48]

Hence Plato says, in *Phædo:* "The philosopher is manifest in this, that he separates the soul more widely from communion with the body than other men." *b* Love (says Jerome) the knowledge of the scriptures, and you will not love the vices of the flesh. The godlike Zenocrates demonstrated this in the firmness of his purpose,

a Literally: as has been proved in the 2d chapter. In the 2d chapter it was attempted to be proved, that the value of books was ineffable. This is therefore probably intended as a free translation of the same reading as that of our text.—*Ed.*

b This follows the Oxford edition. See note 11 opposite page.

tiam scripturarum et carnis vitia non amabis." Demonstravit hoc Zenocrates deiformis in constantia rationis, quem nobile scortum Phrynæ [a] nomine statuam diffinivit non hominem, cum nullis valeret eum illecebris evirare, quemadmodum Valerius libro quarto, cap. tertio, plene refert. Hoc ipsum noster Origenes ostendit qui, ne eum ab omnipotenti femina effeminari contingeret, utriusque sexus medium, per abnegationem extremorum, elegit, animosum quippe remedium nec naturæ tamen consentaneum nec virtuti; cujus est hominem non insensibilem facere passionum, sed subortasa fomite rationis enecare mucrone.

Rursus mundana et pecunias[1] parvipendunt,[2] quotquot amor afficit librorum, dicente Hieronimo ad[3] Vigilantium, epistola LIV. Non est ejusdem hominis aureos nummos et scripturas probare. Unde a quodam metrico sic dictum est. [b]

Nulla libris erit apta manus ferrugine tincta,
Nec nummata queunt corda vacare libris[4]
Nummipete[5] cum libricolis nequeunt simul esse.
Ambos, crede mihi, non tenet una domus.

Nullus ergo potest Mammoni et libris servire.[6] Vitiorum deformitas in libris maxime reprobatur, ut inde dicatur omnimode[7] vitia detestari, qui libros dilexerit perscrutari. Dæmon, [c] qui a scientia nomen habet, per

1 *Mundanas pecunias*, ms. 3352c and Ox. ed.

2 *Parvipendunt ex animo*, mss. and Ox. ed.

3 *Contra*, ms. 797 and Ox. ed.

4 This verse is followed by two others in mss. 797, 3352c and Ox. ed.

Non est ejusdem nummos librosque probare
Persequitur libros grex, Epicure, tuus.

5 *Nummicolæ*, Ox. ed. James gives the variation, *Nummipetæ*.

6 *Deservire*, ms. 797 and Ox. ed.; *Nullus igitur potest libris et Mammone deservire*, ms. 3352c.

7 *Et inducatur*, *omnimode*, mss.; *Ut inducatur*, etc., Ox. ed.

a "Nobilem stoycum phime nomine,"—*Cologne edition.* "Nobile scortum phyrne."—*Paris ed.* The Cologne editor seems to have been at a loss for a name for his Stoic: it is not usual to contract proper names.—*Inglis.*

b In the first edition the two middle lines are omitted: they are taken from John of Salisbury, and are not all together in the original. Many ideas in this book are from the same source—why say "somebody?" the bishop knew whose verses they were.—*Inglis.*

c The *dæmon* appears by the context to be Lucifer. Cornelius Agrippa says: "Some worshipped a serpent as the inventor of science, that is, the devil who taught Eve. Others say that it was a certain spirit called Theutus, an enemy to mankind" (Thoth). It is said by some that the commander sent to the Trojan war from Arcadia was Ornytus; but Homer calls him Teuthis: he is also called Theutis. He wounded Minerva, who appeared to him after his return. Homer had some reason for choosing this name.—*Inglis.*

whom the noble strumpet Phryne defined to be a statue, and not a man, as no enticement was able to shake his chastity; as Valerius relates at large, book IV, chap. iii. Our Origen is another example; who, that he might not chance to be effeminated by omnipotent woman, chose the medium between the two sexes by the abnegation of his extremities. A spiteful remedy truly; neither consonant to nature nor to virtue, whose business is not to make man insensible of the passions, but to check the first efforts of insubordination by the power of reason. Again: All who are affected by the love of books, hold worldly affairs and money very cheap, as Jerome writes to Vigilantius (*Epist.* LIV): [a] "It is not "for the same man to ascertain the value of gold coins "and of writings;" which somebody thus repeated in verse;

No tinker's hand shall dare a book to stain;
  No miser's heart can wish a book to gain;
The gold assayer cannot value books;
  On them the epicure disdainful looks.
One house at once, believe me, cannot hold
  Lovers of books and hoarders up of gold.

No man, therefore can serve mammon and books. The deformities of vice are highly reprobated in books; so that they are thence said to detest vice in all its forms, who delight in perusing books. The demon who is named after science, is most easily triumphed over by the knowledge of books; his numerous versatile frauds and thousand pernicious meanderings, are laid open to the readers of books, that he may not fraudulently circumvent the innocent, by transforming himself into an angel of light. The divine reverence is revealed to us by books; the virtues by which it is cultivated are most expressly divulged, and the reward is described which the truth, which neither deceives nor is deceived, pro-

a An allusion, says M. Cocheris, to the following sentence of Jerome: Non est ejusdem hominis, et aureos nummos et scripturas probare, et degustare vino et prophetas vel apostolos intelligere.—*Ed.*

librorum scientiam potissime triumphatur. Cujus fraudes multipliciter flexuosæ, milleque perniciosi meandri per libros panduntur legentibus, ne se transfigurans in angelum lucis, dolis circumveniat innocentes.

Divina nobis per libros reverentia revelatur, virtutes quibus colitur, propalantur expressius, atque merces describitur, quam quæ nec fallit nec fallitur veritas pollicetur. Imago similima futuræ beatitudinis, est sacrarum contemplatio litterarum, in quibus nunc creator nunc creatura conspicitur; ac de torrente perpetuæ jucunditatis hauritur fides, fundatur potentia litterarum; spes librorum solatio confirmatur, ut per patientiam et consolationem scripturarum, spem habeamus. Charitas non inflatur sed ædificatur per verarum litterarum notitiam, imo super libros sacros constat luce clarius ecclesiam stabilitam.

Delectant libri prosperitate feliciter arridente; consolantur individue nubila fortuna terrente;[1] pactis humanis robur attribuunt, nec feruntur sententiæ graves sine libris.

Artes et scientiæ consistunt in libris, quorume molumenta nulla mens sufficeret enarrare. Quanti pendenda est mira librorum potentia, dum per eos fines tam orbis quam temporis cernimus,[2] et ea quæ non sunt, tanquam ea quæ sunt, quasi[3] in quodam æternitatis speculo contemplamur. Montes scandimus et abyssorum voragines in libris perscrutamur,[4] species piscium, quos communis aer nequaquam salubriter[5] continet, intuemur.[6] Codicibus, fluviorum et fontium et diversarum terrarum proprietates distinguimus, metallorum atque gemmarum genera et mineræ cujusque materias, de libris effodimus. Herbarumque vires arborum et plantarum,[7] prolemque totam pro libito cernimus Neptuni, Cereris

1 *Torrente*, Ox. ed.

2 *Temporis terminum*, mss. 797 and 2454, and Ox. ed.

3 *Et ea quæ non sunt, sicut ea quæ sunt, quasi*, mss. and Ox. ed.

4 *Voragines perscrutamur*, ibid.

5 *Similiter*, Ox. ed.

6 *Communis aer intuemur*, ms. 797.

7 *Plantarum addiscimus*, mss. 797 and 3352c; *Planetarum addiscimus*, Ox. ed.

mises. The contemplation of divine literature, in which the Creator and the creature are alternately beheld, and which is drawn from the eternal stream of pleasure, is a perfect representation of future beatitude. Faith is founded on the power of letters; Hope is confirmed by the solace of books, as we retain it by patience and the consolation of scripture; Charity is not inflated, but edified by the knowledge of true literature; nay, the church appears in the clearest light, to be established upon the sacred books. Books are delightful when prosperity happily smiles; when adversity threatens, they are inseparable comforters. They give strength to human compacts, nor are grave opinions brought forward without books. Arts and sciences, the benefits of which no mind can calculate, depend upon books. How great is the wonderful power arising from books! for by them we see not only the ends of the world, but of time; and we contemplate alike things that are, and things that are not, as in a sort of mirror of eternity. In books, we ascend mountains and fathom the depths of the abyss; we behold varieties of fishes which the common atmosphere can by no means contain in soundness; we distinguish the peculiarities of rivers and springs, and different countries, in volumes. We dig up the various kinds of metals, gems and minerals, and substances of all sorts, out of books; and we learn the virtues of herbs, trees and plants, and behold at leisure the whole offspring of Neptune, Ceres and Pluto; for if we are pleased to visit the inhabitants of Heaven, by walking up Taurus, Caucasus and Olympus, we transcend the kingdoms of Jove, and with lines and compasses measure the territories of the seven planets, and at last survey the great firmament itself, decorated with signs, degrees and configurations in endless variety.

There we survey the antarctic pole, which eye hath not seen nor ear heard, and with delectable pleasure we admire the luminous way of the galaxy, and the zodiac painted with celestial animals. From this we pass on,

et Plutonis. Quod si nos cœlicolas visitare delectat, suppeditantes Taurum Caucasum et Olimpum, Jovis[1] regna transcendimus, et septem territoria planetarum funiculis et circulis emetimur. Ipsum tandem firmamentum supremum, signis, gradibus et imaginibus, varietate maxima decoratum, lustramus. Ibi polum antarcticum, quem nec oculis vidit nec auris audivit, inspicimus; luminosum iter galaxiæ, et animalibus cœlestibus picturatum zodiacum, delectabile jucunditate miramur. Hinc per libros ad separatas transimus substantias, et ut cognatas intelligentias intellectus salutet, primamque causam omnium, aut motorem immobilem infinitæ virtutis oculo mentis cernat, et amore inhæreat sine fine. Ecce per libros adducti, beatitudinis nostræ mercedem attingimus, dum adhuc existimus viatores. Quid plura! procul dubio sicut Seneca docente octogesima quarta epistola quæ incipit. Desii jam de te esse sollicitus . . . didimus, otium[2] sine litteris mors est, et vivi hominis sepultura, ita revera a sensu contrario, litterarum seu librorum negotium concludimus[3] esse vitam. Rursus per libros tam amicis quam hostibus intimamus, quæ nequaquam secure nunciis commendamus: quoniam libro plerumque ad principum thalamos ingressus conceditur, quo repelleretur penitus vox auctoris, sicut Tertullianus in principio[4] *Apologetici* sui dicit. Carceribus et vinculis custoditi, ademptaque penitus corporis libertate, librorum legationibus utimur ad amicos, eisque causas nostras expediendas committimus,[5] quo nobis fieret causa mortis accessus. Per libros præteritorum reminiscimur, de futuris quodammodo prophetamus, præsentia, quæ labuntur et fluunt, scripturæ memoria stabilimus.

Felix studiositas et studiosa felicitas præpotentis eunuchi, de quo *Actuum* octavo narratur, quem amor propheticæ lectionis accenderat[6] tam ardenter, quod nec ratione itineris a lectione cessaret, reginæ Gandacis pala-

1 *Junonis*, mss. and Ox. ed.

2 *Sicut Seneca docente didicimus, otium*, ms. 797 and Ox. ed.; *Sicut Seneca docente addiscimus otium*, ms. 3352c.

3 *Concludimus hominis*, mss. 797, 3352c, and Ox. ed.

4 *Primo*, Ox. ed.

5 *Committimus, atque illuc transmittimus*, mss. 797, 3352c, and Ox. ed.

6 *Quoniam amor propheticæ lectionis, succenderat*, mss. and Ox. ed.

through books, to separate substances; and as the intellect greets kindred intelligences with the eye of the mind, it discerns and cleaves to the first cause of all, the immovable mover of infinite power, in love without end. Behold how, being led on by books, we obtain the reward of our beatitude while we are yet wayfarers: what more can we wish for? Without doubt, as Seneca teaches us in his 84th letter, beginning Desij, "Leisure "without letters is death, and the sepulture of the "living man;" [a] so we justly conclude, from a converse meaning, that to be employed with literature and books is life.

Again, through books we intimate both to friends and enemies things that we can by no means safely entrust to messengers, inasmuch as access to the chambers of princes is generally conceded to a book, from which the voice of the author would be altogether excluded, as Tertullian says in the beginning of his *Apologetics*. When we are kept in prison, in chains, and entirely deprived of bodily liberty, we make use of the embassies of books to our friends, and to them we commit the expediting of our causes, and we transmit them there where access could not be made by ourselves in case of death. By books we remember the past, and in a certain manner prophesy the future, and we fix things present that are vacillating and transient in the memory of writing.

It was a felicitous studiousness and a studious felicity of the powerful eunuch, of whom it is related, in the 8th chapter of *Acts*, that the love of prophetic reading so vehemently excited him, that he never ceased to read on account of traveling: he had given up the form of Queen Candace to oblivion, had removed the treasures he had the charge of from the care of his heart, and was alike regardless of the road, and of the chariot in which he was carried; the love of his book

a Taken, says Cocheris, almost word for word, from Siger de Brabant, mentioned by Dante. The expression of Seneca differs from this somewhat.—*Ed.*

tium[1] oblivioni tradiderat, Gazas, quibus præerat, a cura cordis se moverat, et tam iter quam currum quo ferebatur, neglexerat. Solus amor libri totum sibi vendicaverat domicilium castitatis, quo modo disponente, mox fidei januam meruit introire. O gratiosus[2] amor librorum, qui Gehennæ filium et alumnum Tartari, per baptismalem gratiam, filium fecit regni!

Cesset jam stilus impotens infiniti negotii consummare tenorem, ne videatur aggredi temere, quod in principio fatebatur impossibile cuiquam esse.

1 *Regiam speciosam*, ms. 797; *A legendo cessaret, reginæ Candacis regiam populosam*, mss. 2454, 3352c, and Ox. ed.; *Populosam*, ed. 1476.

2 *Generosus*, Ox. ed.

alone had claimed this domicile of chastity, disposed by which he was already worthy to enter the gate of faith. O gratifying love of books, that by the grace of baptism made this son of Hell and nursling of Tartarus a son of the kingdom of Heaven!

Let the impotent pen now cease to consummate the tenor of an infinite undertaking, lest it may seem rashly to encounter what in the beginning was acknowledged to be impossible for any one to accomplish. [a]

[a] The author, in this chapter, grows warm in praise of books and the influence of letters. Some passages, and especially on page 162, recall to our minds the much more felicitous language of Cicero upon the same subject, in his oration *pro Archia poeta:* Nam cætera, he says, neque temporum sunt, neque ætatum omnium, neque locorum: at hæc studia adolescentiam alunt, senectutem oblectant, secundas res ornant, adversis perfugium ac solatium præbent, delectant domi, non impediunt foris, pernoctant nobiscum peregrinantur, rusticantur.

Macaulay, also, in the closing paragraphs of his review of Mitford's *History of Greece*, is equally eloquent upon a similar theme. Speaking of the literary influence of Athens, he exclaims: "But who shall estimate her influence on private happiness? Who shall say how many thousands have been made wiser, happier, and better, by those pursuits in which she has taught mankind to engage; to how many the studies which took their rise from her, have been wealth in poverty—liberty in bondage—health in sickness—society in solitude. Her power is indeed manifested at the bar; in the pulpit; in the senate; in the field of battle; in the schools of philosophy. But these are not her glory. Wherever literature consoles sorrow or assuages pain, wherever it brings gladness to eyes which fail with wakefulness and tears, and ache for the dark house and the long sleep, there is exhibited in its noblest form the influence of Athens.—*Ed.*

CAPITULUM XVI.

DE LIBRIS NOVIS SCRIBENDIS ET ANTIQUIS REPARANDIS.[1]

SICUT necessarium est reipublicæ pugnaturis militibus arma providere militaria,[2] et congestas victualium copias præparare, sic ecclesiæ militanti contra paganorum et hæreticorum insultus, operæ pretium constat esse librorum sanorum multitudine communire. Verum quia omne quod servit mortalibus, per lapsum temporis mortalitatis dispendium patitur, necesse est, vetustate tabefacta, volumina innovatis successoribus instaurari, ut perpetuitas, quæ repugnat naturæ individui, concedatur[3] speciei. Hinc est, quod signanter dicit *Ecclesiastes*,[4] faciendi plures libros nullus est finis. Sicut enim[5] librorum corpora, ex contrariorum commixtione compacta suæ compositionis[6] continuum sentiunt detrimentum, sic per prudentiam clericorum est reperiri[7] remedium, per quod liber sacer solvens naturæ debitum, hæreditarium obtineat substitutum, et simile semen sacrisacro mortuo[8] sustineatur,[9] verificeturque statim illud *Ecclesiastici*, xxx: "Mortuus est pater illius, et quasi non est mortuus, similem enim reliquit post se filium."[10] Sunt ergo transcriptores veterum, quasi quidam propagatores recentium filiorum, ad quos paternum [11] devolvatur officium, ne municipium[12] minuatur.

1 *Quam sit meritorium libros scribere, et veteres renovare*, ms. 797 and Ox. ed.
2 *Vulcania*, ms. 797 and Ox. ed.; *Vulcana*, ms. 3352c.
3 *Concedatur privilegio*, mss. and Ox. ed.
4 *Dicitur ecclesiastes xii*, ibid.
5 *Enim nec*, Ox. ed.
6 *Ex contrariorum compositione commixta, suæ compositionis*, ibid.
7 *Clericorum, debet reperiri*, mss and Ox. ed.
8 *Semen fratri mortuo suscitet*, mss. 797, 3352c and Ox. ed.; *Semen sacri mortuo*, ms. 2454.
9 *Suscitet*, Ox. ed.
10 *Enim sibi relinquit post se*, mss. and Ox. ed.
11 *Patrum*, Ox. ed.
12 *Ne librorum municipium*, mss. and Ox. ed.

CHAPTER XVI.

OF WRITING NEW BOOKS AND REPAIRING OLD ONES.

AS it is necessary for a state to provide military arms, and prepare plentiful stores of provisions for soldiers who are about to fight, so it is evidently worth the labor of the church militant to fortify itself against the attacks of pagans and heretics with a multitude of sound books. But because everything that is serviceable to mortals suffers the waste of mortality through lapse of time, it is necessary for volumes corroded by age to be restored by renovated successors, that perpetuity, repugnant to the nature of the individual, may be conceded to the species. Hence it is that *Ecclesiastes* significantly says, in the 12th chapter: "There is no "end of making many books." For as the bodies of books suffer continual detriment from a combined mixture of contraries in their composition, so a remedy is found out by the prudence of clerks, by which a holy book paying the debt of nature may obtain an hereditary substitute, and a seed may be raised up like to the most holy deceased, and that saying of *Ecclesiasticus*, chapter 30, be verified: "The father is dead, and as it were not "dead, for he hath left behind him a son like unto him-"self." The transcribers therefore of old books are as it were a sort of propagators of new sons, to whom that paternal duty has devolved, that the common stock may not be diminished. Transcribers of this sort are justly called antiquaries, whose studies Cassiodorus confessed pleased him most of all the things that are accomplished by bodily labor, thus noticing it in his *Institution of Divine Letters*, cap. iii: "Happy science (he says), "praiseworthy diligence, to unfold language with the "fingers, to give salvation to mortals in silence, and to

Sane[1] hujusmodi transcriptores antiquarii nominantur, quorum studia, inter ea quæ complentur labore corporeo, Cassiodorus[2] sibi placere confitetur, *De Institutione Divinarum Litterarum*, xxx capitulo, ita subdens:[3] Felix, inquit, scientia,[4] laudanda sedulitas manu hominibus prædicare, linguas digitis aperire, salutem mortalibus tacitam[5] dare, et contra diaboli temptationes[6] illicitas calamo et atramento pugnare. Hæc ille, porro scriptoris officium Salvator exercuit, dum inclinans se deorsum, digito scribebat in terra, *Johannis* octavo, ut nullus quantumcunque nobilis dedignetur[7] hoc facere, quod sapientiam Dei patris intuetur fecisse.

O scripturæ serenitas singularis, ad cujus fabricam inclinatur Artifex orbis terræ, in cujus tremendo nomine flectitur omne genu. O venerandum artificium, singulariter præ cunctis praxibus, quæ hominis manu fiunt, cui pectus Dominicum incurvatur humiliter, cui digitus Dei applicatur vice calami functus. Ceterum Dei[8] filium vel arasse, texuisse vel fodisse non legimus: nec quicquam aliud de mechanicis decebat divinam sapientiam humanatam, nisi scribendo litteras exarare: ut discat quilibet generosus aut sciolus, quod hominibus digiti tribuuntur,[9] ad scribendi negotium potius quam ad bellum. Unde librorum sententiam[10] approbamus, qua clericum inertem scripturæ, censuerunt quodammodo mancum fore, capitulo sexto supra. Scribit justos in libro viventium Deus ipse; lapideas quidem tabulas, digito Dei scriptas, Moyses accepit. Scribat librum[11] qui judicat, Job proclamat; digitos scribentis in pariete, *Mene, Thecel*[12] *Phares*, Balthasar[13] tremens vidit, *Danielis* quinto. Ego, inquit Jeremias, scribebam in volu-

1 *Scientiæ*, ms. 3352c.

2 *Plinius*, in the first edition. This error probably arises from the word *plus*, which is found in all the manuscripts and in the Oxford edition, and which the compositor would seem to have read *Plinius*. J. Petit, in his edition of 1500, sought to amend this error by inserting *Cassiodorus* and suppressing *plus*.

3 *Scribens*, Ox. ed.

4 *Intentio*, mss. 797, 3352c, and Ox. ed.; *Sententia*, ms. 2454.

5 *Tactu*, Ox. ed.

6 *Surreptiones*, mss. and Ox. ed.

7 *Indignetur*, Ox. ed.

8 *Functus. Sevisse Dei*, mss. 797, 2454 and Ox. ed.

9 *Tribuuntur divinitus*, mss. and Ox. ed.

10 *Sententiam plurimum*, ibid.

11 *Librum ipse*, ibid.

12 *Methel*, ms. 3352c.

13 *Nabuchodonosor*, mss. and Ox. ed.

"fight against the illicit temptations of the devil with "pen and ink!" So far Cassiodorus.

Moreover[48] our Saviour exercised the office of a writer, when stooping down he wrote with his finger on the ground (*John* viii), that no man, however noble, may disdain to do that which the wisdom of God the Father is seen to have done. Oh singular serenity of writing, in the delineation of which the Artificer of the world, at whose tremendous name every knee is bent, bowed down! Oh venerable invention, singularly above all contrivances made by the hand of man, in which the breast of the Lord was humbly inclined, in which the finger of God was applied to perform the office of a pen!

We do not read[48] that the Son of God sowed or plowed, or wove or dug, or that any other of the mechanical arts were becoming to the divine wisdom humanized, [a] excepting to trace letters by writing, that every noble man and sciolist may learn that fingers were given to man for the business of writing rather than for fighting. Wherefore we approve of the opinion of many books, which deem a clergyman unskilled in writing to be in a certain manner maimed,[49] as aforesaid in chapter vi. God himself inscribes the just in the book of the living. Moses indeed received stone tables written upon by the finger of God. Job exclaims: "Let him who gives "judgment write a book." [b] The trembling Balthasar saw fingers writing on the wall, *Mene Techel Phares* (*Dan.* v). "I," says Jeremiah, "wrote in a volume "with ink" (*Jer.* xxx). Christ thus commanded his beloved John: "What you see, write in a book" (*Apoc.* i). The office of a writer was also enjoined by Isaiah and by Joshua, that the practice as well as the skill might be commended to posterity. The King of kings, and Lord of lords, Christ himself, had writing upon his garment and upon his thigh; [c] as without

a The author does not seem to have had any idea of the dignity of labor, so much insisted upon now--a-days. That our Savior did work as a carpenter when a youth, is very probable, and he is often represented by painters as so engaged.—*Ed.*

b *Job*, xxxi, 35. In our version, Job denounces it as a calamity upon his enemies: "Oh that mine adversary had written a book."—*Ed.*

c *Rev.* xix, 6.—*Inglis.*

mine atramento, *Jeremie* xxxvi.[1] Quod vides scribe in libro, Christus Johanni caro suo præcepit, *Apocalipsis* primo. Sic Ysaiæ, sic Josuæ officium scriptoris injungitur, ut tam actus quam peritia[2] futuris in posterum commendetur. In vestimento et in femore scriptum habet rex regum et dominus dominantium Christus ipse, ut sine scriptura nequeat apparere, perfectum omnipotentis regium ornamentum. Defuncti docere non desinunt, qui sacræ scientiæ libros scribunt. Plus Paulus scribendo sacras epistolas ecclesiæ profuit fabricandæ, quam gentibus et Judeis evangelizando sermone. Nempe per libros quotidie continuat comprehensor, quod olim in terra positus inchoavit viator; sicque verificatur, de doctoribus libros scribentibus, sermo propheticus, *Danielis* xii, qui ad justitiam erudiunt multos, erunt quasi stellæ in perpetuas æternitates. Porro sollicitudinem[3] antiquorum, priusquam Deus originalem mundum cataclismo dilueret, adscribendam miraculo non naturæ, catholici decrevere doctores, ut Deus tantum eis vitæ[4] concederet, quantum reperiendis et in libris scribendis scientiis conveniret: inter quas astronomiæ miranda diversitas, ut experimentaliter[5] visui subderetur, sexcentorum annorum periodum, secundum Josephum, requirebat. Verumtamen non abnuunt, quin terra nascentia illius temporis primitivi, utilius alimentum præstarent mortalibus, quam moderni, quo dabatur non solum hilarior corporis endelechia[6] sed etiam[7] diuturnior florens ætas; ad quam non modicum contulit, quod virtuti vivebant, omnimode resecato superfluo voluptatis. Igitur quisquis Dei munere est ditatus[8] juxta consilium Spiritus Sancti, *Ecclesiastici* xxxviii, sapientiam scribe in tempore vacuitatis ut ad præmium tibi cum beatis et spatium[9] augeatur ætatis.

Ceterum si ad mundi principes divertamus sermonem,

1 *xxx*, Ox. ed.
2 *Ut tantæ artis peritia*, ed. 1500, 1610, and 1702.
3 *Pulchritudinem*, Ox. ed.; *Policratudinem*, mss.
4 *Deus ipse tantum vitæ*, mss. 797, 3352c, and Ox. ed.
5 *Experimento*, Ox. ed.
6 *Enechia*, ms. 3352c.
7 *Sed et*, ms. 3352c, and Ox. ed.
8 *Dei munere scientia est dotatus*, Ox. ed.
9 *Ut et præmium cum beatis, et spatium in præsenti*, mss. and Ox. ed.

writing, the perfect regal ornament of the Omnipotent cannot be apparent.

Those who write books of holy science do not cease to teach when dead. Paul did greater service in forming the church by writing holy epistles, than by evangelizing verbally to the Gentiles and Jews; for the compiler continues by books from day to day what the traveler laid in the earth formerly began—and thus the prophetic words about teachers writing books are verified: "They who teach many according to righteousness shall exist like the stars to all eternity" (*Dan.* xii). Moreover, catholic doctors have determined that the deep researches of the ancients, before God deluged the original world by a general flood, are to be ascribed to miracle and not to nature; as God granted them as much of life as was requisite for discovering and inscribing the sciences in books, amongst which, according to Josephus, the wonderful diversities of astronomy required a period of 600 years, that they might be experimentally submitted to observation. But indeed they do not insinuate that the productions of the earth did not afford a more useful aliment to mortals in those primitive times, than they do now; by which not only a more exhilarating energy of body was given, but also a more durable and flourishing age; added to which, it conferred not a little to their strength, that the superfluities of voluptuousness were in every way discarded. *a*

Therefore whosoever thou art, being endowed with the gift of God according to the counsel of the holy spirit (*Ecclus.* xxxviii), write wisdom while you have leisure, that your reward with the blessed and the length of your days may be increased. Now if we turn our discourse to the princes of the world, we find great

a The bishop seems, very sensibly it appears to us, to reject the supposition of the catholic doctors: though it was less absurd, when it was believed that Noah had preserved the result of these astronomical observations (see chapter vii). To prolong the lives of the antediluvians to enable them to obtain this knowledge, and then destroy all by a deluge, would be strange indeed. But we know now, that the observations merely of even a thousand years would give but little knowledge of the movements of the earth or of the heavenly bodies.—*Ed.*

imperatores egregios invenimus, non solum artis scribendi peritia floruisse, sed et ipsius operi plurimum indulsisse. Julius Cæsar, primus omnium et tempore et virtute, *Commentarios* reliquit tam belli Gallici quam civilis, a semetipso conscriptos. Item de *Analogia* duos libros, et *Anticathones* totidem, et poema quod inscribitur *Iter*, et opuscula alia multa fecit; ut tam Julius[1] quam Augustus cautelas scribendi litteram occultarent.[2] Nam Julius quartam litteram posuit[3] loco primæ, et sic deinceps alphabetum expendit: Augustus vero secundam pro prima, et pro secunda tertiam, et ita deinceps usus fuit. Hic in Mutinensi bello, in maxima mole rerum, quotidie et legisse et scripsisse traditur, ac etiam declamasse. Tiberius lyricum carmen scripsit, et poemata quædam Græca. Claudius similiter tam Græci quam Latini sermonis peritus, varios libellos fecit. Sed præ aliis et his, Titus in scribendi peritia floruit, qui cujuscunque volebat litteram mutuavit[4] facilime, unde se fatebatur[5] falsarium maximum, si libuisset, fieri potuisse. Hæc omnia, Suetonius, de *Vita Duodecim Cæsarum*, annotavit.

1 *Iter fecit. Tam Julius*, etc., ms. 3351c, and Ox. ed.

2 *Scribendi litteram pro littera adinvenit, ut quæ scriberent occultarent*, mss. 797, 3352c, and Ox. ed.

3 *Præposuit*, Ox. ed.

4 *Imitabatur*, mss. 797, 3352c, and Ox. ed.; *Mutabat*, ms 2454.

5 *Profitebatur*, mss. and Ox. ed.

emperors not only to have flourished by skill in the art of writing, but for the most part to have indulged in the practice of it. Julius Cæsar, the first of them all as well in time as in virtue, [a] left *Commentaries* upon the Gallic and civil wars, written out by himself: he also made two books of *Analogy*, and as many against Cato (*Anticatos*), and a poem titled *The Journey*, and many other tracts. And Julius, as well as Augustus, invented secret modes of writing letters, that they might conceal what they wrote; for Julius put the fourth letter for the first, and so went through the alphabet; but Augustus put the second for the first, and the third for the second; and such was the custom afterwards. This last is said to have read and written daily, and even to have declaimed, in the greatest pressure of affairs, during the Mutinensian war. Tiberius wrote lyric verse and some Greek poems. Claudius in like manner, skilled both in the Greek and Latin languages, made various books. But in the art of writing, Titus went beyond these and others, who imitated the hand-writing of whomsoever he pleased, with the utmost facility, and therefore confessed that, if he had chosen, he could have become a great forger. All these things Suetonius notices in his *Lives of the Twelve Cæsars.*

a Is not *valor* a closer translation?—*Ed.*

CAPITULUM XVII.

DE LIBRIS MUNDE TRACTANDIS ET COLLOCANDIS.[1]

NON solum Deo præstamus obsequium, novorum librorum præparando volumina, sed et sacratæ pietatis exercemus officium, si eosdem nunc illæse tractemus, nunc locis idoneis redditos, illibatæ custodiæ commendemus; ut gaudeant puritate, dum habentur in manibus, et requiescant secure, dum in suis cubilibus reconduntur. Nimirum post vestes et vascula corpori dedicata Dominico, sacri libri merentur a clericis honestius contrectari, quibus toties eos præsumunt attingere manu fæda.[2] Quamobrem exhortari studentes super negligentiis variis reputamus expediens, quæ mutari[3] faciliter[4] semper possent, et mirabiliter libris nocent. In primis quidem circa claudenda et aperienda volumina, sit matura modestia, ut nec præcipiti festinatione solvantur, nec inspectione finita, sine clausura debita dimittantur. Longe namque diligentius librum, quam calceum convenit conservari.

Est enim scholarium gens perperam educata communiter, et nisi majorum regulis refrænentur infrunitis inscitiis[5] insolescit. Aguntur petulantia, præsumptione tumescunt; de singulis judicant tanquam certi, cum sint in omnibus inexperti.

Videbis fortasse juvenem cervicosum, in studio segniter residentem, et dum hiberno tempore hiems alget, nasus irriguus frigore comprimente[6] distillat, nec prius

1 *De debita honéstate circa librorum custodiam adhibendam*, mss. 797 and 3352c, and Ox. ed.; *De custodia librorum*, ms. 2454.

2 *Toties irrogatur injuria, quoties eisdem apponitur manus fæda*, mss. 797, 3352c, and Ox. ed.

3 *Vitari*, mss. and Ox. ed.; *Imitari*, ed. 1500, 1610, and 1702.

4 *Falliciter*, ms. 3352c.

5 *Infinitis infantiis*, mss. and Ox. ed.

6 *Opprimente*, Ox. ed.

CHAPTER XVII.

OF HANDLING BOOKS IN A CLEANLY MANNER, AND KEEPING THEM IN ORDER.

WE not only set before ourselves a service to God, in preparing volumes of new books, but we exercise the duties of a holy piety, if we first handle so as not to injure them, then return them to their proper places, and commend them to undefiling custody, that they may rejoice in their purity while held in the hand, and repose in security when laid up in their repositories. Truly, next to the vestments and vessels dedicated to the body of the Lord, holy books deserve to be most decorously handled by the clergy, upon which injury is inflicted as often as they presume to touch them with a dirty hand. Wherefore we hold it expedient to exhort students upon various negligencies, which can always be avoided, but which are wonderfully injurious to books.

In the first place, then, let there be a mature decorum in opening and closing of volumes, that they may neither be unclasped with precipitous haste, nor thrown aside after inspection without being duly closed, for it is necessary that a book should be much more carefully preserved than a shoe. But school folks are in general perversely educated, and if not restrained by the rule of their superiors, are puffed up with infinite absurdities; they act with petulance, swell with presumption, judge of everything with certainty, and are unexperienced in anything.

You will perhaps see a stiff-necked youth, lounging sluggishly in his study; while the frost pinches him in winter time, oppressed with cold, his watery nose drops, nor does he take the trouble to wipe it with his hand-

se dignatur emunctorio tergere, quam subjectum librum madefecerit turpi rore. Cui utinam loco codicis, corium subderetur sutoris. Unguem habet fimo fætenti refertum, giganti similimum,[1] quo placentis materiæ signat locum. Paleas dispertitur innumeras, quas diversis in locis collocat evidenter, ut festuca reducat, quod memoria non retentat. Hæ paleæ, quia nec venter libri digerit, nec quisquam[2] eas extrahit, primo quidem librum, a solita junctura distendunt, et tandem negligenter oblivioni commissæ putrescunt. Fructus et caseum super librum expansum non veretur comedere, atque scyphum hinc inde dissolute transferre; et quia non habet eleemosinarum sacculum[3] præparatum, in libris dimittit reliquias fragmentorum. Garrulitate continua, sociis oblatrare non desinit, et dum multitudinem rationum adducit a sensu physico[4] vacuarum, librum in gremio subexpansum, humectat spargine salivarum.[5] Quid plura! statim duplicatis cubitis, reclinatur in codicem, et per breve studium, soporem invitat prolixum; ac pro[6] reparandis rugis, limbos replicat foliorum, ad libri non modicum detrimentum.

Jam imber abiit et recessit, et flores apparuerunt in terra nostra, tunc scholaris, quem describimus, librorum neglector potius quam inspector, viola,[7] primula atque rosa, nec non quadrifolio, farciet librum suum. Tunc manus aquosas et scatentes sudore, volvendis voluminibus, applicabit; tunc pulverulentis undique chirotecis, in candidam membranam impinget, et indice veteri pelle vestito, venabitur paginam lineatam;[8] tunc ad pulicis mordentis aculeum sacer liber objicitur; qui tamen[9] vix clauditur infra mensem, sicque[10] pulveribus introjectis tumescit, quod claudentis instantiæ non obedit.

Sunt autem specialiter coercendi, a contractione librorum, juvenes impudentes, qui cum litterarum figuras

1 *Gagati similimum*, mss. 797, 3352c, and Ox. ed.
2 *Priusquam*, ed. 1702.
3 *Eleemosinarium*, mss. and Ox. ed.
4 *Philosophico*, Ox ed.
5 *Olivarum*, ed. 1702.
6 *Atque*, Ox. ed.; *Ac reparandis*, ms. 3352c.
7 *Violata*, Ox. ed.
8 *Lineatim*, ibid.
9 *Tum*, ibid.
10 *Sed si*, ibid.

kerchief till it has moistened the book beneath it with its vile dew. For such a one I would substitute a cobbler's apron in the place of his book. He has a nail like a giant's, perfumed with stinking ordure, with which he points out the place of any pleasant subject. He distributes innumerable straws in various places, with the ends in sight, that he may recall by the mark what his memory cannot retain. These straws, which the stomach of the book never digests, and which nobody takes out, at first distend the book from its accustomed closure, and being carelessly left to oblivion, at last become putrid. He is not ashamed to eat fruit and cheese over an open book, and to transfer his empty cup from side to side upon it; and because he has not his alms-bag at hand, he leaves the rest of the fragments in his books. He never ceases to chatter with eternal garrulity to his companions; and while he adduces a multitude of reasons void of physical meaning, he waters the book, spread out upon his lap, with the sputtering of his saliva. What is worse, he next reclines with his elbows on the book, and by a short study invites a long nap; and by way of repairing the wrinkles, he twists back the margins of the leaves, to the no small detriment of the volume. He goes out in the rain, and returns, and now flowers make their appearance upon our soil. Then the scholar we are describing, the neglecter rather than the inspector of books, stuffs his volume with firstling violets, roses and quadrifoils. He will next apply his wet hands, oozing with sweat, to turning over the volumes, then beat the white parchment all over with his dusty gloves, or hunt over the page, line by line, with his fore-finger covered with dirty leather. Then, as the flea bites, the holy book is thrown aside, which, however is scarcely closed once in a month, and is so swelled with the dust that has fallen into it, that it will not yield to the efforts of the closer.

But impudent boys are to be specially restrained from meddling with books, who, when they are learning to

effigiare didicerint, mox pulcherrimorum voluminum, si copia concedatur, incipiunt fieri glossatores incongrui, et ubi largiorem marginem circa textum perspexerint, monstruose appareant alphabetum,[1] vel aliud frivolum, qualecunque, quod imaginationi occurrit,[2] incastigatus calamus protinus exarare præsumit. Ibi Latinista, ibi sophista, ibi quilibet scriba indoctus, aptitudinem pennæ probat, quod formosissimis[3] codicibus, quoad usum et pretium, creberrime vidimus obfuisse.

Sunt iterum fures quidam, libros enormiter detruncantes, qui pro epistolarum cartis,[4] schedulas laterales abscindunt, littera sola salva, vel finalia folia, quæ ad libri custodiam dimittuntur, ad varios usus et abusus assumunt.[5] Quod genus sacrilegii, sub interminatione anathematis, prohiberi deberet.

Convenit autem prorsus scholarium honestati, ut quoties ad studium a refectione reditur, præcedat omnino lotio lectionem, ne digitis sagimine[6] delibutis, aut signacula libri solvat, aut folia prius volvat. Puerulus autem lacrimosus, capitalium litterarum non admiretur imagines, ne manu fluida polluat pergamenum: tangit enim illico, quidquid videt.

Porro laici, qui librum æque respiciunt[7] resupine transversum, sicut serie naturali expansum, omnium librorum communione penitus sunt indigni. Hoc etiam clericus disponat, ut olens ab ollis lixa cinereus, librorum folia[8] non contingat, illotus, sed qui ingreditur sine macula, pretiosis codicibus[9] ministrabit.

Conferret[10] autem plurimum tam libris quam scholaribus, manuum honestarum munditia, si non essent scabies et pustulæ, characteres clericales. Librorum defectibus, quoties advertuntur, est citius[11] occurendum: quoniam nihil grandescit citius quam cissura, et fractura, quæ ad tempus negligitur, reparabitur postea cum usura.

1 *Monstrosis apparitant alphabetis*, Ox. ed.
2 *Occurrit*, *celerius*, mss. and Ox. ed.
3 *Firmissimis*, Ox. ed.
4 *Cartulis*, mss. 797, 3352c, and Ox. ed.
5 *Ad varios abusus assumunt*, ibid.
6 *Lotio*, *nec digitus sanguine*, mss. and Ox. ed.
7 *Librum e converso respiciunt*, Ox.ed
8 *Lilia*, mss. 797, 3352c, and Ox. ed.
9 *Manibus*, Ox. ed.
10 *Confert*, ibid.
11 *Otius*, mss. 797, 3352c. and Ox. ed.

draw the forms of letters, if the copies of the most beautiful books are allowed them, begin to become incongruous annotators, and wherever they perceive the broadest margin about the text, they furnish it with a monstrous alphabet, or their unchastened pen immediately presumes to draw any other frivolous thing whatever, that occurs to their imagination. There the Latinist, there the sophist, there every sort of unlearned scribe tries the goodness of his pen, which we have frequently seen to have been most injurious to the fairest volumes, both as to utility and price. There are also certain thieves who enormously dismember books by cutting off the side margins for letter paper, leaving only the letters or text, or the fly leaves put in for the preservation of the book, which they take away for various uses and abuses, which sort of sacrilege ought to be prohibited under a threat of anathema.

But it is altogether befitting the decency of a scholar, that washing should without fail precede reading, as often as he returns from his meals to study, before his fingers besmeared with grease loosen a clasp or turn over the leaf of a book. Let not a crying child admire the drawings in the capital letters, lest he pollute the parchment with his wet fingers, for he instantly touches whatever he sees.

Furthermore, laymen, to whom it matters not whether they look at a book turned wrong side upwards or spread before them in its natural order, are altogether unworthy of any communion with books.[a] Let the clerk also take order that the dirty scullion, stinking from the pots, do not touch the leaves of books, unwashed; but he who enters without spot shall give his services to the precious volumes. The cleanliness of delicate hands, as if scabs and pustules could not be clerical characteristics, might also be most important, as well to books as to scholars, who as often as they perceive defects in books

a This sentence strikingly illustrates the difference between the age in which the author wrote and the present. The ecclesiastical prohibition has indeed been in vain, and the laity have long since ceased to regard it.—*Ed.*

De librorum armariis mundissime fabricandis, ubi ab omni læsione serventur[1] securi, Moyses mitissimus nos informat *Deuteronom.* xxxi. Tollite, inquit, istum et ponite eum in latere archæ fœderis domini Dei vestri. O locus idoneus et bibliothecæ conveniens, quæ de lignis Sethim imputribilibus facta fuit, auroque per totum interius et exterius circumtecta! Sed et omnem inhonestatis negligentiam circa libros tractandos, suo Salvator excludit exemplo, sicut legitur *Lucæ* iv. Cum enim scripturam propheticam de se scriptam, in libro tradito[2] perlegisset, non prius librum ministro restituit, quam eumdem suis sacratissimis manibus plicuisset. Quo facto, studentes docentur clarissime, circa librorum custodiam, quantumcunque minima negligi non debere.

1 *Salventur*, mss. and Ox. ed. 2 *Traditam*, Ox. ed.

should attend to them instantly, for nothing enlarges more quickly than a rent, as a fracture neglected at the time, will afterwards be repaired with increased trouble.

The most meek Moses instructs us about making cases for books in the neatest manner, wherein they may be safely preserved from all damage. "Take this book," says he, "and put it in the side of the ark of the cove-"nant of the Lord your God" (*Deut.* xxxi). Oh, befitting place, appropriate library, which was made of imperishable Shittim wood, and covered all over inside and out with gold! But our Saviour also, by his own example, precludes all unseemly negligence in the treatment of books, as may be read in *Luke* iv. For when he had read over the scriptural prophecy written about himself in a book delivered to him, he did not return it to the minister till he had first closed it with his most holy hands; by which act students are most clearly taught that they ought not in the smallest degree whatever to be negligent about the custody of books.[a]

[a] This chapter is very tersely and vigorously written. The invectives of the worthy bishop upon the abuse of books have not lost their applicability at the present day. All the misuses which he enumerates and rebukes, are at present practiced to the disgrace of scholars. Those who have charge of our public libraries especially can testify to the destruction of many valuable works by the same abuses so truly and bitterly characterized in this chapter.—*Ed.*

CAPITULUM XVIII.

AUCTOR CONTRA SUOS DETRACTORES.[1]

NIHIL iniquius in humanis perpenditur, quam quod ea, quæ geruntur justissime, malignorum obliquiis pervertuntur, et inde reportat quis famam criminis,[2] unde magis meruit speciem[3] honoris. Oculo simplici perpetrantur plurima,[4] nec sinistra dextræ se commiscet, nullo fermento massa corrumpitur, neque vestis ex lino lanaque contexitur; perversorum tamen præstigiis, opus pium mendaciter transformatur in monstrum. Hæc est nimirum peccatricis animæ[5] reprobanda conditio, quod non solum in factis moraliter dubiis, pro pejore[6] sententiat; imo frequenter illa, quæ speciem boni habent, nequitiosa subversione depravat. Quamvis enim amor librorum,[7] ex objecti natura præferat honestatem, miro tamen modo obnoxios nos efficit judiciis plurimorum; quorum admirationibus obtrectati, nunc de curiositate superflua,[8] nunc de cupiditate in illa duntaxat materia, nunc de vanitatis apparentia, nunc de voluptatis intemperantia circa litteras notabamur; quorum revera vituperiis non plus quam caniculorum latratibus movebamur, illius solius testimonio contentati, ad quem renes et corda pertinet perscrutari. Cum enim voluntatis secretæ finalis intentio homines lateat,[9] cordium inspectori, perniciosæ temeritatis merentur redargui, qui humanis actibus, quorum non vident fontale principium, epigramma tam

1 *Quod tantam librorum copiam collegimus, ad communem profectum scholarium, et non solum ad propriam voluptatem*, ms. 797 and Ox. ed.; except the word *voluptatem*, is *voluntatem*, in Ox. ed. and ms. 3352c.

2 *Obloquiis pervertantur, et inde quis reperiat infamiam criminis*, mss. 797, 3352c, and Ox. ed.

3 *Spem*, ms. 3352c. and Ox. ed.

4 *Quam plurima*, mss. and Ox. ed.

5 *Naturæ*, mss. 797, 3352c, and Ox. ed.

6 *Pejore parte*, Ox. ed.

7 *Librorum in clerico*, ms. 797 and Ox. ed.; *Librorum enim in clerico*, ms. 3352c.

8 *Curiosa superfluitate*, Ox. ed.

9 *Lateat, unicoque Deo pateat*, mss. 797, 3352c and Ox. ed.

CHAPTER XVIII.

THE AUTHOR AGAINST DETRACTORS.

NOTHING is held to be more unjust in human affairs, than that those things which are most justly done, should be perverted by the obloquies of the malignant, as if he who reports the news of a fault should thereby deserve the highest degree of respect. Many things are done with an honest intention; the right hand does not interfere with the left; the mass is not corrupted by any ferment, nor is the garment woven of flax and wool. A pious work, however, is mendaciously transformed into a monster by the legerdemain of perverters. This state of a sinful mind is without doubt to be reprobated, because it not only judges for the worst of acts morally doubtful, but even with iniquitous perversity very often depraves those that bear the stamp of goodness.

Now, although the love of books, in a clerical man, from the nature of the object, bears honor in the face of it, yet it made us in a wonderful manner obnoxious to the criticisms of many; traduced by whose wonderings we were sometimes remarked upon for superfluous curiosity, sometimes for earnestness in that matter alone, sometimes for a display of vanity, and sometimes for immoderate pleasure in literature; but in truth, these vituperations no more discompose us than the barking of a lap-dog, being contented with the testimony of Him, to whom alone it belongs to search the reins and heart. For as the final intention of the secret will is concealed from man and exposed to God alone, the inspector of hearts, they deserve to be rebuked for pernicious rashness, who, not perceiving the mainspring of human actions, so readily set the sinister mark of their

faciliter superscribunt sinistrum. Finis enim se habet in operabilibus, sicut principia in speculativis, vel suppositiones in mathematicis, teste philosophorum principe VII *Ethicorum*. Quapropter sicut ex principiorum evidentia, conclusionis veritas declaratur; ita plerumque in agibilibus, ex honesti finis intentione, bonitas moralis in opere sigillatur; ubi alias opus ipsum judicari deberet indifferens, quoad mores.

Nos autem ab olim in præcordiis mentis nostræ propositum gessimus radicatum, quatenus opportunis temporibus exspectatis, divinitus aulam quamdam, in reverenda universitate Oxoniensi, omnium artium liberalium nutrice præcipua, in perpetuam eleemosinam fundaremus, necessariisque redditibus ditaremus, quam numerosis scholaribus occupatam, nostrorum librorum jocalibus[1] super ditaremus,[2] ut ipsi libri[3] et singuli eorundem communes fierent, quantum ad usum et studium, non solum scholaribus[4] aulæ tactæ, sed per eos omnibus universitatis prædictæ studentibus in æternum, secundum modum et formam quam sequens capitulum declarabit. Quapropter sincerus amor studii, zelusque orthodoxæ fidei, ad ædificationem ecclesiæ confirmandæ,[5] pepererunt in nobis sollicitudinem hanc stupendam nummicolis, ut collectos codices undecunque venales, neglectis sumptibus, emeremus, et qui venundari non debebant, transcribi honestius faceremus.

Cum enim delectationes hominum, ex dispositione corporum cœlestium, cui mixtorum complexio frequenter obedit, diversimode distinguantur: ut hi in architectura, illi in agricultura, hi in venationibus, illi in navigationibus, hi in bellis, illi in ludis eligant conversari; cecidit circa[6] nostræ Mercurialis species voluptatis honestæ, quam ex rectæ rationis arbitrio, cujus nulla sidera dominantur imperio, in honorem ordinavimus majestatis supremæ, ut unde mens nostra tranquillitatem reperit requiei, inde devotissime cresceret cultus Dei. Qua-

1 Misprinted *localibus* in ed. of 1473.

2 *Jocalibus ditaremus*, mss. 2454, 3352c and Ox. ed.

3 *Redditibus dotaremus ut ipsi libri*, ms. 797.

4 *Studium scholaribus*, Ox. ed.

5 *Confirmandam*, ibid.

6 *Circa libros*, mss. and Ox. ed.

baneful temerity upon them. For the end, in things practicable, sustains itself like principles in speculative, and assumptions in mathematical propositions, as Aristotle, the prince of philosophers, witnesses (*Ethics*, VII). Wherefore, as the truth of a conclusion is made clear from the evidence of principles, so, for the most part, moral goodness in things practicable is stamped upon the performance by the intention of an honest purpose, where on the contrary the work itself ought to be deemed indifferent as to morals. But we have for a long time held a rooted purpose in the inmost recesses of our mind, looking forward to a favorable time and divine aid, to found, in perpetual alms, and enrich with the necessary gifts, a certain hall in the revered University of Oxford, the first nurse of all the liberal arts; and further to enrich the same, when occupied by numerous scholars, with deposits of our books, so that the books themselves and every one of them may be made common as to use and study, not only to the scholars of the said hall, but through them to all the students of the aforesaid university for ever, according to the manner and form which the following chapter will declare. Wherefore a sincere love of study, and a zeal for confirming the orthodox faith, to the edification of the church, brought forth in us this to money-lovers stupendous solicitude in purchasing such books, collected from all parts, as were to be sold, regardless of the expense, and of causing those that ought not to be sold to be handsomely transcribed. For as the pleasures of men are diversified in many manners, according to the disposition of the heavenly bodies, to which a complexion of mixtures frequently accommodates itself, so that some choose to be conversant with architecture, some with agriculture, some with field sports, some with navigation, some with war, and some with games—so our Mercurial sort of honest pleasure about books fell under the will of right reason (in the control of which no stars are dominant), which we have so regulated in honor of

mobrem desinant obtrectantes,[1] sicut cæci de coloribus judicare, vespertiliones de luce[2] disceptare non audeant, atque trabes gestantes in oculis propriis, alienas festucas eruere non præsumant. Cessent commentis satyricis[3] suggillare, quæ nesciunt, et occulta discutere, quæ humanis experientiis non patescunt. Qui nos fortassis affectu commendassent benevolo, si ferarum venatui, alearumque lusui, dominarum applausui vacassemus.

1 *Obtrectatores*, Ox. ed.
2 *Luminibus*, ibid.
3 *Satyricorum*, ibid.

the Supreme Majesty, that our mind might find the tranquillity of rest, and that the worship of God might most devoutly increase thereby. Wherefore let detractors like the blind desist from judging of colors. Let not bats dare to argue about lights, nor those who have beams in their own eyes presume to pluck the motes out of other people's. Let those cease to defame what they know nothing of with satirical remarks, and to discuss secrets which are not open to human research, who perhaps would have commended us with a benevolent affection, if we had found leisure for hunting wild beasts, playing at hazard, or for the favors of mistresses.*a*

a The custom of abusing and defying critics in anticipation of their malignity, which was universal among authors for many centuries, and of which this chapter is an example, has now happily nearly passed away. The reason cannot be that the critics are less numerous or less severe, but probably lies in the fact that experience has shown the attempt, either to mollify the enemy or forestall public opinion, to be futile.

Some of these tirades against critics however are very witty and amusing, especially those of Cervantes, genial and kindly as they could not help being, despite their professed purpose, and also those of Fielding.—*Ed,*

CAPITULUM XIX.

DE ORDINATIONE PROVIDA QUALITER LIBRI EXTRANEIS CONCEDANTUR.[1]

DIFFICILE fuit semper sic homines limitare legibus honestatis, quin astutia successorum terminos niteretur præcedentium transilire et statutas infringere regulas insolentia libertatis; quamobrem de prudentium consilio, certum modum præfiximus, per quem, ad utilitatem studentium, librorum nostrorum communicationem et usum volumus devenire. In primis enim libros omnes et singulos, de quibus catalogum fecimus specialem, concedimus et donavimus,[2] intuitu caritatis, comitati scholarium in aula[3] Oxoniensi degentium, in perpetuam eleemosynam, pro anima nostra et parentum nostrorum, nec non pro anima illustrissimi regis Angliæ Eduardi tertii post conquestum, et devotissimæ dominæ reginæ Philippæ consortis ejusdem; ut iidem libri omnibus et singulis universitatis dictæ villæ scholaribus et magistris, tam regularibus quam sæcularibus commodentur pro tempore, ad profectum et usum studentium, juxta modum quem immediate subjungimus, qui est talis.

Quinque de scholaribus in aula præfata commorantibus, assignentur per ejusdem aulæ magistrum, quibus librorum[4] custodia deputetur, de quibus quinque personis tres, et nullatenus pauciores, librum vel libros ad inspectionem et usum duntaxat studii valeant commodare: ad copiandum vero et transcribendum, nullum librum volumus extra septa domus concedi. Igitur cum scholaris quicunque sæcularis vel religiosus, quos in præsenti favore ad paria judicamus, librum aliquem commodan-

1 *De modo communicandi studentibus omnes libros nostros*, mss. 797, 3352c and Ox. ed.

2 *Donamus*, mss. and Ox. ed.

3 *Communitati scholarium in aula nostra*, Ox. ed.

4 *Omnium librorum*, mss. and Ox. edition.

CHAPTER XIX.

A PROVIDENT ARRANGEMENT BY WHICH BOOKS MAY BE LENT TO STRANGERS.

IT was always a difficult matter so to limit men to the rules of honesty, that the knavery of the last generation might not overstep the boundaries of its predecessor, and infringe established rules by the licentiousness of liberty. Wherefore by the advice of prudent men we have devised beforehand a certain method by which we wish the communication and use of our books to descend to the service of students. In the first place, therefore, we have conceded and given with a charitable view, to a company of scholars residing in a hall at Oxford, as a perpetual alms-deed for our own soul and for the souls of our parents, as well as for the souls of the most illustrious king of England, Edward the Third, after the conquest, and of the most devout Lady Philippa his consort, all and singular the books of which we have made a special catalogue,[a] that all and singular the said books[b] may be lent out for a time to the scholars and masters, as well regulars as seculars, of the university of the said city, for the advantage and use of students, according to the manner immediately subjoined, which is to this effect.

Five of the scholars dwelling in the aforesaid hall are to be appointed by the master of the same hall, to whom the custody of the books is to be deputed. Of which five, three, and in no case fewer, shall be competent to lend any books for inspection and use only; but for copying and transcribing we will not allow any book to pass without the walls of the house. Therefore when

[a] Cocheris says in his preface that this catalogue has never been found. —*Ed.*

[b] The text is: the said books to all and singular the scholars and masters, &c.—*Ed.*

dum petiverit, considerent diligenter custodes, an librum talem habuerint duplicatum, et si sic, commodent ei librum cautione recepta, quæ librum traditum in valore transcendat, judicio eorum; fiatque statim tam de cautione quam de libro commodato memorialis scriptura, continens nomina personarum, quæ librum tradunt, et illius, qui recepit, cum die et anno Domini, quo contingit fieri commodatum. Si vero custodes invenerint, quod ille liber qui petitur, duplicatus non fuerit, talem[1] librum non commodent[2] cuicunque nisi fuerit de comitiva scholarium dictæ aulæ, nisi forte ad inspectionem infra septa domus vel aulæ prædictæ, sed non ad ulterius deferendum. Scholari[3] vero cuilibet prædictæ[4] aulæ, liber quicunque per tres[5] de prædictis custodibus valeat commodari, nomine tamen suo, cum die, quo librum recipit, primitus annotato. Nec tamen ipse possit librum sibi traditum alteri commodare, nisi de assensu trium de custodibus supradictis, et tunc deleto nomine primi, nomen secundi, cum tempore traditionis scribatur.

Ad hæc omnia observandum, custodes singuli fidem præstent, quando eis custodia hujus modi deputatur. Recipientes autem librum vel libros, ibidem jurabunt, quod eum vel eos ad alium usum, nisi ad inspectionem vel studium, nullatenus applicabunt, quodque illum vel illos,[6] extra villam Oxoniensem cum suburbio, nec deferent nec deferri permittent.

Singulis autem annis, computum reddent prædicti custodes magistro domus et duobus,[7] quos secum duxerit de suis scholaribus assumendum, vel si eidem non vacaverit, tres deputet inspectores alios a custodibus, qui librorum catalogum perlegentes, videant quod eomns[a] habeant vel in voluminibus propriis vel saltem per cautiones præsentes. Ad hunc etiam[8] computum persolvendum, tempus credimus opportunius, a kalendis Junii

a This is unquestionably a misprint for *omnes.—Ed.*

1 *Nullatenus talem*, mss. and Ox. ed.

2 *Librum nullatenus commodent*, ms. 3352c.

3 *Scholarium*, ms. 797 and Ox. ed.

4 *Dictæ*, ms. 3352c.

5 *Per aliquem*, Ox. ed.

6 *Ipsum, vel ipsos*, ibid.

7 *Ducibus*, ibid.

8 *Autem*, mss. 797, 3352c and Ox. ed.

any scholar, whether secular or religious, whom we have deemed qualified for the present favor, shall demand the loan of a book, the keepers must carefully consider whether they have a duplicate of that book; and if so, they may lend it to him, taking a security which in their opinion shall exceed in value the book delivered; and they shall immediately make a written memorandum both of the security and the book lent, containing the names of the persons who delivered the book, and of him who received it, with the day and year of our Lord on which the loan took place. But if the keepers shall find that there is no duplicate of the book demanded, they shall not lend such book to any one whomsoever, unless he be of the company of scholars of the said hall, except as it may happen for inspection within the walls of the aforesaid hall, but not to be carried beyond them. But to every scholar whatever of the aforesaid hall, any book whatever may be available by loan; his name, and the day on which he received the book, being first noted down. He however is not to have the power of lending the book delivered to him, to another, without the assent of three of the aforesaid keepers, and then the name of the first borrower being erased, the name of the second, with the time of delivery, is to be inscribed. For observing all these conditions each of the keepers shall pledge his faith, when a custody of this kind is deputed to him. But the receivers of a book or books shall swear in like manner that he or they shall in no way apply a book to any other use but to inspection or study, and that they will neither carry nor permit it to be carried without the city of Oxford and the suburbs. And the aforesaid keepers must render an account every year to the master of the house, and two of his scholars to be selected by him; or if he has not leisure, he shall depute three inspectors, not being keepers, who reading over the catalogue must see that they have the whole, either in the books themselves or at least in the securities representing them.

usque ad festum sequens gloriosissimi martyris sancti Thomæ.

Hoc autem omnino adjicimus, quod quilibet, cui liber aliquis fuerit commodatus, semel in anno librum præsentet custodibus, et suam, si voluerit, videat cautionem. Porro si contingat[1] fortuito per mortem, furtum, fraudem vel incuriam librum perdi, ille qui perdiderit,[2] vel ejusdem procurator, seu etiam executor, pretium libri solvat, et ejusdem recipiat cautionem. Quod si qualitercunque custodibus ipsis lucrum evenerit, in nihil[3] aliud quam in librorum reparationem et subsidium convertatur.[4]

1 *Contingit*, ed. 1702.

2 *Perditum esse ille qui perdidit*, Ox. ed.

3 *Eveniat, nihil*, mss. 797, 2454 and Ox. ed.

4 *Hic multas librorum conditiones circam librorum custodiam prætermitto, eo quod mihi pro præsenti videatur inutile talia recitare*, ms. 797 and Ox. ed.

We also think the most convenient time for settling this account will be from the kalends of June to the subsequent feast of the most glorious martyr St. Thomas. But we have to add this, that every person, in every instance, to whom any book has been lent, shall exhibit the book once in the year to the keepers, and if he wishes it he shall see his security. Moreover if any book should happen to be lost, through death, theft, fraud or carelessness, he who lost it or his administrator or executor shall in like manner pay the price of the book and receive the security; but if profit should in any way arise to the keepers themselves, it is not to be converted to any other purpose than to the aid and repairing of the books.

Here we pass over many particulars relating to the care of books, because it appears unnecessary to detail them at present.

CAPITULUM XX.

AUCTOR PETIT ORATIONES ET NOTABILITER DOCET ORARE STUDENTES.[1]

TEMPUS jam efflagitat terminare tractatum, quem de amore librorum compegimus; in quo contemporaneorum nostrorum admirationibus, de eo quod tantum libros dileximus, rationem reddere nisi sumus. Verum quia vix datur aliquid[2] operari[3] mortalibus, quod nullius pulvere aspergatur[4] vanitatis; studiosum amorem, quem ita[5] diuturnum ad libros habuimus, justificare penitus non audemus, quin fuerit forsitan nobis quandoque occasio[6] alicujus negligentiæ venialis, quamvis amoris materia sit honesta, et intentio regulata. Si namque cum omnia fecerimus, servos nos inutiles dicere teneamur; si Job sanctissimus sua opera omnia verebatur; si juxta Ysayam, quasi pannus menstruatæ, omnes sunt justitiæ nostræ: quis de perfectione cujuscunque virtutis præsumat jactare? quin ex aliqua circumstantia valeat reprehendi, quæ forsitan a se ipsa non poterat deprehendi. Bonum enim ex integris causis, malum autem omnifarie, sicut Dionisius, *De Divinis Nominibus*, nos informat.

Quamobrem in nostrarum iniquitatum remedium, quibus nos omnium Creatorem crebrius offendisse cognoscimus, orationum suffragia petituri, studentes nostros futuros dignum duximus exhortari, quatenus sic, tam nobis quam aliis eorumdem futuris benefactoribus fiant grati, quod beneficiorum nostrorum providentiam spiritualibus retributionibus recompensent. Vivamus in eorum me-

1 *Exhortatio scholarium ad rependendum pro nobis suffragia debitæ pietatis*, mss. 797, 3352c, and Ox. ed.
2 *Dicitur aliquod*, Ox. ed.
3 *Opera*, ms. 2454.
4 *Respergatur*, Ox. ed.
5 *Jam*, ibid.
6 *Forsan nobis interdum occasio*, ib.

CHAPTER XX.

THE AUTHOR DESIRES TO BE PRAYED FOR, AND NOTABLY TEACHES STUDENTS TO PRAY.

TIME now urges us to finish the tract we are tagging together, about the love of books, in which we have endeavored to account for the amazement of our contemporaries at our taking such great delight in books. But because scarcely anything can be said to be performed by mortals that has not some sprinkling of the powder of vanity in it, we will not attempt entirely to justify the zealous love we have so constantly had for books, as it may perhaps at times have been the cause of some venial neglect on our part, although the object of our love were honorable, and the intention regulated. For may we not still be bound to call ourselves unprofitable servants, when we shall have done all these things? Indeed if the most holy Job was fearful in all his works; if, according to Isaiah, all our righteousness is as a menstruous cloth, who shall presume to boast of the perfection of any virtue whatever? or shall not deserve to be reprehended for some circumstances which perhaps he was not able to perceive of himself? For good arises out of pure causes; but evil is omnifarious (as Dionysius instructs us, on *Divine Names*).

Wherefore, being about to demand the aid of prayers as a remedy for the sins by which we acknowledge ourselves very often to have offended the Creator of all things, we have thought proper to exhort our future students, that they may in so far become grateful as well to ourselves as to their other future benefactors, as to recompense our providential benefactions by spiritual retributions, that we may live entombed in their memo-

moriis funerati, qui in nostris vixerunt benevolentiis nondum nati, nostrisque nunc vivunt beneficiis sustentati. Clementiam Redemptoris implorent instantiis indefessis, quatenus negligentiis nostris pareat, peccatorum reatibus pius Judex indulgeat, lapsus nostræ fragilitatis[1] pallio pietatis operiat, et offensas quas et pudet et pænitet comisisse, benignitate divina remittat; conservit in nobis, ad sufficiens spatium pænitendi, suarum numera gratiarum, fidei firmitatem, spei sublimitatem,[2] et ad homines[3] latissimam caritatem; flectat superbum arbitrium ad culparum suarum lamentum, ut deploret transactas elationes vanissimas, et retractet indignationes amarissimas ac delectationes insanissimas detestetur. Vigeat[4] sua virtus in nobis, cum nostra defecerit, et qui nostrum ingressum sacro baptismo[5] consecravit gratuito, nostrum processum[6] ad statum apostolicum sublimavit.[7] Laxetur a nostro spiritu amor carnis; evanescat penitus metus mortis, desideret dissolvi et esse cum Christo. Et in terris solo corpore constituti, cogitatione et aviditate in æterna patria conversemur. Pater misericordiarum et Deus totius consolationis, filio[8] de siliquis revertenti benignus occurrat; drachmam denuo repertam recipiat, et in thesauros æternos per sanctos angelos transmittat. Castiget vultu terrifico, exitus nostri hora, spiritus tenebrarum, ne latens in limine portæ mortis Leviathan, serpens vetus, insidias improvisas calcaneo nostro paret. Cum vero ad terrendum[9] tribunal fuerimus advocati, ut cuncta, quæ[10] corpore gessimus, attestante conscientia referamus, consideret humanitas juncta Deo effusi sui sancti sanguinis pretium, et advertat divinitas humana carnalis naturæ figmentum, ut ibi transeat fragilitas impunita, ubi clemens pietas cernitur infinita; et ibi respiret spiritus miseri, ubi exstat judicis proprium misereri. Amplius refugium spei nostræ post Deum,

1 *Nostri fragilitatem pallio*, Ox. ed.
2 *Suavitatem*, ibid.
3 *Omnes homines*, mss. and Ox. ed.
4 *Urgeat*, Ox. ed.
5 *Sacramento baptismatis*, ibid.
6 *Progressum*, mss. and Ox. ed.
7 *Sublimavit immerito, nostrum dignetur egressum sacramentis idoneis communire*, ibid.
8 *Filio prodigo*, ibid.
9 *Tremendum*, ms. 797, and Ox. ed.
10 *Quæ in*, Ox. ed.

ries, who being yet unborn lived in our benevolence, and now live supported by our benefactions.

Let them, with unwearied importunity, implore the clemency of our Redeemer, to the end that he may spare our neglects; that the pious Judge may be indulgent to the guilt of our sins; that he may throw the cloak of charity over the omissions of our frailty, and through his divine benignity remit the offences which with shame and repentance we acknowledge ourselves to have committed; that he may preserve in us sufficient time for repentance, for returning thanks for his gifts, for the confirmation of our faith, for the exaltation of our hope, and for the most unbounded charity towards all mankind; that he may incline our proud will to lament its errors, to deplore its former most vain elations, retract its most bitter indignations, and detest its most insane pleasures; that his strength may grow in us as our own decays, who alike gratuitously consecrated our entrance into holy baptism, and undeservedly exalted our progress to the apostolical state. That the love of the flesh may be weakened in our spirit, and the fear of death entirely vanish from it; that it may desire to be set at liberty, and to be with Christ; and that when in body alone we are placed in the earth, we may dwell in thought and earnest desire in the eternal country!

May the Father of mercy and the God of all consolation run to meet the prodigal son returning from the husks! May he receive the drachm found again, and transmit it by holy angels into the eternal treasury! May He, with terrific countenance, castigate the spirit of darkness in the hour of our departure, that the old serpent Leviathan, lurking at the threshold of the gate of death, may not prepare unlooked for snares for our feet! But when we shall be called up to the tremendous tribunal, that we may relate everything that we did in the body (our conscience bearing witness), may humanity joined to God consider the price of his holy blood poured out for us! and may divinity made man advert

virginem et reginam theotocam benedictam, nostri semper studentes salutationibus satagant frequentare devotis, ut qui propter nostra facinora triplicata meruimus judicem invenire turbatum, per ipsius suffragia semper grata mereamur eundem reperire placatum. Deprimat pia manus brachium æquælibræ,[1] qua nostra tam parva quam pauca merita pensabuntur, ne, quod absit, præponderet gravitas criminum et dampnandos dejiciat in abyssum.

Clarissimum autem meritis[2] Cuthbertum, cujus gregem pascendum indigni suscepimus, omnium cultu studeant venerari, devote rogantes assidue, ut suum quidem licet indignum vicarium, precibus excusare dignetur feliciter, et quem[3] successorem admisit in terris, procuret effici confessorem in cœlis. Puris denique tam mentis quam corporis precibus rogent Deum, ut spiritum ad imaginem Trinitatis creatum, post præsentis miseriæ incolatum, ad suum reducat primordiale prototypum, ac ejusdem concedat perpetuum fruibilis faciei conspectum,[4] per dominum nostrum Jesum Christum. Amen.

1 *Æquilibre*, mss. and Ox. ed.
2 *Clarissimum meritis confessorem*, ibid.
3 *Dignetur, et quem*, ibid.
4 *Conspectum. Amen.* The ms. and Oxford edition terminate thus.

EXPLICIT PHILOBIBLON.

to the composition of carnal nature, that its fragility may pass on with impunity to that place where clement piety is declared to be infinite, where the spirit of mercy breathes, and where the peculiar office of the Judge is to be exceedingly merciful! Furthermore, the refuge of our hope, next to God and the Blessed Virgin and Queen Mother, is that our students may always be careful to reiterate devout salutations, that we who deserve to meet an angry Judge may be made worthy to find him appeased by their ever grateful suffrages! May a pious hand depress to an equipoise the scale in which our merits, as small as few, shall be weighed, lest (which God forbid!) the weight of crime may preponderate, and cast us to be damned in the abyss! Moreover, let them be devoutly anxious to venerate the merits of St. Cuthbert the confessor, whose flock we, though unworthy, took upon ourselves to feed, earnestly praying that he may favorably condescend to exculpate his vicar, though indeed undeserving, and that he may bring it about that the successor he admitted on earth, may be made a confessor in heaven!

Finally, let them beseech God with holy prayers, as well bodily as mental, that he may bring back the spirit created in the image of the Trinity, after its sojourn in this life of misery, to its primordial prototype, and grant it a perpetual view of his rejoicing countenance, through our Lord Jesus Christ! Amen.

Here endeth the Philobiblon, or Book upon the
Love of Books, Printed at Cologne
in the year of our Lord
M.CCCC.LXXIII.

NOTES.

BY JOHN B. INGLIS.

---

1. Page 41. *Deliberate choice.*

The English translation of προαίρεσις is substituted for the *consilium* of the monks, which does not give the effect of the compound word *preference*, that is, deliberate and not accidental choice. The allusion to Aristotle in this place is not much to the purpose.

2. Page 41. *Septiform spirit.*

If the reader can make out from the following quotations, what this spirit is, he will be much edified; if not, he may invoke it himself, or consult Astexanus, Aquinas, the *Salisbury Horæ*, and many other like authorities. The septenary number in the new law designates what the decenary does in the old. The seven gifts of the Holy Ghost are designated in the *Decalogue;* viz: wisdom, understanding, knowledge, council, mercy, fortitude, fear. This septiform grace, according to the seven properties or effects of fire, which signifies the Holy Ghost, occasions the diversity of gifts in the said spirit. The seven effects of fire are, destruction, as of sin by wisdom; illumination, as enlightening the understanding; conjunction, as of the knowledge of many; ascension, as of the mind by council; melting, as to mercy; consolidation, as producing fortitude; fervency, as in contemplation and the fear of God.

3. Page 43. *Elegorum quin potius electorum.*

The bishop never misses an alliteration, even to punning: *elegorum* may have a different meaning from what is here given to it; but it may also be derived from some old law term, as we have *utlegary* for outlawry in the *Vieux Abrigement.*

4. Page 43. *Want of oil.*

Tertullian says the wild olive springs from the stem of the true tree, and the wild fig from the seed of the fruitful tree. This appears to be reversing the order of nature. The wild plant must be the original, though fruit may be improved by cultivation; the plant may however degenerate by neglect.

5. Page 45. *Meteor.*

Naturam et speciem veræ stellæ præcedens subito decidit et fit a sub. The various readings are, prætendens, decidens, assub. This passage is rather paraphrased than translated; the allusion is evidently to what is called a shooting star; but *fit a sub* is said of a comet, describing it as a meteor formed in a lower sphere than that of the planets, and as a thing that will burn out and be extinguished: "Stella crinita—nubes ignea "accensa—vapor terrenus grossus." Ptolemy and others are quoted for these descriptions.

6. Page 45. *Liberty of the church.*

An inexhaustible subject, though it may be cut very short, by allowing the said liberties to have no limits. In 1491, while his holiness was standing on the pinnacle of the glorious edifice his predecessors had raised, taking a view of the world over which he meant to extend his sway, as opportunity offered, and little dreaming how soon he might have a fall, his prothonotary, John Lupus (an awkward name in a sheepfold), was writing a book, *De Libertate Ecclesiastica,* &c.; that is, on ecoclesiastical liberty, and on the confederation of princes, together with certain golden questions most worthy of notice. Such is the title; the effect is to show that the pope is lord of the creation. The book was printed at Strasburg in 1511, perhaps before. If the reformers had translated it into every European language, with a proper comment, as a warning to princes and people, we should by this time have known little about spiritual lords temporal, church and state, and many other absurdities that have made the Christian religion a name with no other definition than what every individual or sect chooses to give it, while no two can agree about what it ought to be. To some it is a burthen they bear for the sake of Christianity; and some have shown a disposition to shake off Christianity itself, on account of the mass of rubbish it is encumbered with, and which they know not how to separate from it. A disputed brief of Pius II is taken as a text and pretext for writing this tract. What is said of it is of no consequence; whether spurious or not, the church had a right to give it. There are about seventy questions in the tract, and about as many leaves: it would have made a ponderous volume if the authorities referred to had been given at length. Q. 2. Whether the liberty of churches and priests is of right divine? Answered in the affirmative. Q. 3. Whether the pope can dispense contrary to divine law? Whether tithes are of natural or divine right: how they are comprehended under the moral precepts; and whether the pope can give dispensation for not paying tithes? All affirmed, though not without qualification; rights may be declared either human or divine, as may appear most convenient, and are therefore easily disposed of; but whether even the pope can give up so divine a right as tithes is a serious question. "Dum tangit Dei honorem;" so says Solomon, *Prov.* iii, "Honora Dominum de tua substantia." It touches the honor of God; this was Solomon's feeling when he said, "Honor "the Lord with thy substance." King James's bishops have added five marginal references to this verse, one of them in favor of tithes, *Malachi* iii, 10. The last is rather unfortunate, but he was an honest man who made it, *Luke* xiv, 13. "But when thou makest a feast, call the poor, the maimed, "the lame, and the blind," and "thou shalt be recompensed at "the resurrection of the just." Was it not once the law that part of the tithes should go to the poor? We are nowhere told by the church, though it is a self-evident fact, that under a government entirely ecclesiastical (a warlike one at times), like that of the Jews, the tithes were the revenue of the state, for the church was the state. 1 *Samuel* viii, 14 to 17, says, if you have a king he will tithe you, speaking of it as a grievance. This proves one of three positions: either that no tithes were paid in his time; or, that no other government taxes were paid; or, that the church would not give up its tithes, even though it kept them for private use; for it would have been no grievance to the people to pay the king instead of the church, if they paid no more than they did before. It shows also why David was so anxious about building the temple, and making himself the head of it; why he called Solomon a priest and a tithe collector, for he could have addressed the 110th psalm to nobody else; why Solomon built the temple at the seat of government, where it ought not to have been; why the Jews built another in what they considered the right place, and made a schism that weakened the empire, and was one of the causes of its fall. It is true that the tithes were given to the Lord, or to the Levites—the words are used separately and jointly. But who were the people given to? Were they not the Lord's, and did they not hold themselves to be under his peculiar government spiritually and temporarily? Who ordered them to make war and peace? the church; and the church must have paid: Jews do not fight for nothing. Q. 7. Admitting, though it is not conceded, that a community may receive taxes from the clergy, can such taxes be augmented? non licet hodie clericis augmentare. The allusion is to tolls taken at the gates of cities, or in markets upon commodities brought for sale, of which the produce of church lands, tithe in kind, &c., were no small portion. Ans. If such produce pays toll from custom, the toll cannot be augmented on the clergy. It is certain a community may augment its toll on the people, and the clergy their taxes, but no notice is taken of this—the church only protects itself. Q. 11. Part 2. From whom did ecclesiastical liberty emanate? and what such liberty and immunity is. It would take a fortnight to read the three pages of this chapter with all the references, if the books were at hand. "That we may better understand this matter, it is to be in-"quired what is properly called ecclesiastical liberty, &c. "Et. glo in. c. cũ devotissima xij. q. ij. ait;" that is, "And the gloss on chapter beginning *Cum devotissima*, dis-"tinction xii, question ii, says:" The author is sometimes named, but oftener not, being supposed to be known from the subject. This gloss says: "Immunity is the privilege the "church enjoys," i. e. it keeps all it has got, and takes as much more as it can get, and so the privilege is always good. Chrysostom says: "The greatest care has been taken by God "not to surround the church with mountains, but to fence it "round with faith; for heaven is stretched out, the air ex-"panded, the sea poured out, and paradise planted for the "church; for on account of the church the only begotten son "of God was made man, who himself says, 'I who founded "heaven and created the angels established her; but I was not "crucified on account of heaven, I did not receive a celestial "body on account of heaven, nor assume the nature of angels.' "Wherefore Isaiah, alluding to the same words of the Lord, "says, 'quasi sponsa posuit mitra mihi, et quasi sponsus or-"navit me ornamento:'" which quotation disagrees with four

Bibles, that all disagree with each other. The turn given to it seems to be, that the bride, or church, puts a mitre on the bridegroom, who in return adorns the bride. The conclusion is, that the Roman church is called catholic, and the head of other churches. There is a shuffle about the word *universal*, but that is claimed afterwards. "It obtained the primacy from "the voice of our Lord and Saviour, who created it upon the "rock of the rising faith. Solomon claimed immunities for the "temple—Exaudivi orationem, 'I have heard your prayer.' "God promised to give Moses immunities (*Exodus* xxi); God "gave cities, &c. (*Joshua* xx), and made them free from all "subjection, jurisdiction, and exactions of temporal princes. "God says, 'All the earth is mine' (*Exodus* xix); the Psalmist "adds, 'and the plenitude thereof.' From these and many "other authorities that it would be tedious to quote, it appears "that churches and their priests, ministers and tithes, are ex- "empted by Almighty God himself from all superiority and ju- "risdiction of temporal rulers and other seculars; and so it is "interpreted by holy men and supreme pontiffs." He should have said (for the quotations include it), because all the world, &c., belongs to the church. There is one more question that confirms the whole: Whether kings can be compelled at the instance of pontiffs to defend the church, &c.? They can. Indeed they now know what it is to turn knights-errant for the church. "Being the minister of peace and the head of "all nations, it is proper that the sovereign pontiff should cor- "rect by evangelical denunciation, paternal admonition, cen- "sure and penalties; but as he cannot assist one party (with "force) without injuring another, it is more convenient he "should assist neither than that one should be aggrieved." That is, the church should make no enemies for itself, though it may artfully and secretly throw the onus of discord upon whoever will take the risk of it. What has it gained by it? What has any nation gained by setting itself up as the arbiter of the rights of others, and the rectifier of political wrongs that did not concern itself? Mordecai, who sits at the king's gate, can answer the last question for all Europe. His old clothes bag, filled to the brim with pawned crowns, presents a better moral and political lesson than even the history of his race. Wars are expensive: the church knew it; but it could find no divine authority for paying; its greatest and best privilege is to be a receiver. There can be no greater treason against the human race, than a false arrogation of divine authority, nor a more dangerous power than that which is assumed under it. It is not in the nature of man not to abuse unlimited power, because he has not unlimited wisdom to control it. Neither does such power accord with the nature of man as a social being, for society is a nullity without the seal of reciprocity; the ruler and the ruled must be of one accord, or there can be no peace between them, and no stability in their institutions. The church of Rome, in assuming unlimited power under the *new law*, was compelled to look to the *old* for its authority, though it made no scruple of abolishing that, wherever it was found unprofitable. Its head calls himself, what the gospel commands him to be, Servus servorum Dei. It is the business of a church to govern its own servants or priests and nobody else. It is the business of a Christian priest to do the duties of his office, to instruct the people in theirs, to persuade and exhort them to attend to it; and to do all this as the most humble servant of the servants or people of God. It is for the interest of civil society to provide priests with a moderate competency, but not to support them in idleness, and luxury, nor to give to any priest more than is necessary for his individual support: if he requires more on account of his family, he may earn it honestly, as many do, in a becoming manner. He is educated for a teacher; he gets a preference oftener than he deserves it, and in that respect is better off than the multitude, who know not where to look for the means of subsistence. Overlooking all these things, to say nothing of the poverty enjoined in the gospel, the church of Rome (and every church will do the same if it can) assumes the right of disposing of the souls, bodies, and possessions, of all the people in the world, at its own will and pleasure. Not finding sufficient authority for its pretensions, even by misinterpreting the *Old Testament*, it quotes (in Lupus's treatise and elsewhere) Pharaoh and Mahomet, the priesthood of Egypt, Greece, and Rome, its own barbarians, and traditions of all sorts, of which nobody knows the origin. Long as this note is, it is to the purpose of the *Philobiblon*, the author's objects being to promote the church of Rome, to increase its love of literature, and diminish its love of wealth. Whether the love of money will not always be the ruling passion of a political church, is a problem not difficult to solve, if experience is worth anything in the solution. As to literature, what church has not corrupted its own and every other branch of knowledge it had the teaching of?

7. Page 53. *Ferrules.*

Omitted in ed. 1599. The worst scholars know best what this means.

8. Page 57. *Reward for wisdom.*

Aristotle says, the judges of intellectual contests should be wiser than those they judge of. If the wisest contended, who could decide? Such contests would be a source of enmity. In bodily contests, men are not indignant against the judges, but they are apt to be angry with anybody that thinks them less wise than themselves.

Qui docet indoctos, licet indoctissimus esset,
Ipse brevi reliquis doctior esse queat.—*Lilly.*

9. Page 59. *Virtue.*

Al. *veritatem.* Not so in Aristotle.

10. Page 63. 72,000 *sesterces.*

Aristotle left his library to Theophrastus, who left his to Neleus; he carried it to Scepsis (Palæscepsis, or Scaptis), where, being placed in the hands of ignorant men, it was shut up and neglected; but it being known that the kings of the Attali, under whom these men lived, were desirous of founding a library at Pergamus, the books were concealed in a cellar under ground (probably for fear of seizure), till they were damaged by moths and damp. They afterwards came into the hands of Apelicon, who gave a large sum of money for the works of Aristotle and Theophrastus: but Apelicon, like many we know in our times, was more fond of books than of learning; and being desirous to have perfect copies, he caused them to be transcribed; but the lost writing not being properly supplied, he edited books full of errors. After the death of Apelicon, Sylla (who took Athens) brought his library to Rome, where Tyrannion the grammarian, a great admirer of Aristotle, ingratiating himself with the librarian, caused them to be reedited; but still less correctly, owing to certain inferior writers being employed, and their copies not being duly collated. If then the Greek copies were corrupted, what is to be thought of the Latin translations, especially the earlier ones? which those who read them labor not so much to know what is said in them, as what ought to be said. Truly, if Aristotle were to revive, he would deny many things attributed to him; but he has fared better than some whose works have perished entirely, though he is partly the cause that many have perished, having drawn the glory of others to himself. Ruet etiam ipse quamvis magnus.—*Pius II.*

11. Page 67. *Babbling accents.*

Pius II says: It may be asked why, amongst all the barbarous nations that came to the assistance of Priam, Homer calls the Carians alone barbarous of speech. Strabo thought, from the name being first conferred on them, that those who spoke with difficulty, harshly, or in an uncultivated manner, were called barbarians, such as we call *blæsos* and *balbos*, lispers and stammerers, for we (Romans) also are ingenious in contriving names akin to things. All those, therefore, who spoke confusedly were called barbarians; such were all nations except the Greeks; the name, by misuse, came to signify all other nations. The apostle Paul calls all people barbarians who do not understand each other's language: "If I "know not the meaning of the voice (is this a barbarous trans- "lation?) I shall be unto him that speaketh a barbarian, and "he that speaketh shall be a barbarian unto me," 1 *Cor.* xiv, 11. This does not prove that the world is not older than Homer: its origin may be the *ba, ba,* of children; and that appears to be the meaning of it here. May it not have represented the *burr,* or imperfect guttural pronunciation of the letter R, common in the North of England, in France, and perhaps elsewhere?

12. Page 67. *Four wings.*

See note 13, pp. 66, 68.

13. Page 69. *Lost, or rejected.*

That is, the Trinity was overlooked; for John was not asked to explain what his witnesses bore witness to, and it would have been entirely lost but for the controversies of the clergy. This is true; but the controversy began about words, and ended in the discovery of a trinity, and an accumulation of blunders about it, from which the church could not extricate itself. The *Athanasian Creed* was intended by the church to make an end of the question, by forcing its blunders on the people with all their inconsistencies, upon pain of damnation: it never thought the people worth throwing away an argument upon. A similar controversy took place about the immaculate conception of the Virgin Mary: the church refused to decide it. The controversy about the proper time for keeping Easter lasted 1200 years: the church had the worst of it; their opponents were the Jews. The day was at last fixed at a wrong time, for the sake of convenience. It was this dispute that finally brought about the change of style, by detecting the error in the common era, which was first done at Rome, though not perfectly. The merit of it belongs to Paul (a Jew) of Middelburg, not of Burgos. It has been attributed to somebody else.

14. Page 69. *People of the acquisition.*

This word, used in the Rhemish *New Testament*, was objected to by Fulke, as unintelligible to the vulgar reader; if it is a good word, that is a bad reason: it is certainly not synonymous with *peculiar*, nor does peculiar mean *purchased*. See 1 *Peter*, ii, 9, and the margin. If *peculiar* is not in the original text, what right had our translators to put it there! Were the Christians intended to be a universal or a peculiar people?

15. Page 69. *Placed behind.*

See note *b*, p. 68.

16. Page 69. *After the order of Melchisedech.*

It was the anonymous author of the *Epistle to the Hebrews* who first applied this to Jesus, taking it from the 110th Psalm. The councils of the church found something in this epistle that suited their purpose, and therefore put it into the *Canon*, and endeavored to pass it off as a production of Paul. But to say nothing of other evidence, Paul knew better than to address a letter to the Hebrews, who are never once mentioned in any other book in the *New Testament;* and for a very good reason, namely, there had been no people who went by that name for 500 years before this writer's time. Josephus says they were called Jews after the return from Babylon, 461 B. C.; and so he and every body else who knew any thing about them called them from that time. The probability is, the church wished to preserve some of the doctrines of the epistle; but having no partiality for the writer or those he wrote to (perhaps the Ebionites or some other sect), altered the address, and concealed the name of the author. What occasion had this author, in applying the words of the psalm to Jesus, to repeat them six times over, and to lay such a stress upon tithes? See chap. vii, 2, &c. But the 8th verse has been enforced by the church of England, "he *receiveth them* of whom "it is witnessed that he liveth," the italics denoting an interpolation. Is this true or false of Jesus, or who is it spoken of? "Levi paid tithes in Abraham, for he was yet in the loins of "his father when Melchisedech met him." It has been argued whether a child could be baptized in the womb; but nobody else ever thought of taxing a man in his father's loins, though "the child that is yet unborn" has been taxed by those who neither thought of nor cared for the consequences. The importance of Melchisedech to the church is, that he was a king, a priest, and a tithe-collector. It is for the churches that sanction this application of the text to Jesus to give satisfaction upon that head. The author before us applies it also to priests and tithe-collectors; so far, well: but what makes priests kings? They are kings when kings are weak enough to be ruled by them, and to believe they strengthen their political government by an alliance with them—blind enough not to see when they are undermining their thrones by oppressing and irritating their subjects, and that all their acts of legislation are for their own benefit—church and state being a partnership in which the principal of the firm receives all the profit, the junior stands all the loss, and no little risk of going into the gazette solus. It is a partnership between man and wife, with a settlement on the wife: this has been verified to the letter in Spain; but there may be cases where the wife would not even contribute to the personal support of her husband if he had the misfortune to stand in need of it, and still less to discharge the debts of the firm. Let us suppose a church and state to enter into a war for the sake of religion and morality. Who were most likely to have advised such a war? Who pays for it? Who profits by it—not only by the rise in the value of its possessions, tithes, &c., &c., but actually demands increase of salaries on account of the increased expense of living? The war ends in something like bankruptcy, or in the impoverishment of the people; does the church lower its increased rates, or give up any thing? Has it not even in a calamitous peace in some instances raised its demands, sought out an old act of parliament to make 2*s* 9*d* the tithe of 20*s*, and raised the tax on a parish from £250 a year to £2500. Now, if a parish can afford to pay £2000 a year more than it formerly paid, why not pay it to the impoverished state, and not to a pampered individual, perhaps the holder of two livings, and a magistrate, in a place connected with neither—a man who studies the value of brick and mortar, watches every nail that is driven in his parish, and tithes every paltry improvement to the last farthing! As to tithes, it is an absurdity to say they cannot be abolished without injury to anybody; and a greater to leave the commutation of them to the church, which will only contrive something that will ultimately turn to its own advantage. This was the case with the act above alluded to; it was meant to fix the tithe upon the rent of the day, never to be raised; it was purposely not enrolled, and probably falsified; for the ministers of state at the time were churchmen. Does any church care whether it is held in respect or not, while it can tax even those who are disgusted with its abuses and leave it on that account? Is it likely to recall them by erecting new buildings at their expense, taxing them at the door for entering them; not even exempting children at school from an enormous charge, and publicly avowing pecuniary advantage to be all its object, by setting up a shop-board in front of them, with "Orders taken in here?" Verily the handwriting is already on the wall!

17. Page 77. *25th Eccles.*

It has been said that if lions were painters there would be more pictures of lions killing men than of men killing them. Women have written less than men, upon a subject they could certainly have given another turn to. It is no proof of the boasted superiority of man, and still less of the superior learning and sanctity of the clergy, that they have not entered into a controversy upon it. But why has a clergy sworn to celibacy and chastity, shown itself to have known more of the secrets of women, and of the worst class of them, than all other writers? Or where did it get the knowledge but by illicit intercourse, which it appears rather to have gloried in than endeavored to conceal. A book, called *De Remedio Amoris*, written by one Andreas, chaplain to Pope Innocent IV, 1243-53, contains all that can be said in abuse of women, and more than anybody else ever thought of. It is in the catalogue of manuscripts appended to the Oxford edition of this work; but the editor does not say whether these were the bishop's books. It is also in print; but I only know of one copy, very old, without date.

18. Page 83. *Every artificer, &c.*

"The height of prudence," *Ecclus.* xxxviii, 25, &c. "How "can he get wisdom that holdeth the plough?" The monks read, for wisdom, &c., money, and holdeth not. The church makes others hold the plough for them.

19. Page 91. *Offscourings of the world.*

Peripsema, an elegant Greek word, for the preservation of which we are indebted to Paul, whose vocabulary in this way is copious. See 1 *Tim.*, i, 10; *Ephes.* v, 5; 1 *Cor.*, vi, 9, &c., where "*some of* you," is a mistranslation. Jerome introduced *peripsima* into Latin; Erasmus follows his orthography; Trithemius corrects it. His works, *De Statu et Ruina Monas-*

tici Ordinis; De Triplici Regione Claustralium, &c., are worth consulting: his editor calls them not less useful than pleasant and necessary. It was found necessary to remind the monks of the twelve degrees of humility; but twelve verses upon that subject being found too much for their memories, they were reduced to four:

"Cerne deum: nec velle tuum fac: te regat alter.
Dura feras: nil corde tegas: sed in infima queras.
Esto peripsema: solivagus non: obstrue linguam.
Risus parcus: sermo gravis: gestus humiles sint."

The humility of a monk was chiefly required towards his superiors; it consisted in the most passive obedience, and rigid observance of rules. It was part of Augustine's rule, that no monk should go out of his convent alone; "two or more," that their conduct might always be under watch.

20. Page 91. *In suffering.*

Si penuriam patientes, animas vestras scitis in patientia possidere. The real meaning of this passage is, perhaps: If you know how to retain self-possession. It alludes to what may be a garbled quotation, in *Luke* xxi, 16 to 19, where the context is: "Ye shall be betrayed—put to death—but there "shall not a hair of your head perish." Upon which our translators add, "In your patience possess ye your souls." Here it has been asked what the vulgar understand by *patience:* some indeed, not of the vulgarest, can make nothing of this translation. Jerome reads, "In your suffering you "shall possess." "Viriliter feras quod necesse est, dolor pa-"tientia vincitur," says a school book called *Seneca's Moral Sentences*. To such works the knowledge of our translators was confined.

21. Page 93. *Lenity.*

The old edition *levitatis*. From this and other similar errors, it is inferred, that as no pains were taken to correct errors, none were taken to alter the text, and that it is therefore upon the whole more genuine than the Oxford edition. The edition 1473 was printed 129 years after the work was written, and the manuscript was probably of much earlier date. See note *a*, page 80.

22. Page 93. *The order of preachers.*

Dominic was the founder of the order of Preachers, but rather at an unfortunate time; for the 4th Lateran council had just prohibited the erection of any new religious order, which he was not aware of till after he had matured his, and associated himself with sixteen others for the purpose of carrying it into effect: this was in 1215. The pope died soon after, and his successor, Honorius III, is pretended to have confirmed the order in 1216. But the constitutions of the order, revised and published in 1515, are satisfied with something short of a positive assertion on that head, hinting at but concealing the truth. Butler, much against his will, alludes to a verbal confirmation. The fact is, Innocent III, the predecessor of Honorius, was well inclined towards Dominic, but could not break the order so recently established; he had, however, a correspondence with him, and while on a journey, in which he died at Perugia, he ordered his secretary to write a letter according to his dictation. The secretary being ready to begin, his holiness said, "Write to Friar Dominic and the Preaching "Friars"—here he made a long pause, being unwell and not able to collect his ideas. The secretary in the mean time wrote the superscription. The pope at last recovering himself began again, repeating the last words to keep up the connection: but not exactly recollecting them, he said, "and the "Friars Preachers." The secretary, who was in Dominic's interest, and had his wits about him, saw that this was a good title; he therefore took a fresh paper, and began again: the letter was finished and properly signed, and Dominic and his associates did not fail to take advantage of it. Honorius appointed Dominic master of the sacred palace, with liberty to serve by deputy. Either owing to the interference of one of these deputies, or because Innocent had done so before him, Honorius continued to call the friars *Prædicatores*—confirming the name, but not the order. When Dominic was canonized in 1234, the pope (Gregory IX) desired the notary to put the word *Prædicantes* into the act of canonization, but he wrote *Prædicatores;* and when called to account for it, maintained that *Prædicantes* was ungrammatical in the place in question, as it had an adjective signification, applicable only to persons in the act of preaching; while the bull meant to commend the saint for having founded an order of preachers. The word was therefore allowed to remain, and the order was considered as confirmed by the bull. Dominic originally observed the rule of Augustine, and it was always prefixed to his own; hence the double rule, and the reference to Augustine. There were other friars appointed to preach against the heresies of the times, but they were not preachers by profession; and moreover, there were some who associated the idea of prophet with the word prædicator. See p. 91, where "divinely sub-

"stituted" applies to the Preachers. The order was founded to oppose the Albigenses and other heretics. The church was better pleased to occupy the people with its ceremonies than with preaching, which had nearly got into disuse. Luxury and ease were the objects of the clergy, and if heresy could have been overcome by force, doctrine might have gone to sleep: the bishop, indeed, proves that it was sufficiently neglected. That there was a great scarcity of preachers long after this time is certain. The archbishop of St. Andrew's in Scotland published a catechism in 1552, in which he says: "And to be short and plain with all you that are spiritual "curates under us, our whole intention (as we take God to "witness) is to help as much as lies in us the Christian people "your parishioners out of blind and dangerous ignorance, and "to bring them to the knowledge of things that belong to their "salvation. And therefore every Sunday and principal holi-"day, when there comes no preacher (or traveling monk) to "them, to show them the word of God, this catechism may be "used and read to them instead of preaching, till God of his "goodness provide a sufficient number of catholic and able "preachers, which shall be within few years, as we trust in "God, to whom be honor and glory for ever. Amen."

It would appear that these Roman Catholic preachers were yet to be taught, though John Knox was at the church door. In 1538 Dean Thomas Forrest, vicar of Dolour, was called before the bishop of Dunkeld, for preaching every Sunday on the epistles and gospels of the day, and desired to forbear, as it brought him under suspicion of heresy; but if he could find a good gospel or epistle that made for the liberty of holy church, he might preach that. The dean said, he had read the *Old* and *New Testament*, and had never found a bad gospel or epistle in either. The bishop said, Thank God, I have lived well these many years, and never knew of the said testaments; and if you, Dean Thomas, leave not these fantasies, you will repent when you cannot mend it. The dean neglected the warning, and was burnt. The bishop's notion of a gospel, &c., seems to have been derived from the portions selected for church service.

23. Page 93. *Study of holy writ.*

Some objected, though improperly, to the Preachers and Minors, because they did no manual labor. Those who labored became cultivators of land, and not of religion. See note 18.

24. Page 93. *Certain tracts.*

The lives of Christ, the virgin, and of the saints, as written by the Roman Catholics, are taken from the tracts here alluded to. Some of them are very ancient, and some bear marks of being altered from legends even older than Christianity; for there were monks in all ages, especially in the east, whose acts were sufficiently remarkable to deserve a record. Even in the lives of the primitive fathers there are some extraordinary allusions: "This new sect of philosophy "(the Christian) which we profess, heretofore flourished "amongst the barbarians. Afterwards, under the reign of "Augustus (who died in the 13th year of Jesus), it spread it-"self over the provinces of your (the Roman) empire." The writer was Melito, bishop of Sardis about the year 170. The Nazarites could have been nothing but monks (see *Num.* vi.). In *Matth.* ii, 23, read Nazarite, for so the prophet spoke. The quotation is from *Judges* xiii, 5 and 7.

25. Page 103. *Permanent form.*

Ylen endelecheia—entelecheia would be perfect. These words were introduced into Latin by the old translators. "*Hyle. es. en.*—primordial matter—something between some-"thing and nothing, between substance and no substance, in-"corporeal body, the receptacle of forms." Calcidius on Plato says, seeing darkness we see nothing, and hearing nothing we hear silence; so by understanding nothing (or what it means) we understand *hyle.* Augustine says: I conceive something shapeless before I can understand what nothing is. The wise men of Gotham found a lobster on Salisbury plain; after due consultation about what it might be, they came to the conclusion that it was something, or something else. Hermolaus Barbarus could not discover what Aristotle meant by *entelecheia,* without consulting the devil. Perhaps he was not aware of two words having different derivations and meanings, for there seems to be some uncertainty whether both were formerly used. *Entelecheia,* or the intellect of matter, may apply to the earth as a whole, the mass remaining the same in quantity, though its parts undergo change, having their origin, perfection and decay. But their perfection has not *endelecheia,* for they are not permanent in any state: in this way *entelecheia* is applicable also to perishable animate nature. Amongst the various and often improper attributes men think proper to give to the great first cause of all (for they multiply them in the ratio of their own ignorance) *endelecheia* is perhaps one of the least objectionable, if it means intellect itself, without qualification; that is, the perfect (range of) idea and comprehension, that has so arranged the universe that it can go on for ever as a whole, without the possibility of obstruction or destruction from the changes and convulsions its parts may be liable to: it is also the soul of the whole, for it lives with it, and the whole would not exist without its cause. This, if we can find no better, we may call the attribute of divinity; it is superior to reason, which belongs to inferior nature and not to divinity; for reason is useless where there is no possibility of error, it is a guide where the perfect foreknowledge and intelligence of *endelecheia* is wanting. If there is anything intuitive in man, it may be a slight emanation, an extra portion of soul, given to him to teach him to value and make a good use of his other gifts. After all, there was no occasion for making two words of endelecheia, unless it was for technicality; for permanence and perfection, as they relate to matter, must be subject to the same limited meaning. The Egyptians seem to have considered chaos as a fluid mixture of all substances. Plato's *hyle* was their first form on being separated; they are now called primitive, which may answer well enough for distinction; but how can that be primitive, which is composite?

26. Page 105. *We lament Pythagoras.*

There may be an omission here of what was said of Pythagoras. Orpheus was lacerated by Ciconian women, but there is no authority for any such story of Pythagoras

27. Page 105. *We pity Zeno.*

Nearly the same story is told of Anaxarchus: his name is accidentally omitted in the first edition 1473; but the words "heu jam rursus" show that it must have been in the original text.

28. Page 119. *Never having disdained....preference to any.*

There is a particular reason for these remarks. The great quarrel between the monks and parochial clergy was warmly carried on at this time. In page 93 the Preachers are called coadjutors: as teachers they were so: but they also took the offices of the church upon themselves, received confessions, &c., and were no doubt paid for it. This took the people from the church, many of whom never even received the sacrament in it, though the rule of the church for doing so, and previously confessing at least once a year, to the parochial clergyman, was peremptory. The convent had many attractions for the people; they were educated in it, attended its chapel, and above all made companions of the monks, with whose conversation and stories they were much delighted. Richard Fitz-Ralp, archbishop of Armagh, was the principal mover in this controversy, though Wickliff's name is better known in it, owing to the effect his writings had in Bohemia, and perhaps to his translation of the *Bible*. Fitz-Ralp translated it into Irish, if not into English: it is certain there are two distinct translations of the time, and equally certain that there was an understanding between the translators. This is now known to a learned antiquary, who may perhaps be able to make further discoveries. The partiality shown to the Mendicants, in page 123, is reasonable: the author does not spare the idle part of them in other places. See page 101.

29. Page 121. *The aforesaid paupers.*

Alludes to the Mendicants; as also the "eleventh hour," in page 123. See also note on page 93, "study," &c.

30. Page 129. *Ovid, De Vetula.*

A poem in three books, formerly attributed to Ovid, and printed in some of the early editions of his works. Those who reject this as a monkish performance may be very good critics; but why overlook *Metamorphosis* and *Metempsychosis?* If the soul of Ovid passed into a monk, there let it remain; indeed there never was a soul more likely than his to pass into the body of a monk. The monks were Ovids in everything but poetry. Unluckily there are no English translations of these and some other verses in this work; the translator was therefore obliged to take Mr. Tonson's method, of getting them done by various hands, and after all to take a bit from one and a bit from another. Molière, or somebody else, speaks of a poet who could make a thousand first verses, but not one to rhyme to any of them. Poets who complain of poverty mistake their calling; they should write by the fathom, and leave writing by the foot to those who were born, like Pope, with a tongue in their head of the exact measure.

31. Page 129. *Euclid.*

This story has been doubted. Aulus Gellius does not say he went every night, nor how he traveled; the danger was greater than the labor: 20,000 paces are less than 20 English miles.

32. Page 131. *Perihermenias.*

Περι Ἑρμενειας, *On Interpretation;* a logical treatise which follows that on the *Categories.* "In his heart's blood:" this is a corruption of the eulogy bestowed on Aristotle by a Greek writer, who says "he dipped his pen in intellect."

33. Page 131. *Baneful diploma.*

"Passing through a dangerous abridgement of the regular "course of study, they take out a baneful diploma:" the translation should have been more to this effect.

34. Page 133. *Dark waters.*

1 *Corinthians*, x, 1, 2.

35. Page 133. *Show herself indebted.*

Se debitricem ostendat. Query, show herself to England, replete with the knowledge of all nations. The whole sentence is carelessly written. The Parisian school was spoken of with contempt by many about this time, and more so afterwards. Its doctors excommunicated Thomas Aquinas, who laughed at them for their pains: the sentence remained on record, till after he was a canonized saint in heaven; when somebody happening to notice it, the doctors stupidly reversed it by a public decree, instead of privately cancelling it and concealing their own folly and ignorance.

36. Page 137. *Tegni.*

One of Galen's tracts is so called.

37. Page 137. *Horace.*

The name of Horace is inserted here, though omitted in all the editions.

38. Page 137. *Treatisers.*

Tractatores, of the orthodox faith. "This black-mouthed treatiser," says an old writer. Such are the orthodox in general, for their faith is their own, and they have an evil word for all who do not adopt it. The bishop meant to speak no better of them.

39. Page 139. *Theotoctos.*

According to the doctrine of the Athanasian creed, the virgin is the mother of God: she is expressly called his wife and mother in the *Horæ* for the use of Rome. Bonaventure made a *service* for her, in which not only the *Psalms* but the *Athanasian Creed* is parodied: "Whosoever will be saved, "before all things it is necessary that he must hold a firm "faith in Mary, which unless he shall preserve entire and "unviolated, without doubt he shall perish to all eternity," &c. As Bonaventure was canonized, the church denies that he wrote this; but the proof is extant: it would not have been questioned but for the reformers.

40. Page 147. *Exotic words.*

The bishop's glossary, mentioned in Chap. xii, ought to have been preserved, as well as his amended books.

41. Page 149. *Youth.*

Cheerfulness gives energy to labor, as beauty adds perfection to youth—is Aristotle's meaning.

42. Page 149. *To allure children.*

Ut pueris, olim dant crustula, blandi doctores, elementa velint ut discere prima.

43. Page 151. *Helleflight.*

Ellefuga.—This word was a *pons asinorum* to some good Grecians—but that is probably its meaning; at least making it the name of a problem gets over all difficulty. The allusion is to the flight of Helle, who turned giddy in taking a flying leap, mounted on a ram; and fell into the sea; so a weak head fails in crossing the *pons.* The problem was invented by Pythagoras, "and it hath been called by barbarous writers of the "latter time dulcarnon."—*Billingsley.* This name may have been invented after our author's time. Query, δολκαρηνον.

44. Page 151. *That son of inconstancy.*

There may be others to whom this would apply, but Nigellus is probably the person alluded to. He converts himself into an ass, and takes a fancy that his tail is not long enough; that is, a monk who wished, or whose friends wished him, to be an abbot or bishop, He went to Paris for his education, but he could not learn. He associated with the English, of whom he says:

"Morsibus egregij verbis vultuq; venusti.
"Ingenio pollent, consiloq; vigent.
"Dona pluunt populis et detestantur avaros
"Fercula multiplicant, et sine lege bibunt."

It would not all do. "Cum nihil ex toto quodcunq; (docente "magistro aut socio) potuit discere præter A. B." It is impossible to give an idea of the curious book containing the adventures of this worthy in a note. It was written about the end of the 12th century by an English monk named Wereker—if that is not a mistake for Yorick.

"Et si contigat me pontificalibus uti
"Quo poterit capitis mitra sedere loco."

If it had rained mitres, none of them would have fitted his head.

45. Page 151. *Turbat acumen.*

Desij, p. 163.—A mode of reference very convenient in old books that are not paged, &c.

46. Page 153. *Venerable Bede.*

Bede, is more quoted, and for a greater variety of learning, than any other writer. The name of *Venerable* was given him by common consent. One of the popes was long after asked to canonize him; he said, "he had done it better for himself, "and the church could do him no greater honor."

47. Page 153. *Maro.*

Mr. James puts Varro in the margin. The story may be found in Donatus's preface to Virgil.

48. Page 171. *Moreover—we do not read.*

We have only the authority of John for what the author first alludes to; but *John* vii, 15, allows the Jews to say "Jesus "never learnt letters or learning," without contradiction. In this place learning, and not writing, is the question: the word *wrote*, in *John* viii, 6, should perhaps have been translated, *marked* or *drew*, which it also means. If he wrote, why not tell us what? Translators need not make the apostles contradict themselves. *Mark* vi, 3, does not contradict the Jews, who ask "Is not this the carpenter?" They knew he was. Indeed, if he did not study, how was he employed till he was thirty years old? Many churchmen differ in opinion from the bishop on this subject.

49. Page 99, 171. *Maimed.*

And therefore disqualified by the canonical law.

50. Page 197. *Duly closed.*

There is no better preservation for a large book than a clasp, as it keeps out dust; but if hard substances are put into it they spoil it—a very curious pair of scissors for instance, rusty and adhering to the leaves. Some old volumes are so heavy that they will not keep in shape without clasps. Erasmus says, "As for Thomas Aquinas's *Secunda Secundæ*, "no man can carry it about, much less get it into his head." To add to the weight of such a volume, there are generally five large brass nails on each side, corners of the same, and four pegs to stand on; the title is on one of the sides (outside), written on parchment, with a piece of transparent horn over it, and a frame: some have an iron chain attached to them, perhaps to fasten them to a desk. The anathema, recommended in page 181, is often to be found on the first leaf: "Cursed be he who shall steal or tear out the leaves, or in "any way injure this book."

51. Page 181. *Laymen.*

The Church of Rome always had that sort of dread of books coming into the hands of laymen that marks a guilty conscience. But what is a layman? Albertus Magnus, commenting on *Isaiah* i, 3, "The ox knoweth his owner, and the ass his "master's crib"—says, "The ox is the priest who cultivates "the soil of the hearts of the faithful;—the ass is the layman "that carries the burthen of his master; he carries his pack-"saddle, and carries his master, that food may be set before "him in his manger." Our Author says (in page 97), "Oxen "plough and asses feed by them." *Job* i, 14. Still calling the layman an ass:—it was a standing joke, and is yet so, even out of the Church of Rome. The very name of layman was invented as a mark of contempt, to denote an inferior animal, which the word *people* would not do without an offensive adjective. Every thing that the Roman churchmen do and say is full of contradiction and perversity, because something sinister lurks under their acts and sayings, that even they, the most artful of men, cannot help mixing up with them. It was a bungle to call a priest an ox, for it is written, "The ox shall do no work on the sabbath." Isaiah never meant to say that an ox did not know his master's manger as well as an ass, nor that the ox and the ass did not both work in their way for the same master, but neither solely to feed the other. Albertus Magnus was, in the opinion of some, the greatest man the church ever produced; that is, that he was equal if not superior to Thomas Aquinas in learning; though one of the popes said Aquinas was superior in sanctity, and therefore decreed that his works should be received as the highest authority, next to the gospel. The fact is, Albertus was far superior to Aquinas in secular learning. They may both have been good moral men, but they taught nothing to the people, unless it were their duty to a church that was any thing but Christian; to believe in the church and not in the gospel, which they universally perverted, and consequently found it necessary to withhold from public inspection, though it was intended to be the people's own book, and to be adapted to the understandings of men, women, and children, of all conditions. Our author says, "The clergy ought to teach by "sound doctrine, and by the example of their lives." Of their example generally, John of Salisbury says, "Terret me "Aggeus, parabola mystica sacerdotij periculum exprimens et "manifeste docens, quia populus sacerdotum moribus facilius "vitia contrahit quam virtutes."—*Policrat.* vi, 7,—"because "the people more readily contract vice than virtue from the "manners of the priesthood." So say all the Roman Catholic writers, and so they would have it, because the sins of the people must all be confessed and redeemed by large gifts to the church. So say all sectaries—they alone know the road to salvation—it is through their meeting, which he who would be saved must patronize. A national church would stand clear of such an imputation, if it enforced no incredible or absurd doctrines; if its priests were clean-handed, and as moral as those who are considered good members of society; if they received their salaries from a fund, without being their own collectors; and above all, if their body had no political character, and the individuals composing it, would abstain from forcing themselves into judicial situations. Truly, it is a very suspicious mark of the merciful feelings of a parson, to commit his parishioner and pupil, to prison, to be tried for life or death, who would perhaps not have been a criminal if he had been better instructed; and whom he ought rather, if possible, to save and restore to virtuous habits, that he may not only make his peace with the society he has injured, but thereby more certainly insure his peace with God. "Father, "forgive them, for they know not what they do."

52. Page 181. *Scullion.*

The monks in many monasteries performed all the menial offices—it was a proof of humility. When the pope sent two nuncios to Bonaventure with a cardinal's hat, they found him in a convent, where he was only a visitor, washing dishes.

Quisquis theologus, quisquis legista peritus
Vis fieri ; multos semper habeto Libros
Pristina gestorum quæ condita vulgus haberet
Cum legis in charta, mens tua commemorat
Non in mente manet quicquid nos vidimus ipsi,
Quisque sibi libros vendicet ergo. Vale.

THE END.

APPENDIX.

EXTRACTS FROM ANCIENT RECORDS CONCERNING RICHARD DE BURY.

I. DE RICARDO DE BURY.[1]

RICARDUS de Bury natus fuit in quadam villula prope Edmondis Bury, patre Domino Ricardo Awngeville milite; et a suo avunculo domino Johanne de Willyby rectore exhibitus est primo ad scolas grammaticales, et postea ad studium Oxoniæ, per aliquod certum tempus; deinde assumptus ad instruendum Edwardum de Wyndesor, tunc principem, qui postmodum dictus Edwardus tertius; postmodum ordinatus est principalis receptor patris ejusdem Edwardi in Wasconia. Quo tempore dictus Edwardus fugit cum matre Parisius; quibus expensis deficientibus, venit ipse Ricardus clam cum magna summa auri quam collegit in officio prædicto. Qua de causa insequebatur eum locumtenens Regis cum viginti quatuor lanceis usque Parisius; ubi, præ metu mortis, ab-
Post hæc ordinatus est Coferarius Regis, deinde Thesaurarius
sconditus est in campanili Fratrum Minorum per septem dies.
de wardrop, postea clericus privati sigilli, per quinque annos. Quo tempore bis adiit summum Pontificem Johannem. Et primo tempore, quo sibi advenit, ordinatus est ad ipso Capellanus principalis capellæ suæ; et recepit ab eo rochetam in loco bullæ, pro proximo episcopatu vacante ex post in Anglia. Et eo tempore promotus est de beneficiis ecclesiasticis; [ad] quod potuit expendere ad valorem quinque millia marcarum.

1 This chapter commences the Chronicle of William de Chambre, inserted at the end of the Chronicle of Robert de Graystanes. See *Publications of the Surtees Society*, Lond., 1839, p. 127 et seq.—*Cocheris.*

Et secundo tempore quo [prædictum] summum Pontificem adiit, adeptus est ab eo trescentas gratias [et septem] pro clericis promovendis. Et omni tempore quo venit ad præsentiam summi Pontificis sive Cardinalium, venit ipse cum viginti clericis suis in vestibus unius sectæ, et triginta sex armigeris alterius sectæ. Post hæc, cum rediret Angliam, audiens Parisius de morte Lodowici, episcopi Dunelmensis, et regem misisse literas ad summum Pontificem pro ipso episcopatu sibi adquirendo, multum dolebat. Insuper cum quidam clericus ipsius, nomine Willielmus de Tykall, rector de Stanhop, instigaret eum mittere literas ad Cardinales et ad alios amicos suos in Curia, pro prædicto episcopatu habendo, respondit se nec pro illo episcopatu nec pro aliquo alio literas missurum. Dominica ante Natale, xlvi ætatis suæ anno, consecratus est episcopus Dunelmensis ab archiepiscopo Cantuariensi, Johanne Stretford, in abbathia Nigrorum Monachorum de Cherdsay. In qua consecratione episcopus Lincolniæ, Henricus Burwesch, fundebat omnes expensas, jussu domini Regis. Post hæc, factus est thesaurarius Angliæ ; et eodem anno [quinto die Junii, per Willelmum Cowton, priorem Dunelmensem] est installatus. In qua installatione fecit grande convivium ; ubi interfuerunt Rex et Regina Angliæ, mater regis Angliæ, Rex Scotiæ, duo archiepiscopi et quinque episcopi, septem comites cum uxoribus suis, et omnes magnates citra Trentam, multi milites et armigeri, plures etiam abbates et priores et viri religiosi, cum innumera multitudine communitatis. Eodem anno institutus est Cancellarius Angliæ. Et infra triennium ex post ter adiit Regem Franciæ, Parisius, in nuncio regis Angliæ, ad vendicandum regnum Franciæ. Postea adiit Handewarpe, et alia vice ad Braban ; et ita fatigatus fuit per diversa loca pro prædicta legatione novem annis. Et medio tempore fuerunt omnes libertates Dunelmensis ecclesiæ conservatæ sine aliquo detrimento. Post hæc Angliam rediit.

Multum [enim] delectabatur de [comitiva] clericorum; et plures semper clericos habuit in sua familia. De quibus fuit Thomas Bradwardyn, postea Cantuariensis archiepiscopus, et Ricardus Fyzt Rauf, postmodum archiepiscopus Armachanæ, Walterus Burley, Johannes Maudit, Robertus Holcot, Ricardus de Kylwyngton, omnes doctores in theologia; Ricardus Benworth, postea episcopus Londoniensis, et Walterus Segraffe, postea episcopus Cicestrensis. Et quolibet die in mensa solitus erat habere lectionem nisi forte per adventum magnatum impediretur ; et post prandium singulis diebus disputationem cum clericis prænominatis, et aliis suæ domus, nisi major causa impediret. Et, aliis vicibus, aut servitio divino aut libris vacabat: nisi foret ex causis arduis impeditus. Omni etiam septimana distribuit in cibos pauperum octo quartaria frumenti pista, præter fragmenta solita domus suæ. Et, si plures supervenirent, post distributionem dictæ eleemosinæ, contulit singulo obolum. Præter hæc, veniens aut rediens à Novo Castro usque Dunelmum, aliquando duodecim marcas contulit in eleemosynis, etiam à Dunelmo usque Stokton quandoque viii marcas, et à Dunelmo usque Aukland v marcas à Dunelmo usque Middellam c solidos. Post ejus obitum inventa fuit una de suis capsellis plena lintheaminibus, camisiis et braccis cilicinis, in qua putabatur thesaurum inveniri.

Præterea præfatus dominus Ricardus, in floribus vitæ suæ, contulit duo vestimenta ecclesiæ, unum rubeum de velveto, cum tribus capis ejusdem sectæ, subtiliter broudatis, et aliud de nigra camica, cum tribus capis ejusdem sectæ, cum largis orariis decenter ornatis: plura proponens ecclesiæ reliquisse, videlicet unum de rubeo velveto, quod sui executores vendiderunt domino Radulpho de Neville, qui postea, conscientia motus, illud reddidit ecclesiæ;[2] aliud etiam dedit, de alba camica, cum tribus capis ejusdem sectæ, quod fecit in honore sanctæ Mariæ, nobiliter broudatum, quod sacrista, post ejus mortem, de ejusdem executoribus cum multa difficultate conquisivit.[3] Item, in exequiis ejus, sicut patet per instrumentum publicum inde factum, habuit sacrista duos equos magnos portantes corpus ejus in lectica, et unum equum mulum portantem capellam.[4] Habuit etiam idem sacrista duas cistulas, unum baculum pastoralem, unam mitram, annulum et sandalia, duo candelabra argentea, unum thuribulum argenteum et deauratum, cum una navicula, item ix bawdkyns de panno serico rubeo cum vitibus [et literis] intextis, item ix pannos sericos cum quadrupedibus habentibus pedes et capita deauratos, item unum pannum viridem cum gallis albis et rubeis intextum. Ex quibus omnibus facta sunt vestimenta ad magnum altare et alia altaria in ecclesia. Item ex quatuor si-

2 This garment of red velvet was given to the church by Raoul de Nevill, in 1355. See the following passage from the Chronicle of William de Chambre, relative to that gift. Nevill was the first layman interred in the church of Durham —*Cocheris.*

"Anno domini MCCCLV dominus Radulphus de Nevill, qui primus fuit sæcularis, exceptis episcopis, qui in ecclesia Dunelmensi habuit sepulturam, dedit sancto Cuthberto et ecclesiæ unum vestimentum de rubeo velveto, [auro et serico et magnis parlis cum imaginibus sanctorum in tabernaculis stantibus ditissime brudatis; viz. unam casulam cum duabus tunicis, et una capa, et duobus pannis pro altari, et una alba, et una stola, et manipula, quod habuit in cautione ab executoribus domini Ricardi Burye, episcopi Dunelmiæ, pro centum libris argenti; et quod idem episcopus pro magno altari illud ordinavit; ille, post mortem ejusdem episcopi eidem altari et ecclesiæ illud libere condonavit."]—*Hist. Dunelm. script.*, p. 134.

3 See No. XIV of this appendix.

4 See appendix, No. XIII.

gillis ejusdem factus est unus calix deauratus; ut patet per hos versus sub pede ipsius inscriptos:

RI. DVNELMENSIS, QUARTI, NATV BVRIENSIS.
HIC CIPHVS INSIGNIS FIT PRÆSVLIS EX TETRA SIGILLIS.[5]

Item, dum, quadam die, sederet ad mensam, apud Eboracum, cum vii comitibus, subito superveniens dominus Johannes Wawham, nunciavit sibi dominum Robertum de Graystanes fore defunctum; qui tantum de ejus morte condoluit, quod præsentiam nunciantis ferre non potuit. Quem cum comites interrogarent, quare tantum doleret de morte ejus, "Certe" inquit, "si tam bene novissetis industriam ejus, quantum ego "novi, credo quod tantum quam ego doleo, doleretis." Et addidit "fuit enim habilior ad papatum, quam ego vel omnes "mei consimiles ad dignitatem minimam in ecclesia sancta "Dei." Multum etiam affectabat retinere secum in familia filios generosorum episcopatus sui. Quod factum nutrivit magnam amicitiam inter ipsum et ipsius patriæ generosos; et monachos Dunelmensis ecclesiæ semper habuit in maximo honore.

Item Ricardus de Bury fuit sufficientis literaturæ, in regendo familiam discretus, in convivando extraneos dapsilis, in erogando eleemosinam sollicitus. Iste, audito quod displicuit, fuit faciliter provocatus, sed facillime revocatus. Iste summe delectabatur in multitudine librorum. Plures enim libros habuit, sicut passim dicebatur, quam omnes pontifices Angliæ. Et, præter eos, quos habuit in diversis maneriis suis, repositos separatim, ubicunque cum sua familia residebat, tot libri jacebant [sparsim] in camera qua dormivit, quod ingredientes vix stare poterant vel incedere, nisi librum aliquem pedibus conculcarent. Iste ornamenta ecclesiastica quamplurimum pulchra et decentia contulit ecclesiæ Dunelmensi; plura proponens, si vixisset diutius, contulisse. Cum, igitur, episcopatum Dunelmensem, quem habuit ex provisione apostolica, rexisset in tranquillitate competenti, cæteris partibus Angliæ contribu-

5 In an act of February, 1496, in which the chancellor of the church of Durham acknowledges the receipt of the silver seals of John Sherewood, bishop deceased, is cited apropos of the use that should be made of them, the inscription placed upon the foot of the chalice of Richard de Bury; as it does not exactly conform to that given by the chronicler, we reproduce it here:

"Et pro certa et veridica attestacione deliberacionum sigillorum episcorum primitus habitorum hujusmodi versus insculpti sunt in pede unius calicis compositi ex sigillis Ricardi de Bery, quandam Dunelmensis episcopi, sub tenore qui sequitur:

Ri. Dvnelmensis qvarti natv beriensis."
Hic calix insignis fit præsvlis ex tetra signis

According to a marginal note written upon the same act, we observe that the chalice was used at the altar of Thomas Hatfeld, and that it had disappeared sixteen years before, that is in 1480. (See *Hist. Dunelm. scrip. tres*, app., p. CCCLXXXVIII.) The seals which he made use of are given in fac simile in the first volume of the *History of Durham*, by Surtees, Lond., 1816, folio.—*Cocheris.*

tionibus et angariis multipliciter fatigatis, per xi annos, duos menses, et xii dies; in anno duodecimo, longa infirmitate decoctus, apud Aukland diem clausit extremum, xiv die Aprilis, anno Domini MCCXL quinto, qui xxi die ejusdem mensis fuit, quodammodo honorificè, non tamen cum honore satis congruo, coram altari beatæ Mariæ Magdalenæ ad australem angulum Dunelmensis ecclesiæ tumulatus.[6]

II. DE ELECTIONE FRATRIS DOMINI ROBERTI DE GRAYSTANES.[7]

PETITA a domino Rege eligendi licentia et obtenta, vocatisque fratribus in cellis, et infra, Idus Octobris, Die ad hoc statuto, per compromissarios electus est dominus Robertus de Graystanes, supprior domus et doctor theologicus, in episcopum Dunelmensis ecclesiæ et pastorem. Nomina vero compromissariorum hæc erant; Galfridus de Burdon, quondam prior Dunelmensis, tunc vero pro provisione habens cellam de Wermuth (cum decimis ejusdem villæ, et de Fulwell), Willielmus de Dunelmo sacrista, Johannes de Seton prius et post supprior Dunelmensis; Gilbertus de Ellewyk, prior insulæ sacræ paginæque professor; Emericus de Lumley, prior de Lythum; Thomas de Lund, prior de Fincale, doctor theologicus; Johannes Fossour, prior Sancti Leonardi justa Stanford; Alexander de Lamesley, magister de Jarow; Petrus de Hilton, Feretrarius, Walterus de Scaresbek hostillarius; Johannes de Beverlaco, prior Oxoniæ et bacularius theologicus; Willielmus de Dalton, et ipse electus tertius decimus. Publicata electione et ab omnibus approbata, ipse electus in itinere versus regem obtinuit literas proclamatorias ab archiepiscopo Eboracensi et diem pro confirmatione habenda, v idus Novembris. Rex vero, inventus apud Lugo tersale, penultimo die

6 In chap. iii of the same chronicle, entitled *Of Thomas Hatfeld, Bishop of Durham*, William de Chambre thus recurs to the death of Richard de Bury:

"Anno Domini MCCCXLIIIII (1345) xiii die Aprilis, obiit Ricardus de Bury, episcopus Dunelmensis, apud Auklande, et xxi die mensis ejusdem in ecclesia Dunelmensi coram altari B. Mariæ Virginis (*sic*) Magdalenæ, in australi angulo ejusdem ecclesiæ, est sepultus."

His burial is thus described in a document of the end of the sixteenth century, printed by the Surtees Society, under the title *Description of all the ancient monuments, rites, and customs belonging or being within the monastical church of Durham, before the suppression. Written in* 1593.

"Richard de Bury, Bishopp of Durham, lyeth buried before this altar under a faire marble stone, whereon his owne ymage was most curiously and artificially ingraven in brass, with the pictures of the twelve apostles decided imbordered [devided and bordered] of either side of him, and other fine imagery worke about it, much adorninge the marble stone."—*Cocheris.*

7 What follows is taken from the Chronicle of Graystanes, edited by the care of the Surtees Society, with the Chronicle of William de Chambre. See *Hist. Dunelm. scriptores tres*, p. 120 et seq.—*Cocheris.*

octobris, tale responsum dedit. "*Intelleximus quod dominus* "*papa de illo episcopatu providit domino Ricardo de Bury familiari* "*clerico nostro; nec ipsum Papam offendere volumus: ideo electioni* "*tuæ consentire nequimus.*" Dominus enim rex pro præfato clerico non solum Papæ sed etiam Priori et Capitulo scripserat, ipsos rogando ut eum eligerent, ipsum ut episcopatum reservando ei conferret. Rediit ergo electus Eboracum; et non obstante quod non intervenisset consensus regius, deliberatione habita cum canonicis ecclesiæ Eboracensis et utriusque juris peritis, consentientibus etiam priore et conventu Dunelmensi, quarto Idus Novembris in ecclesia beatæ Mariæ Eboraci est confirmatus, et dominica proxima sequente, scilicet xviii kl. Decembris, per venerabiles patres Eboracensem, Karleolensem, Armanachanum, in capella Archiepiscopi in palatio consecratus; et die Jovis proxima subsequente, in octavis scilicet sancti Martini, Dunelmi installatus. Acceptaque obedientia a subditis, et vicario generali ibi dimisso, iter arripuit episcopus versus regem, temporalia petiturus. Sed rex cum eo loqui noluit, sed per thesaurarium suum respondit; quod invisum erat ante illud tempus, quod aliquis in Anglia absque consensu regio in episcopum consecraretur vel electus confirmaretur; et ideo super tam arduo et inaudito noluit rex inconsulte respondere; et ad proximum parliamentum distulit respondendum. Interim tamen domino Ricardo de Byry, cui ad rogatum regis, Papa episcopatum contulerat, uno die ante electionem de ipso Roberto factam, scilicet pridie Idus Octobris, Rex temporalia episcopatus Dunelmensis dederat; ex hoc delationem ad parliamentum non nisi in sui illusionem factam episcopus advertebat.

DE RICARDO DE BURY.

Venerunt ergo clerici domini Ricardi de Bury Dunelmum cum Bullis et literis regiis; et in possessionem temporalium statim inducitur. Archiepiscopus vero Eboracensis, visis bullis, et intellectis comminationibus regiis, de temporalibus suis in manu regis capiendis, inductus per regales, clero et populo Dunelmensi scripsit, ut Ricardo de Bury obedirent, non obstantibus prioribus literis eis pro Roberto episcopo destinatis. Unde et iv Idus Januarii clerus et populous Dunelmensis dioceseos Ricardo de Bury obedientiam juraverunt. Et sic Robertum episcopum, non vocatum, non monitum nec contumacem, spoliarunt; cum tamen jus commune habuisset pro eo, et contra impetrationem Ricardi et provisionem, legitimas defensiones debuit habuisse. Et cum satis haberet quod contra provisionem Ricardi objiceret; condescendens tamen statui domus et prioris, qui propter guerram et casus varios depauperati sustinere non potuerunt onera litis, maxime contra regem, habentem Papam ita sibi propitium, et contra Ricardum, qui jam eis præerat in temporalibus et spiritualibus; et etiam quia contra quemcunque objicere est vile et odiosum: elegit potius dissimulando voluntatem Dei cum patientia expectare, quam finam litis, quæ dubios solet habere exitus, quærere per objectus; maxime cum sanctum Cuthbertum et plerosque alios [sanctos] episcopos legimus renunciasse episcopatibus pacifice jam possessis; sed paucos vel nullos sanctos circa episcopatus per objectus legimus litigasse. Color pro Roberto fuite iste. Papa episcopatum Dunelmensem unica vice et non semper suæ dispositioni reservavit, et de eodem disposuit ante electionem Roberti, quia per unum diem ante, ut patet ex dictis. Cum igitur disponere sit verbum facti et non juris; per provisionem factam Ricardo expiravit reservatio quæ præcessit. Non enim stant simul, quod Papa disposuit, et quod reservatio facta suæ dispositioni adhuc in suo robore mansit. Posset enim tunc papa de eodem episcopatu iterato disponere, virtute reservationis prædictæ. Tempore ergo electionis Roberti nulla reservatio fuit, ergo electioni suæ nihil obstitit nisi provisio facta domini Ricardo. Si ergo illa posset infici per objectus; foret jus Roberti clarum. Item ita clarum jus habet capitulum ad eligendum, sicut aliquis clericus ad quodcunque beneficium, quia collatum sibi a rege et per multos Papas confirmatum. Quare igitur potest magis auferre ab eis electionem suam, sibi a Regibus concessam et per Papas confirmatam, quam alteri clerico beneficium sibi a suo episcopo collatum, maxime sine causæ cognitione, et eorum negligentia hoc nullantenus promerente! Item maxime est hoc in præjudicium Regis; quia eadem ratione posset Papa reservare omnes episcopatus Angliæ et eos conferre Cardinalibus vel aliis extra regnum commorantibus; et depauperaretur regnum per abductionem pecuniæ, et periclitaretur propter defectum consilii, quod vigere solet in episcopis regni: vel alienigenis conferre posset, qui in terra remanerent. Et adhuc foret Regi periculum, quod tot extranei occuparent episcopatus in Anglia, castra et alia eis pertinentia, quia insurgerent cum alienigenis contra Regem. Rex etiam juratus est ad magnam cartam; cujus unus articulus est, ut electionis sint liberæ. Multa erant alia, quæ majores regni monebant ad loquendum de ista materia.

III. AD PAPAM, LITERÆ PROPRIA REGIS MANU SCRIPTÆ, PRO RICARDO DE BURY.[8]

A. D. 1330.
An. 4 Edwardi III.

PAPÆ Rex, devota pedum oscula beatorum. Pater desideratissime, ob affectionis intimæ puritatem quâ personam dilecti clerici et secretarii nostri, magistri Ricardi de Bury, amplectimur in visceribus caritatis, fructuosa obsequia quæ nobis, à pueritia nostra, impendit multipliciter laboribus indefessis, et indiès impendere non desistit, nostro assiduè lateri assistendo, nec non ipsius merita probitatis et industriæ magnitudinem contemplando, ipsum vestræ clementiæ nostris literis, conscriptis propria manu nostra, ut cordis nostri desiderium super hoc benignitati vestræ plenius nudaretur, recommendavimus vicibus iteratis.

Et præter hoc, dilectum et fidelem nostrum, Willielmum de Monte Acuto, quem nuper unà cum aliis fidelibus nostris, pro quibusdam nostris negotiis, ad vestræ sanctitatis presentiam destinavimus, oneravimus, ut ipse eundem clericum nostrum commendaret vestræ beatitudini ex parte nostra; cui vestra tunc, ut nobis retulit, sanctitudo respondit, quòd de statu suo disponere volebatis tempore oportuno.

Verum quia ejusdem clerici nostri promotionem, præ cæteris nostris clericis, peroptamus eo quod novimus ipsum virum in consiliis providum, conversationis et vitæ munditia decorum, literarum scientia præditum, et in agendis quibuslibet circumspectum;

Sanctitati vestræ votivis affectibus supplicamus, quatinùs, nostram in eodem clerico nostro, si placet, contemplantes personam, ei præbendas illas, quas magister Gilbertus de Middleton, archidiaconus Northampton, jam defunctus, habuit in ecclesiis cathedralibus Hereford', London', et Cicestr', et quarum provisio ac aliorum beneficiorum quæ idem Gilbertus habuit in diversis partibus regni nostri, dum adhuc viveret, fuit dispositioni vestræ et sedis apostolicæ, ut dicetur, specialiter reservata.

Conferre dignemini de nostræ apostolicæ plenitudine potestatis, literasque vestras apostolicas gratiosas inde jubere fieri, nobisque, per præsentium bajulum, destinari, non obstante quòd idem Ricardus quandam exilem præbendam obtinet in

8 This document is printed in the *Fœdera, Conventiones*, etc., of Rymer, Lond. ed., vol. II, part 2, p. 804.—*Cocheris.*

dicta ecclesia Cicestr', quam paratus erit demittere, juxta juris exigentiam in eventu.

Conservet, etc.

Datum apud Guldeford', xvii die decembris.

IV. BULLA JOHANNIS XXII PAPÆ, DE CENSU UNIUS ANNI ET DIMIDII REGNI ANGLIÆ ET TERRÆ HIBERNIÆ, AB AMBASSIATORE REGIS RECEPTO.[9]

A. D. 1333.
An. 7 Edwardi III.

JOHANNES episcopus, servus servorum Dei, carissimo in Christo filio, Edwardo, Regi Angliæ illustri, salutem et apostolicam benedictionem.

Cum censum annuum mille marcharum Sterlingorum argenti, pro regno Angliæ, ac terris tuis Iberniæ, nobis et ecclesiæ Romanæ solvere annis singulis tenearis;

Censumque hujusmodi videlicet;

Mille marchas sterlingorum argenti pro uno anno, terminato in festo apparitionis beati Michaelis, de anno Domini millesimo trecentesimo tricesimo.

Nec non et ulterius, de eodem censu, pro termino sexti Resurrectionnis Dominicæ, de anno Domini millesimo trecentesimo tricesimo primo, quingentas marchos sterlingorum argenti.

Per manus dilecti filii, magistri Richardi de Bury, decani ecclesiæ Wellensis, capellani nostri, tuique ambassiatoris et nuncii, in sex millibus florenorum auri, singulis marchis pro quatuor florenis auri computatis, die datæ præsentium, nostræ cameræ persolvi feceris, ac etiam assignari;

Nos, tuis in hac parte volentes indempnitatibus præcavere, solutionem et assignationem hujusmodi ratam et gratam, habentes;

Te, fili carissime, ac regnum et terras tua prædicta de dictis mille et quingentis marchis sterlingorum, in dictis sex millibus florenorum auri, sicut et prout exprimitur superiùs, solutis et assignatis, absolvimus imperpetuùm et quitamùs.

Datum Avinione, iii nonas julii, pontificatus nostri anno decimo septimo. *Sub filis canabeis.*

9 See *Fœdera*, etc., ibid., p. 864.

V. DE MAGNO SIGILLO LIBERATO.[10]

A. D. 1334.
An. 8 Edwardi III.

MEMORANDUM quod venerabilis pater J. Cantuariensis archiepiscopus tocius Angliæ primas, cancellarius domini Regis, vicesimo octavo die Septembris, anno Regni dicti regis octavo, horâ vesperarum, in camera ipsius Regis in palacio suo apud Westm', liberavit magnum sigillum suum, in quadam bursa sigillo ipsius archiepiscopi consignata, in præsencia venerabilis patris H. Lincoln' episcopi, thesaurarii ipsius regis, Johannis comitis Cornub', Ricardi comitis Arundell', magister [sic] Roberti de Stretford archidiaconi Cantuar', domini Roberti de Taunton, et aliarum tunc ibidem existentium;

Et idem dominus Rex sigillum illud a præfato archiepiscopo recepit, et illud venerabili patri R. Dunolmensi episcopo, quem cancellarium suum ibidem constituit, liberavit;

Et idem epsicopus sigillum illud a domino Rege recepit, et debitum juramentum ibidem præstitit;

Et die Jovis proximo sequenti idem Cancellarius sigillum prædictum in capitulo Fratrum Prædicatorum London' apperuit, et indè brevia fecit consignari.

VI. DE MAGNO SIGILLO LIBERATO JOHANNI ARCHIEPISCOPO CANTUARIENSI.[11]

A. D. 1335.
An. 9 Edwardi III.

MEMORANDUM, quod venerabilis pater R. Dunolm' episcopus, Cancellarius domini regis, sexto die Junii, anno regni dicti Regis nono, horâ nonâ, in camera Fratrum Minorum de Eborum, ubi idem dominus Rex hospitabatur, liberavit eidem domino Regi magnum sigillum suum, in quadam bursa, sigillo ipsius episcopi consignata, in præsencia venerabilis patris H. Lincoln' episcopi, thesaurarii ipsius domini Regis, dominorum Johannis de Warenna comitis Surr', Radulphi de Nevill' senescalli hospicii ipsius domini Regis, Galfridi le Scrop', ac Magistri Willielmi la Zousche, et aliorum tunc ibidem existencium;

Et idem dominus Rex sigillum illud a præfato episcopo

10 This act may be found in the *Fœdera*, p. 893.—*Cocheris.*

11 *Fœdera*, p. 909.—*Cocheris.*

recepit, et sigillum illud venerabili patri J. Cantuar', archiepiscopo, tocius Angliæ primati, quem cancellarium ibidem constituit, liberavit; et idem archiepiscopus sigillum illud a domino rege recepit, et debitum juramentum ibidem præstitit;

Et eadem die post prandium magister Robertus de Stretford, archidiaconus Cantuar', frater ipsius archiepiscopi, sigillum illud ad ecclesiam abbaciæ beatæ Mariæ Eborum, de mandato ipsius archiepiscopi detulit, et illud ibidem aperuit, et indè brevia fecit consignari.

VII. PRO EPISCOPO DUNOLMENSI SUPER EXPENSIS IN AMBASSIATA SUA.[12]

A. D. 1336.
An. 10 Edwardi III.

REX, thesaurario et baronibus de Scaccario, ac camerariis suis, salutem.

Cum, duodecimo die Julii, proximò præterito, miserimus venerabilem patrem R. episcopum Dunolmensem, ad partes Franciæ, ad tractandum cum magnifico principe domino Philippo, Rege Franciæ illustri, consanguineo nostro carissimo, super quibusdam negotiis, nos tangentibus;

Et ei concesserimus, pro singulis diebus, quibus in hujusmodi obsequio nostro staret, usque ad reditum suum; quinque marcas pro vadiis suis percipiendas, eique diversas summas pecuniæ, super expensis suis, in itinere illo fecerimus liberari;

Ac idem episcopus jam nobis supplicaverit ut, cum ipso, tam de vadiis suis prædictis quam de expensis, per ipsum circa passagia sua maritima, eundo versus dictas partes, et exindè redeundo, factis, computari, et sibi ulteriùs indè fieri faciamus quod est justum;

Nos, supplicationi suæ in hac parte annuentes, vobis mandamus quod compotum prædicti episcopi, in hac parte, audiatis, et allocetis sibi quinque marcas pro singulis diebus, quibus sic stetit in obsequio nostro, videlicet, a prædicto duodecimo die Julii (eodem die computato) usque vicesimum nonum diem Septembris, tunc proximò, sequentem, quo die ad nos rediit (eodem die similiter computato) id quod sibi, per compotum prædictum, tam pro dictis vadiis suis diurnis quam pro expensis, circa passagia sua factis, ultra prædictas sum-

12 This document as well as the following, is inserted in the *Fœdera*, p. 950.—*Cocheris.*

mas receptas, deberi inveniri contigerit, vos, præfati thesaurarie et camerarii, de thesauro nostro, solvatis.

Teste Rege, apud Stryvelyn, iv die Novembris.

Per ipsum Regem.

VIII. DE EXPENSIS PER CURSORES SUOS.

A. D. 1336.
An. 10 Edwardi III.

REX, eisdem, salutem. Supplicavit nobis venerabilis pater R. episcopus Dunolmensis, ut, cum ipse nuper (tempore quo ipsum misimus in nuncium nostrum ad partes Franciæ) diversos cursores suos, tam ad nos, ad partes Scotiæ quam alibi ad partes Allemanniæ et Britanniæ, pro quibusdam negotiis nostris ibidem, prout idem episcopus per nos oneratus extitit, per diversas vices transmississet, et eis diversas pecuniarum summas, de denariis propriis, pro vadiis et expensis suis, in hac parte, liberasset;

Velimus ei de eisdem summis solutionem fieri jubere, nos, supplicationi suæ hujusmodi annuentes, ut est justum, vobis mandamus quod eidem episcopo, de summis, quos bona fide asserit se pro obsequiis nostris prædictis solvisse, ut est dictum, vos, præfati thesaurarii et camerarii, solutionem celerem, de thesauro nostro, habere faciatis.

Teste ut supra.

Per ipsum Regem.

IX. DE PASSAGIO JOHANNIS, ARCHIEPISCOPI CANTUARIENSIS, ET RICARDI, EPISCOPI DUNOLMENSIS, AD PARTES TRANSMARINAS.[13]

A. D. 1338.
An. 12 Edwardi III.

REX, dilecto et fideli suo Willielmo de Clynton, comiti Huntyngdon', constabulario castri sui Dovorr' et custodi Quinque Portuum suorum, vel ejus locum tenenti in portu Dovorr,' salutem.

Cum venerabiles patres J. archiepiscopus Cantuariensis, totius Angliæ primas, et R. episcopus Dunolmensis, ad partes transmarinas, pro quibusdam arduis negotiis nostris, unâ cum venerabilibus patribus sanctæ Romanæ ecclesiæ cardinalibus, de mandato nostro, proficiscantur.

13 *Fœdera*, etc., 1045.

Vobis mandamus, quod eisdem archiepiscopo et episcopo, cum ad dictum portum Dovorr' declinaverint, naves, competentes et benè munitas pro passagio suo, et familiarium, equorum, hernesiorum, et rerum suorum, habere; navesque illas, unâ cum ipsis, ad partes prædictas proficisci faciatis, prout iidem archiepiscopus et episcopus, vel eorum alter, vobis scire faciet ex parte nostra;

Ita quod pro defectu navium hujusmodi, negotia nostra prædicta infecta seu retardata, non remaneant ullo modo.

Teste Rege, apud Walton, xxiii die Junii.

Per ipsum Regem.

X. LITERA AD DEPRECANDUM PRO DOMINO REGE.[14]

Jul. 1340.
An. 14 Edwardi III.

RICARDUS, permissione divina Dunolmensis episcopus, dilectis filiis priori et conventui ecclesiæ nostræ cathedralis Dunolmensis, cum sinceræ caritatis augmento, benedictionem. Quantis et qualibus periculorum procellis et invasionum horroribus regnum Angliæ subjacuerit, temporibus retroactis, vestram discrecionem credimus immo scimus certitudinaliter, non latere; sed, ecce, ubi plus timebatur adversitas ibi subito, benedictus Altissimus! Versa est vis turbinis in tranquillum. Jam enim ex literis domini Cantuariensis, omni hesitacione semota, recepimus, quod justus Dominus et misericors, cui non est in tibiis viri beneplacitum, nec in fortitudine equi voluntas[15] nos de affligentibus nos salvavit, et odientes nos inimicos, videlicet notros Francigenas, per manum famuli sui domini nostri Angliæ et in mari conclusit[16] Quocirca caritati vestræ firmiter injungimus et mandamus, quatenus, hac instanti sexta feria, coacta processione solempni, ac laxatis vocis organis, in laudum præconiis, Altissimo pro tanta triumphi gracia humili et sincero corde offeratis victimam labiorum.

Valete.

Scripta apud Middelham. 3 Jul. 1340.

14. This letter appears in the Surtees Collection, vol. XXI, entitled Depositions and other ecclesiastical proceedings, 1311 to the reign of Elizabeth, edited by Raine.

15 Psalm cxlvi.

16 The king came in person to destroy the French fleet lhe 24th of June preceding, on St. John Baptist's day.

XI. PRO EPISCOPO DUNOLMENSI, SUPER BALŒNIS ET STURIONIBUS INFRA DOMINIUM CAPTIS.[17]

A. D. 1343.
An. 17 Edwardi III.

REX, dilectis et fidelibus suis, Ricardo de Aldeburgh, Alexandro de Nevill, Willielmo Basset, Thomæ de Metham, et Thomæ de Fencotes, salutem.

Ex gravi querela, venerabilis patris, Ricardi episcopi Dunolmensis accepimus quod, cùm nos nuper susceperimus in protectionem et defensionem nostram ipsum episcopum, homines, terras, res, redditus, et omnes possessiones suas, omnibus et singulis inhibentes nè quis eis, in personis, ant rebus suis, injuriam, molestiam, dampnum inferret aut gravamen;

Idemque episcopus habeat, et habere debeat, ipseque et prædecessores sui, quondam episcopi loci prædicti, à tempore quo non extat memoria, habere consueverint wreccum maris infra dominium manerii sui de Hoveden, tam de piscibus regalibus, quam de aliis rebus quibuscumque, ad terram ibidem projectis;

Quidam malefactores, et pacis nostræ perturbatores, duo cete et duos sturiones, pretii trium milium librarum, ad terram, ad terram, infra dominium ipsius episcopi prædictum, per maris intemperiem projecta, quæ ad prædictum episcopum, tanquam wreccum suum, pertinere debent, dum idem episcopus in diversis obsequiis nostris, tam in transmarinis quam cismarinis partibus, et sub protectione nostra prædicta fuit, vi et armis ceperunt et asportaverunt, et alia enormia ei intulerunt ad grave dampnum ipsius episcopi, et contra protectionem, nostram prædictam, ac contra pacem nostram;

Et quia transgressiones prædictas, si taliter perpetratæ fuerint, relinquere nolumus impunitas, assignavimus vos quatuor, tres et duos vestrum (quorum vos, præfate Willielme, unum esse volumus) justiciarios nostros ad inquirendum, per sacramentum proborum et legalium hominum de comitatu Eborum, per quos rei veritas melius sciri poterit, de nominibus malefactorum prædictorum, qui transgressiones prædictas perpetrarunt, et de transgressionibus illes plenius veritatem, et ad easdem transgressiones audiendum et terminandum secundum legew et consuetudinem regni nostra Angliæ:

Eet ideò vobis mandamus quod ad certos dies, etc., quos, etc... quorum, etc... ad hoc provideritis, inquisitionem illam

17 This curious document may be found in the *Fœdera*, II, 1225.

faciatis, et transgressiones prædictas audiatis et terminetis in forma prædicta, facturi, etc... salvis, etc.

Mandavimus enim vicecomiti nostro comitatus prædicti, quod ad certos, etc... quorum, etc... ei scire faciatis, venire faciat coram vobis, etc... tot, etc... per quos, etc... et inquiri.

In cujus, etc.

Teste Rege apud Westm'. xx die Maii.

Per ipsum Regem.

XII. CAPELLA RICARDI BYRY EPISCOPI.[18]

IN exequiis domini Ricardi Byry episcopi, habuit ecclesia [Dunelmensis] tres equos deferentes corpus ejusdem at capellam a manerio suo de Aukland usque Dunelmum et ex ejus capella, unum vestimentum de alba camica, substiliter brudata, cum ii tunicis et iii capis et ii pannis pro altari ejusdem brudaturæ, cum historia navitatis (sic) dominicæ et Dormicionis et Assumpcionis ejusdem matris gloriosæ; quod viz vestimentum idem episcopus fieri fecerat in honorem virginis Mariæ pro eodem altari; et ii curtinas albas stragulatas, pro cornibus altaris; et i pannum aureum, viridis coloris pro tumba ejusdem; unam mitram brudatam cum multis parvis perlis diversi coloris et cathenis et nodis aureis; unum baculum pastorale argenteum cum capite deaurato; cerotecas et sandalia; et unum thuribulum argenteum et deauratum; et unum pannum longum de rubea camica cum vinea et literis intextis; ex quo facta sunt quatuor vestimenta et i casula; ex quibus unum ad magnum altare pro Dominicis, cum duabus tunicis et ii capis, et iv albis; cætera altaribus in ecclesia sunt distributa. Item, ex dono dicti domini Ricardi diu ante mortem suam, vi panni aurei marmorei coloris cum leonibus et cervis viridis coloris intextis et unus pannus viridis cum albis gallis et viridibus intextis, ex quibus facta sunt vestimenta diversis altaribus in ecclesia. Item, ex dono ejusdem, ii vestimenta, i de nigra camica, cum iii capis cum largis orariis decenter brudatis, aliud de rubeo welveto, cum multis ymaginibus Sanctorum in tabernaculis stantibus, cum auro et serico nobiliter brudatis; et ii panni pro altari de eodem panno et brudatura: sed et unum aliud vestimentum ejusdem panni et coloris, sed et multo dicioris brudaturæ, cum i capa et duobus pannis pro altari, proposuit ecclesiæ reliquisse, sed necessitate coactus, posuit illud in caucionem

18 See Surtees Society publications, volume entitled Wills and Inventories, etc. of Northern Counties of England, part I, chap. xxii, p. 25.

domino Radulpho de Nevyll pro centum libris; qui Radulphus postea sancto Cuthberto optulit. Post mortem Ricardi Byry episcopi, fracta fuerunt iiii sigilla ejusdem, et sancto Cuthberto oblata, ex quibus Ricardus de Wolveston feretrarius fecit unum calicem argenteum et deauratum qui est ad altare sancti Johannis Baptistæ in Orientali parte ecclesiæ: sub cujus calicis pede sculpti sunt hi duo versus subscripti.

Hic ciphus insignis fit præsulis ex tetra signis
Ri: Dunelmensis quarti, natu Byriensis. [19]

XIII. INSTRUMENTUM DE EQUIS PORTANTIBUS LITERAM ET CAPELLAM EPISCOPI.[20]

A. D. 1345.

IN Dei nomine, amen. Appareat, quod anno ab incarnatione Domini MCCC quadragesimo quinto, die vicesima mensis Aprilis, in meis Symonis de Charryng notarii publici et testium præsentia subscriptorum, infra prioratum ecclesiæ Dunelmensis, in quodam stabulo inter magnam portam et bracinum prioratus ejusdem constructo, constitutus personaliter venerabilis vir et discretus magister Johannes de Whytchyrche, rector ecclesiæ de Seggeffeld, Dunolmensis diocesis, executorem testamenti domini Ricardi de Bury, nuper episcopi Dunolmensis se dicens, liberavit executorio nomine supradicto, ut dicebat, et tradidit fratri Waltero Gategang monacho et sacristæ ipsius ecclesiæ Dunelmensem, præsenti tunc ibidem, duos equos magnos griseos, quiliteram, in qua jacebat corpus dicti domini episcopi tunc defuncti, portabant ad ipsam ecclesiam Dunolmensem, ecclesiasticæ tradendum ibidem sepulturæ; et eciam unum equum mulum, videlicet qui capellam dicti defuncti ad ecclesiam portabat eandem; quos omnes tres equos memoratos idem magister Johannes asserebat ex consuetudine debitos esse priori et conventui ecclesiæ Dunolmensis occasione portacionis et sepulturæ prædictarum. Præsentibus tunc ibidem Willielmo Pichecoc capellano, ac Petro de Clif, Thoma Brounesgrove et Willielmo Page testibus.[21]

19 This is a third reading of this inscription, which I have quoted above.—*Cocheris.*

20 See *Dunolmensis historiæ scriptores tres*, append., p. cxxxii.—*Cocheris.*

21 Ibid, p. cxxxiii.—*Ib.*

XIV. LITERA DIRECTA EPISCOPO, PRO VESTIMENTIS, QUÆ NOBIS CONTULIT DOMINUS RICARDUS DE BURY, EPISCOPUS DUNOLMENSIS.

A. D. 1345.

PATEAT universis, per præsentes, quod cum quædam contencio fuisset mota inter nos priorem et conventum ecclesiæ Dunolmensis super vestimentis quæ nuncupantur alba et serico brudata, videlicet una casula, una dalmatica et una tunica, tribus capis et duobus frontellis, ex largicione Ricardi de Bury, dudum Dunolmensis episcopi, ad nos et ecclesiam Dunolmensem pertinentibus, et in possessione nostra existentibus, quæ præfato domino Ricardo, dum vixit, pro vita sua gratanter accomodavimus, et qua dominus Robertus Calne, Willielmus de Hemmyngton et Willielmus de Assh, executores testamenti dicti defuncti occupant et detinent minus juste, petentes, ex parte una, et dictos executores contradicentes, ex altera, conquievit in hunc modum; videlicet quod dicti executores omnia vestimenta et frontalia supra dicta nobis traderent, restituerent, et de eisdem satisfacerent ad plenum; ita quod nos ipsos executores erga quoscumque, occasione premissorum, conservaremus indempnes. Cujus concordiæ pretextu dicti executores nobis vestimenta prædicta cum frontellis supra dictis tradiderunt et liberaverunt; et nos eodem pretextu cavemus et obligamus nos per præsentes ad conservandum dictos executores semper indempnes racione hujus deliberacionis dictorum vestimentorum cum frontellis, ut præmittitur, erga omnes. In cujus rei testimonium, sigillum nostrum commune præsentibus est appensum. Data Dunolmi, xxi die mensis Septembris, anno MCCCXL quinto.

INDEX

TO

NAMES OF PERSONS, PLACES AND BOOKS.

www.ingramcontent.com/pod-product-compliance
Lightning Source LLC
LaVergne TN
LVHW010242110826
845151LV00004B/1367

* 9 7 8 1 4 2 5 5 2 4 2 4 1 *